Development Theory and Practice

Development Theory and Practice

Critical Perspectives

Edited by

Uma Kothari
and
Martin Minogue

palgrave

First published 2002 by
PALGRAVE
Houndmills, Basingstoke, Hampshire RG21 6XS
Companies and representatives throughout the world

PALGRAVE is the new global academic imprint of
St. Martin's Press LLC Scholarly and Reference Division
and Palgrave Publishers Ltd (formerly Macmillan Press Ltd).

ISBN 0–333–80070–2 hardback
ISBN 0–333–80071–0 paperback

This book is printed on paper suitable for recycling and made from fully managed
and sustained forest sources.

A catalogue record for this book is available from the British Library.

Library of Congress Cataloging-in-Publication Data
Development theory and practice : critical perspectives / edited by Uma Kothari
and Martin Minogue.
        p. cm.
    Includes bibliographical references and index.
    ISBN 0–333–80070–2 – ISBN 0–333–80071–0 (pbk.)
    1. Economic development. I. Kothari, Uma. II. Minogue, Martin.

HD75 .D498 2001
338.9–dc21

                                                                    2001036096

10   9   8   7   6   5   4   3   2   1
11   10   09   08   07   06   05   04   03   02

Copy-edited and typeset by Povey–Edmondson
Tavistock and Rochdale, England

Printed in China

For my parents Tara and Shanti Kothari
For Molly and Paddy

Contents

Preface

The contributors to this book have been engaged in teaching, researching, and advising on development issues for the past two decades or more. In that time the 'development agenda' has been substantially transformed by rapid political and economic changes, which in turn have radically altered the thrust and focus of teaching and research on development. It therefore seemed to us an appropriate time to take stock of the development studies field, and in particular to evaluate the dominant ideas that appear to govern development practice and to consider the extent to which alternative ideas (and practices) might challenge the prevailing orthodoxies. We thank the many colleagues – not only at our own university but also in a number of other universities, countries and development agencies – who have helped to shape the ideas and interests of the contributors to this book. We also owe thanks to the truly international body of students who bring to our courses real experience and understanding of development practice, and from whom we constantly learn.

We are particularly grateful to our Publisher Steven Kennedy, who always gave sympathetic encouragement to our project; and to Karen Hunt, who worked wonders to produce a respectable typescript at very short notice.

Uma Kothari
Martin Minogue

Notes on the Contributors

Paul Cammack is Professor of Government at the University of Manchester and Director of Graduate Studies, Graduate School of Social Sciences, University of Manchester.

Jocelyn DeJong is a Lecturer at the Institute for Development Policy and Management, University of Manchester. Her specialist area is the Middle East, and she has a particular interest in health and development, and global and social policy.

Paul Francis is a social anthropologist and has worked on the institutionalization of social analysis for the World Bank, the DFID (UK) and various United Nations agencies. Currently a Senior Lecturer in Social Development at the School of Development Studies, University of East Anglia, he has published on social aspects of rural development, agricultural research, forestry, primary education, involuntary resettlement and participatory development.

Maia Green is Lecturer in Social Anthropology at the University of Manchester. She is a social development consultant, specializing in Africa, and was formerly a Social Development Adviser at the DFID (UK).

Uma Kothari is Senior Lecturer in Social Development at the Institute for Development Policy and Management, University of Manchester. She teaches on development theory and practice, and gender and development. Her research interests are migration processes, colonialism and development studies, industrialization and export-processing zones, and agrarian change.

Rosemary McGee was formerly a Research Associate at the University of Manchester and is now a Fellow of the Institute of Development Studies at the University of Sussex, where she is a member of the Participation Group. She began her contribution to this book while serving as Policy Officer at Christian Aid. She has conducted extensive field research on poverty, gender and participation in Latin America, and the focus of her current work is the promotion of participatory policy processes in developing countries.

Martin Minogue is a Senior Research Fellow at the Institute for Development Policy and Management, University of Manchester. From 1984 to 1996 he was Director of the University's International Development Centre. He has published extensively in the area of comparative public policy and development, and has undertaken consultancies for the United Nations Development Programme, the Asian Development Bank, the British Council, the UK's Department for International Development, and the UK Economic and Social Research Council.

Philip Woodhouse is Senior Lecturer at the Institute for Development Policy and Management, University of Manchester.

1

Critical Perspectives on Development: An Introduction

UMA KOTHARI AND MARTIN MINOGUE

What We Are Trying To Do in This Book

Development is ridden with paradoxes. The first is that, while it appears on the face of things to be very much characterized by a set of highly practical concerns, few subjects are more bedevilled by contested theories. The second is that while development undoubtedly takes place in some places, as measured by shifts in economic growth, relative poverty and inequality have also increased. Perhaps a third paradox is that the more precisely we try to identify coherent theories and measure practical changes, the less confidence we have in the predictability of future events, particularly on a global scale.

The development agenda has changed dramatically in the last few decades, as is clear from a perusal of Leeson and Minogue (1988). The latter text examines the contributions made to development analysis by the various social science disciplines (economics, politics, sociology, anthropology, history), and an attempt is made to examine the problems of interdisciplinarity and to suggest ways forward in the pursuit of a distinctive cross-disciplinary perspective on development thought and practice. The emphasis, though, is undeniably theoretical and draws attention to the intellectual conflicts that characterized most development studies literature in the 1980s. As the introductory chapter shows (ibid., 1988), the bulk of this literature presented two main paradigms (one neo-Marxist, the other representing neoclassical economics), between which there was a tremendous gulf, with each camp talking past the other. At the same time each camp was

1

characterized by significant internal differences, and these intellectual divisions divided the development literature into specific disciplines. At the time Leeson called for efforts to construct a more cohesive interdisciplinary perspective, but it is worth noting in the light of subsequent developments his prescient comment that 'the role played by Marxism in ... development studies should not ... cause nervous colleagues to have sleepless nights' (ibid., p. 41).

Perhaps it is the World Bank and other major players in the development industry who should cause us sleepless nights now, since while they may appear to accommodate different views of what should constitute development, they give active support to a particular, capitalist-friendly, neoliberal version. The present development agenda is very much the practical agenda set out in the programmes of major multilateral and bilateral aid donors. Few of the issues on this agenda could be said to be entirely new: economic growth, poverty reduction, the reform of trade regimes, the reduction of international debt, decentralization, democratization, social development and environmental issues have been standard priorities for at least three decades. More recent priorities, such as good governance, privatization and economic transition, owe more to the political collapse of socialism than to clearly thought out intellectual perspectives. Efforts to reconceptualize the field have arguably led to some shift in perspective by practitioners in relation to, for example, gender, environmental sustainability and social capital. The contemporary development agenda is therefore a combination of old and new, but it might be seen as being realized within a global framework that in political terms at least has changed dramatically.

The chapters in this book present the main issues on the agenda, and analyze the dominant framework within which the development agenda is articulated and implemented. They also seek to explain the persistence of old orthodoxies and the construction of new ones, while presenting the case for alternative approaches where the dominant orthodoxies (whether old, new or in combination) are open to criticism either for their partiality or their ineffectiveness.

Has Development Failed?

In this book we do not assert that development has been a success, rather we argue that there has been a failure of the postwar development project. As Sachs (1992, p. 1) writes,

The idea of development stands like a ruin in the intellectual landscape. Delusion and disappointment, failures and crime have been the steady companions of development and they tell a common story: it did not work.

Despite some gains in social and economic development, the persistence of poverty and inequality, particularly in the midst of economic affluence, continues to be one of the most problematic issues in development today (Hanmer *et al.*, 1997). The balance sheet of human development (Table 1.1) highlights the fact that while progress has been made in some social development spheres for some people, for others there has been increased deprivation and inequality in the distribution of benefits.

Figure 1.1 illustrates the increasing income inequalities between rich and poor countries. What the figures clearly demonstrate is that while development has occurred in terms of absolute growth, the disparities between countries and between the people within them have widened. At the very least this should cause us to question the particular notion of development with which we are working and the criteria used to assess success.

Despite the optimism and confidence amongst officials in bilateral and multilateral agencies that 'aid matters' and can bring about successful development (see Therien and Lloyd, 2000), there have recently been challenges to this consensus, particularly in relation to the links between poverty and development. These critiques have largely been brought about by the recognition that much development planning has failed to reduce inequalities and alleviate poverty (see Thomas, 2000). Schuurman (1993) suggests that development reached an impasse in the mid 1980s because of a crisis at two levels: a crisis in the Third World in terms of increasing levels of poverty, exclusion and inequality; and a crisis in development thinking, with the dominant theories and paradigms that had dominated our understandings and explanations of the world being challenged and subsequently losing their hegemony (Schuurman, 1993, 2000). The critiques of these hegemonic discourses, articulated in much development theory, arose partly because of a commitment to orthodox ideas of development that were too deterministic and dogmatic. Schuurman (2000, p. 9) writes:

In the 1980s development pessimism had already set in because it was realized that the gap between poor and rich countries continues to widen, that where economic growth had occurred it had

TABLE 1.1 *A balance sheet of human development, 1990–97*

Indicator	Development	Deprivation
Health	In 1997 the people of 84 countries enjoyed a life expectancy of more than 70 years, up from 55 countries in 1990. The number of developing countries in the group more than doubled from 22 to 49. Between 1990 and 1997 the share of population with access to safe water nearly doubled from 40 per cent to 72 per cent	During 1990–97 the number of people infected with HIV/AIDS more than doubled from less than 15 million to more than 33 million. Around 1.5 billion are not expected to survive to the age of 60. More than 800 million people lack access to health service, and 2.6 billion access to basic sanitation
Education	From 1990–97 the adult literacy rate rose from 64 per cent to 76 per cent. During 1990–97 the gross primary and secondary enrolment rate increased from 74 per cent to 81 per cent	In 1997 more than 850 million adults were illiterate. In industrial countries more than 100 million people were functionally illiterate. More than 260 million children are out of school at the primary and secondary levels
Food and nutrition	Despite rapid population growth, food production per capita increased by nearly 25 per cent during 1990–97	About 840 million people are malnourished. The overall consumption of the richest fifth of the world's people is 16 times that of the poorest fifth
Income and poverty	During 1990–97 real per capita GDP increased at an average annual rate of more than 1 per cent. Real per capita consumption increased at an average of 2.4 per cent during the same period	Nearly 1.3 billion people live on less than a dollar a day, and close to one billion cannot meet their basic consumption requirements. The share in global income of the richest fifth of the world's people is 74 times that of the poorest fifth

Women	During 1990–97 the net secondary enrolment rate for girls increased from 36 per cent to 61 per cent. Between 1990–97 women's economic activity rate rose from 34 per cent to nearly 40 per cent	Nearly 340 million women are not expected to survive to the age of 40. A quarter to one half of all women have suffered physical abuse by an intimate partner
Children	From 1990–97 the infant mortality rate fell from 76 per 1000 live births to 58. The proportion of one-year-olds immunized increased from 70 per cent to 89 per cent in the same period	Nearly 160 million children are malnourished. More than 250 million children are working as child labourers
Environment	Between 1990 and 1997 the share of heavily polluting traditional fuels in total energy use fell by more than two fifths	Every year nearly three million people die from air pollution and more than five million die from diarrhoeal diseases as a result of water contamination
Human security	Between two thirds and three quarters of the people in developing countries live under relatively pluralist and democratic regimes	At the end of 1997 there were nearly 12 million refugees

Source: UNDP (1998b).

FIGURE 1.1   *The incomes of rich and poor countries continue to diverge*

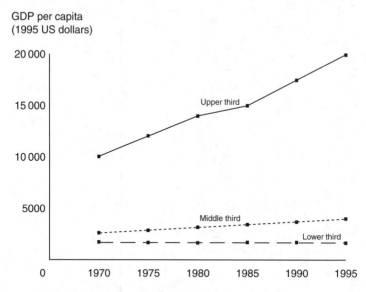

GDP per capita
(1995 US dollars)

Source: Adapted from World Bank (1999).

catastrophic effect on the environment and that the end of real-existing socialism had removed socialist-inspired development trajectories from the academic and political agendas.

Schuurman (1993, p. 10) posits a number of reasons for this impasse, including the following:

- The growing gap between rich and poor.
- A preoccupation with short-term policies aimed at debt management.
- The devastation of the environment in the pursuit of economic growth.
- The deligitimisation of socialism.
- The fact that the global economy could not be approached through national policies.
- The recognition of differentiation, which reduced the usefulness of global theories or metatheory.
- The advances made by feminism, postmodernism and post-colonialism.

It is now widely acknowledged in the development industry that the postwar development strategies have failed to bring the intended benefits to much of the world's population, and hence there is a need to devise new meanings, agendas, processes and targets for development. This is evident from the unevenness of the development process over time and between and within countries, and from distorted development in terms of the coexistence in some places of economic development and social deprivation. In addition there is increasing uncertainty about the global environment from the perspective of many developing countries (Hanmer *et al.*, 1997). Furthermore 'anti-development' and 'postdevelopment' proponents (see Sachs, 1992; Escobar, 1995; Rahnema and Bawtree, 1997; Rist, 1997) suggest that 'Development . . . is rejected not merely on account of its results but because of its intentions, its world-view and mindset' (Pieterse, 2000, p. 175).

What is needed is a clearer understanding and explanation of the reasons for and forms of this failure so that we can begin to resolve the problems, rethink development strategies and look to the future. Most importantly we need to explore ideas about what development constitutes and the important relationship between theory and practice.

Our starting point, which diverges from that of those who analyze the failures of development in terms of factors external to the ideas/ concepts of development (see Rahnema, 1997), is that the problems of development theory and practice are firmly located within the dominant, almost universal ideologies that have long shaped and continue to inform development theory, policy and practice.

Modernization: The Metatheory of Development

While not wanting to deny that the history of the development discourse over the past 50 years has been complex, we assert that the modernization project continues to underlie any apparent change in the development project. That is to say, the mainstream, dominant and powerful development ideology remains within the framework of neoclassical economics. In response to the question of whether neoliberalism is simply a reformulation of modernization theory, then, we would have to answer 'yes', even though we recognize that they propound different roles for the state and the market and view the relationship between them differently. Despite widespread development failures and sustained critique, the principles of modernization theory and neoclassical economics have remained intact (Simon and Narman, 1999, p. 270). While not wanting to present this dominant paradigm as monolithic, and acknowledging the existence of divergent views even amongst those who promote neoliberalism, the basic tenets of modernization and the notions of progress that underlie them endure.

Simon and Narman (ibid., p. 271) suggest that the reasons for the survival of modernization theory are complex, but they offer four general points:

- It remains consistent with the dominant neoclassical economic ideology of development within the US and most of Western Europe.
- It is a very simple and universalistic formulation.
- There have always been sufficient apparent successes to point to as sources of vindication.
- The astonishing speed and inventiveness with which the Bretton Woods institutions rally to its defence, even in the face of overwhelming odds.

The dominant discourse of neoliberalism, that continues to argue that the development project has been successful, remains fundamentally unchallenged, and with the collapse of socialism there appear to be few alternatives, so the orthodoxy persists. Indeed we can go further and say that with the demise of socialism the neoliberal development project has expanded beyond the 'developing world' into a much larger domain, which now encompasses the former socialist states, known tellingly as the 'transitional economies', made up of Eastern Europe and the former Soviet republics. The development project is expansionist and has found new territory.

While postmodernist convention requires us to suggest that everything is diverse, complex and differentiated, we would like to restate the notion that there is a singular, though not always homogeneous, development project that propels us towards modernization.

Having said that, there have been sustained critiques and debates within the field of development about the dominance of a particular ideology, the exclusion of certain groups of people from the project (because of gender, ethnicity, religion or class) and the processes and procedures of development (for example top-down, bottom-up, participative). Some of these have been presented as development alternatives and have played a significant role in drawing attention to some of the problems of development. John Brohman's book *Popular Development: Rethinking the Theory and Practice of Development* (1996) is divided into two parts: the first deals with mainstream theories and practices, and the second with alternative theories and practices, leading to a new framework that he calls 'popular development'. In this way he sets up a false dichotomy, by suggesting that there is a clear distinction between the mainstream and alternatives even though it is now evident that the adoption of alternative approaches by the mainstream has lead to a blurring of the boundaries between them.

Development alternatives have not remained alternative for long – many of them have been successfully and often quite rapidly absorbed into the mainstream. The alternatives are presented as popular and people-centred, including approaches such as gender and development, participatory development and sustainable development. In Pieterse (1998) there is an interesting discussion of the relationship between mainstream and alternative approaches to development. Pieterse argues that there is no alternative development paradigm, but rather that the key elements of alternative development – which is concerned with introducing alternative practices and redefining the goals of development – have successfully been incorporated, adapted and co-opted by the mainstream. Hence there are no simple dichotomies between mainstream and alternative, modern and antimodern. Pieterse stresses that:

Alternative development has been concerned with introducing alternative practices and redefining the goals of development. Arguably this has been successful, in the sense that key elements have been adopted in mainstream development. ... By the same token this means that alternative development has become less distinct from conventional development discourse and practice, since alternatives have been absorbed into mainstream development (ibid., p. 344).

As we can see from successive World Bank reports, forms of alternative development have become institutionalized as part of mainstream development and some have been developed further within the mainstream discourse (see Chapter 9 of this volume). It might be said that the alternative development approaches have often been co-opted to the point where there remain few real alternatives.

A series of modifications have been made to official mainstream policies in an effort to:

Overcome past shortcomings and to meet changing perceptions or priorities ... so as to project a progressive and responsive image. Ironically and probably inevitably, however, the selective adoption of radical alternatives has seen their emasculation, rendering them increasingly less radical and more accommodationist (Simon and Narman, 1999, p. 271).

An important question that Pieterse (1998, p. 345) raises is whether alternative development really presents an alternative way of achieving development; that is, whether it broadly shares the same goals as mainstream development but uses different means that are participatory and people-centred. If this is the case, then alternative development does not redefine development but instead questions its modalities, agency and procedures.

> The pendulum is beginning to swing back towards softer, more socially sensitive and nuanced approaches, but there is little sign that the fundamental ideology of development embodied by the multilateral agencies and some major donors is changing (Simon and Narman, 1999, p. 271).

It is still ultimately about the achievement of Western modernity by developing and transitional countries.

We believe that it is important to dissect, explain and challenge the ways in which this modernization orthodoxy has been constructed and translated into powerful policies and practical interventions. It is particularly important to mount this critique because of the contradiction between its triumphalist claims and the evident facts of development failure. Each of the chapters in this book examines a particular area of development theory and practice, presents a critique of the dominant model in that area, and suggests alternative approaches. While each of the authors may take a different approach to the understanding of development failure, common themes emerge among the chapters.

There is a considerable body of recent literature that charts the history of development from the establishment of the Bretton Woods institutions, through growth and modernization theory, dependency and world systems theories to neoliberalism and so-called 'alternative' development approaches (see Hettne, 1990; Preston, 1996). In the present book, rather than provide a comprehensive history of the development discourse we have selected particular issues that we feel bring out the tensions between theory and practice in general, and specifically between the dominance of the neoliberal paradigm, and the achievement of social progress and poverty reduction. Furthermore the issues covered in this book reflect the increasing attention paid to social development issues since it was recognized that development is about much more than economic growth, and that while progress in social development and economic growth have often been assumed to be positively correlated, this has not always been borne out and there is no automatic causal link between the two. Many of the approaches discussed here emerged out of a need to challenge the dominant economic focus in development thought and practice and to question the historical and theoretical underpinnings of development. However they have subsequently been co-opted onto the development agenda, where they now appear in the mainstream despite the fact that some have their origins in radical discourses. This process of conscription of critical discourses into the mainstream has often been accompanied by a watering down of the challenges and political commentary that went with their construction. It is the consequences of this process that are highlighted in this book. The focus is on the continual need for public engagement and critique of development orthodoxies, whatever their origins, as 'nothing seems more legitimate than to spotlight what a discourse has been trying to hide, or take a position on the consequences flowing from it' (Rist, 1997, p. 3).

We also feel that there is little to be gained from struggling through the different definitions of development to arrive at some overarching meaning, and instead acknowledge that the various actors in development have divergent conceptions and interpretations and attach different meanings to development. According to Rahnema (1997, p. ix) there are at least three different sets of actors, each with their own aspirations and interests: leaders and elites in Third World countries, the masses within those countries, and former Western colonialists who seek to maintain their economic and geopolitical dominance/presence in other parts of the world.

Within the development industry itself there are a variety of actors who also inevitably have divergent agendas, although these may operate broadly within certain (modernist) boundaries. This makes it even more necessary to interrogate the relationship between theory and practice, and to investigate how theories are converted into practice.

This book, then, takes as its starting point the continuing dominance of the neoliberal paradigm within development, and the practical possibility of achieving the Development Assistance Committee targets for 2015, as agreed and supported by its members (OECD, 1996).

- Reduce extreme poverty by one half.
- Ensure universal primary education and eliminate gender disparity in education.

- Reduce infant and child mortality by two-thirds and maternal mortality by three-quarters, while providing universal access to reproductive health services.
- Implement worldwide national strategies for sustainable development and reverse the loss of environmental resources.

We interrogate the orthodoxy from different perspectives and argue that it is unlikely to result in the achievement of these ambitious targets. Furthermore the very existence of these targets is in part a further expression/indication of the past failure of development and the modernization project. They further reflect the futurist approach to development, which has consistently avoided the messy and problematic present, and has been slow to feed the lessons learned and best practice into future development design. Instead it has quickly moved on to formulate the next plan, develop policies for the future and implement the next project. In this respect the development agencies are highly unreflexive. There is little evidence of present (mal)practice informing future policy and even less likelihood of it influencing theoretical and conceptual frameworks of development.

Vattimo (quoted in Pieterse, 1998, p. 349) goes as far as to suggest that this is the case even with 'alternative' development, which continuously 'replicates "the value of the new" reflecting a pathos of modernity; alternative development then partakes of the momentum of modernity and the everlasting hope that the future will redeem the present'.

Whose Development?

Development is an idea, an objective and an activity. These are all interrelated. When we examine the idea of development we are exploring an area of theory. When we attempt to establish objectives we are delineating the process by which the ideas are turned into practice. An examination of actual practice entails detailed analysis of the activities. Such an analysis should tell us whether the objectives have been met, and in turn whether the theory has been realized.

But this rational formulation conceals a host of difficulties. First, it is clear that there is not one idea or theory of development but a plurality. What constitutes the 'idea' of development is disputed territory, much fought over. This affects our perception of both objectives and activities. The objectives of development must be incorporated into the idea of it; different ideas produce different sets of objectives. Similarly, different objectives will produce different practices. So we are faced with the possibility that not only is there more than one theory of development, but there is also more than one practice. Practice is not a given; it is the outcome of the attempt to realize a particular idea.

This brings us to the notion of 'agency'. By this is meant the network of institutions and actors that through their actions and interactions 'produce' development. The analysis of agency is crucial because it allows us to capture the complexities of the process by which ideas are mediated into objectives and translated into practice. We are then in a better position to understand which ideas and objectives prevail over others, and why they do so. In relation to practice, the analysis of agency also directs us to actors who are often neglected: the recipients of development interventions, who may be either beneficiaries or victims. The concept of development agency is most valuable in revealing the 'open secret' of development, that its character and results are determined by relations of power, not by the rhetoric of fashionable populist labels such as 'participation', 'civil society' or 'poverty reduction'. As Korten (1990, pp. 144, 214) says: 'The heart of development is institutions and policies. ... The most fundamental issues of development are, at their core, issues of power'.

How might we represent the interaction of development agency with development ideas to throw light on the complexities of practice? One approach is through a development triad or triangle, representing the crucial components as state, market and community or civil society. Development is the product of collaboration and interaction between these three sets of institutions. The three alternatives might then be labelled 'state-led', market-led' or 'community-led', indicating alternative models for development practice. Crudely these would correspond to traditional state-planned modernization, neoliberalism and economic globalization, and alternative populism.

The devil lies in the detail, or perhaps in the crudeness of the categories. The concept of 'the state' has been as variously interpreted as the concept of development. Marxist theory, for example, assigns an insignificant role to the capitalist state as mere superstructure, while modernization perspectives assume that the state will be the lead player. Neoliberalism wants the best of both approaches, reducing the direct responsibilities of the state but retaining its responsibility for supporting market institutions.

But as Pieterse (1998, p. 356) suggests, development, 'even though it hinges on theory as the beacon of policy, is more concerned with policy than explanatory frameworks'. It may therefore be acceptable to limit analysis of the state, initially at least, to the development strategies and policies that are designed and implemented by state agencies. This may still give us evidence for an estimation of dominant discourse (and theory) if we agree with Korten (1990, pp. 113–14) that it is 'impossible to be a true development agency without a theory that directs action to the underlying causes of underdevelopment ... an organization cannot have a meaningful development strategy without a development theory'. Since the state must engage with the economy, and take up a position in relation to the non-state sector, this will produce an array of policies and actions that will reveal a network of interactive relationships, and will also allow some perception of relations of influence and relative power. This is not a new thought – Myrdal (1968) identified such relations as a crucial dimension of effective development policy over thirty years ago in his notion of the 'soft state'. But it is just as essential now to identify these relationships, which are expanding and branching into ever more complicated institutional networks, partnerships and con-tractual arrangements in ways that give greater weight to 'market' agency in the process and practice of development policy.

What of the third element of the triad: 'community' or 'civil society'? Despite the considerable attention paid to this element in the development literature and the substantial recognition afforded to it by official development agencies, it is difficult to think through what would be the positive and collaborative relationship the com-munity would have with the market, given the ample evidence across all types of political economy of the deeply damaging effects on communities of market failures and imperfections. It was precisely to remedy such damage that the state was given a leading role in development in the past, but with the new formulation of the state-market partnership, who will protect the community?

An alternative formulation would see the triad of state, market and community dissolved in favour of a representation of the means by which theory is converted into practice, with institutions acting as a bridge between the two. There would be no particular need to define the boundaries between state, market and community; the focus would be on real development policies and strategies, their imple-mentation by a wide array of competing or collaborative institutions, including community institutions, and upon the real effects and results. This would enable some estimation of developmental change and its impact on communities, while still permitting some attention to dominant ideas and the degree to which they are translated into practice.

Any of these representations of development theory and practice seem likely to be more productive than the rather tired rehearsal of historical antagonisms. It is surely preferable to link theory and practice on the basis of more grounded analysis and agreement on a common agenda of development issues, even if the appropriateness of the solutions on offer remains contested.

This book is organized around a number of key themes or issues that might stand as a set of 'key words' for the field of development studies, as distilled from current preoccupations in development theory and practice. The next chapter provides an overview of contemporary debates on globalization in order to set the context within which the other chapters are located. This exploration of global processes and the ways in which they are understood and analyzed, together with the implications for development, offers a macro-level framework for reading the subsequent chapters, which focus on specific spheres of development thought and practice.

2

The Political Economy of Globalization

UMA KOTHARI, MARTIN MINOGUE
AND JOCELYN DeJONG

On a political map, the boundaries between countries are as clear as ever. But on a competitive map, a map showing the real flows of financial and industrial activity, those borders have largely disappeared (Ohmae, 1990, p. 18).

Capitalism is, and will remain, a national phenomenon (Rodrik, quoted in Mittelman, 2000).

The debate on globalization fits well with the approach of this book, which is that development debates have been framed by a series of theoretical disputes that have had the effect, intentionally or otherwise, of obscuring the essential continuity of the long modernization project of the 'short twentieth century' (Hobsbawm, 1994a). It has been suggested that development itself was a myth, constructed by Western states in the post-1945 period to disguise the continuation of exploitative economic relations with former colonies, and resting on the premise that these structures of economic control and modernization would contain and promote political modernization in the form of Western liberal democracy (see Crush, 1995). Ironically the preferred means was national, centralized, state-led economic planning, the primary instrument also of the socialist model, which offered to new states an alternative model of political economy. Until the 1980s this global beauty contest was the most influential factor in shaping relations between Western and non-Western countries, development aid and strategies being largely employed as a Cold War weapon. The collapse of the socialist states in the former Soviet Union and Eastern and Central Europe not only appears to have resolved this contest, but to have led to the presumption that there are now no obstacles, or overarching alternatives, to the world-wide extension of the modernization project, a presumption that finds its principal expression in the globalization debate. This chapter is divided into two main sections. The first, rather than attempting to provide a comprehensive picture of globalization or offer a definitive definition of the term, introduces the different ways in which the processes of globalization have been understood and analyzed. The second section focuses more specifically on the political economy of globalization and its implications for development. These two sections are clearly linked as any conclusions or generalizations about the existing relationships among national economies in the international system will be shaped by the particular perspective adopted on globalization itself. It is also clear that both economic and political relationships have to be analyzed, since the position taken on, for example, economic issues will determine views about the political relations of states in the international system, and even about the meanings we should now attach to 'the state' and 'international relations'.

What is Globalization?

Globalization is a highly contested concept in terms of its meaning, form and implications, with more fundamental questions being raised about the extent to which globalization is actually taking place and, if it is occurring, the nature of its genealogy. The term has also been used to describe and explain a range of contemporary cultural, economic and political phenomena, resulting in the concept becoming almost meaningless through overuse. Consequently the literature on globalization is large and diffuse.

Although there is much evidence to suggest that the context of development is now dramatically different because we are living and working in the context of globalization (McMichael, 1996; Hoogvelt, 1997; McGrew, 2000a), there are some who believe that globalization is in fact a myth, or at least exaggerated in terms of its intensity and impact (see Wade, 1996; Weiss, 1998; Hirst and Thompson, 1999). Furthermore, for those who believe that it is happening there is confusion about the causes and effects of globalization. Is globalization the driving force of cultural, economic and political changes, or is the mutual reinforcement of these processes producing globalization? Furthermore if it does exist, what are its origins? When did globalization start and how does it differ from previous periods of global interconnectedness? How can the processes of global change be managed in order to benefit the poor? We begin with an exploration of the forces that are presumed to be driving globalization, and then examine the different perspectives on its positive and negative implications for development.

Is globalization myth or reality? The question here is the extent to which globalization has created a context that is significantly different from earlier historical periods. Is the current interconnectedness substantially different, for example, from what Hobsbawn (1994b) described as the 'Age of Empire', when the spread of colonial economic and political power created elaborate networks of trade, thereby bringing together different peoples and cultures in unprecedented ways? As will be discussed later, Hirst and Thompson (1992) argue that the Gold Standard era from the late nineteenth century to 1913 equalled if not surpassed the current period of economic openness and integration. It has also been suggested that the impact of the telegram in the nineteenth century was as intense as the current globalization of communications (Held *et al.*, 1999).

While the processes of globalization therefore have significant antecedents, and there is acknowledgement that the earlier stages of economic, political, and cultural interconnectedness – through, for example, colonialism – provided vital precursors for the current era, these previous periods were arguably very different from the current one. Held (2000) argues that what distinguishes the current period is the speed, intensity and penetration of global forces. Today there is much more interaction throughout the world and over a shorter timeframe, thus the impact of what happens in one region is now felt much more strongly in far distant ones. Will Hutton, in *The State We're In*, says that '[w]hether in trade, finance or the speed and scope of communication, the degree of interpenetration of financial markets and cultures is unprecedented' (Hutton, quoted in Hirst and Thompson, 1999).

The current period has also witnessed the emergence of new international actors and institutions such as the UN, the World Bank, the IMF, transnational corporations and the growth of other intergovernmental organizations (see Held *et al.*, 1999). These are global in composition and have global reach through the development and promotion of policies. New global actors such as the World Trade Organization and regional blocs such as the European Union are similarly exerting increasing influence on national policy making.

Furthermore new abilities and inclinations for civil society to organize and forge links across national borders present opportunities for influencing national politics in unprecedented ways. But if we agree that the current period is distinctly different, then when did it begin? This continues to be an area of debate in which there is no consensus on which world events were most influential in forging the present globalization era. Was it the abandonment of the gold standard that brought in an era of fluctuating exchange rates, or the growing interdependence of countries as a result of the oil crises of the 1970s and the subsequent debt crisis of the 1980s? Or was it more generally the increasing openness of economies and the liberalization of capital markets following the adoption of monetarism in the UK and the US, and the pervasiveness of the structural adjustment programmes of the 1980s?

There is general agreement that there are several, mutually reinforcing processes of globalization; however there is disagreement about whether these are causes of globalization or the outcome of the extension and intensification of global processes. These driving forces include technological innovations, economic and political shifts and cultural changes. Clearly one of the most potent driving forces has been the speed and spread of communications and the increasing ease and decreasing cost of travel (UNDP, 1999). Economic transformation has included rapid and colossal growth in financial flows following the deregulation of capital markets around the world, much of it speculative and with the potential to destabilize national economies, as the East Asian crisis so poignantly illustrated. The latter trend has reinforced the growing transnationalisation of production that was precipitated by the shift to post-Fordist production and the proliferation and dominance of transnational corporations.

Political shifts are evident in the decline in state intervention and the emphasis on deregulation, privatization and liberalization, and are therefore closely connected to economic changes. These political forms of globalization have led to a reconsideration of the appropriate role of the nation-state and, as we shall see, the specific role that the state should play in the promotion of development.

There is widespread consensus across different perspectives that globalization is reducing the scope and power of the nation-state to direct national development strategies, or at least fundamentally to transform the parameters within which states make decisions and policy choices. While nation-states continue to be significant, their power is increasingly sandwiched between powerful pressures from

above and below, creating a complex system of 'multilayered governance' (McGrew, 2000a). As Held *et al.* (1999, p. 28) note, this has
implications for the transformation of power relations:

> In fact, the stretching of power relations means that the sites of
> power and the exercise of power become increasingly distant from
> the subjects and locales which experience their consequences. ...
> Political and economic elites in the world's major metropolitan
> areas are much more tightly integrated into, and have much greater
> control over, global networks than do the subsistence farmers of
> Burundi.

The question then becomes, what political mechanisms exist to
demand the accountability of global actors, and in whose interests
is this new global infrastructure working? The WTO in many ways
symbolizes these trends and the mutual reinforcement of economic
and political shifts. Unlike its precursor, the General Agreement on
Trade and Tariffs (GATT), it has unprecedented power to demand
changes in national legislation in the interests of free trade. Questions
therefore remain about the potential for democratic regulation of its
actions. As Sell (2000) clearly illustrates, multinational corporations'
increasing dominance and their transnational lobbying shapes, to
varying degrees of success, the ultimate direction of WTO measures.
    Cultural changes are closely linked to technological, political and
economic shifts and have led to unprecedented interaction between
cultures and societies across the globe (see Cochrane, 1995; Massey
and Jess, 1995; Waters, 1995; Tomlinson, 1996; Robins, 1997; Lechner and Boli, 2000; Mackay, 2000). There has also been a rise in
global social movements, and increasing awareness of global issues
and problems is uniting concerned people beyond national boundaries on issues such as the environment, conflict and war, and
migration. All this means that there has been an increase in the
speed, intensity and quantity of flows of information, capital, goods
and, to a lesser extent, people around the globe.
    However, at the same time it is clear that the various aspects of
globalization are proceeding at different paces and thus have a
differential impact on individuals and groups. The fastest developments, for example, have been in the sphere of financial flows, and
perhaps the slowest have been in the free movement of labour. This
latter point raises questions about the uneven distribution of the
benefits of globalization. While neoclassical economists have

espoused the benefits of opening international borders to permit the freer movement of capital, trade, services and technology, increasing restrictions have been placed on the movement of people (Weiner, 1990). Weiner (ibid., p. 160) suggests that there are 'two diametrically opposed world trends. One is for greater openness of international borders. ... The other is for greater restrictiveness.'

It is clear from the above 'that globalization is not a singular condition, a linear process or final end-point of social change' (Held *et al.*, 1997, p. 258), and this point is reinforced in the following discussion on the different ways in which global processes are understood.

Understanding, Interpreting and Analysing Globalization

In the literature, globalization is understood in diverse ways depending on the particular disciplinary emphasis and perspective. For example, the specificities of interpreting global processes depend partly on whether the focus is on the sociology, the economics or the politics of globalization. While these are clearly interconnected, specific disciplinary and ideological perspectives highlight or emphasize particular understandings of processes and relations embedded and articulated by globalization. For example, from a sociology of globalization perspective Robertson (1992) talks about 'world compression', suggesting that the way we live in one part of the world has repercussions for people living in other parts, and that this has implications for the construction or intensification of 'global consciousness'. Giddens (1990) similarly talks about 'time–space distanciation', in which distance or constraints of space are becoming less relevant for social interaction. Massey (1991) suggests that globalization disembeds social processes from localities, relocating them elsewhere, and hence there is a changing sense of place whereby 'place' becomes the site of social interactions and relations regardless of the space people occupy.

When economics is the centre of analysis the discussion focuses more on the globalization of capital, transnational forms of production, the increased integration of economies and the interdependence of trade. The literature on the politics of globalization tends to analyze the changing nature and role of the nation-state and the extent to which it continues to constitute a relevant unit of analysis. Here there is a debate between those who hold the view that the declining role and reduced autonomy of states means that states have become victims of globalization, and those who suggest that states remain significant actors, affecting political outcomes by perpetuating globalization and conditioning the effects of global developments on their citizens. As Giddens writes, 'in circumstances of accelerating globalization, the nation-state has become too small for the big problems of life, and too big for the small problems of life' (Giddens, quoted in McMichael, 1996, p. 149). Examples of such global problems are environmental damage, international migration and refugees, and transnational crime.

As mentioned above there are many different conceptualizations of globalization. Here we offer two that we feel provide a good framework for understanding and analyzing global processes. Appadurai (1990) suggests that we can comprehend globalization as a series of global, disjunctive flows that create different 'scapes'. He identifies five main flows within globalization:

- Mediascapes: images and narratives globally transmitted through, for example, television, film, news and other forms of media.
- Ideoscapes: the transmission across space of ideas and ideologies via, for example, mediascapes or indeed within academia.
- Ethnoscapes: the movement of people such as migrants, refugees, development workers and business travellers.
- Technoscapes: these refer to the increasing ease and speed of travel, access to information and the technological revolution.
- Financescapes: these incorporate global institutions such as the IMF and transnational corporations, and capital flows through various forms of investment.

Held *et al.* (1999) offer a typology of perspectives on globalization in which there are three distinct positions: *globalists* (who are in turn divided between those who are optimistic and those who are more pessimistic about the potential for and form of change), *global sceptics* and *transformationalists*. For globalists (Ohmae, 1995), glo-balization is an inevitable development and cannot be resisted by human intervention and certainly not by traditional political institutions such as the nation-state. Amongst the globalists are those who point to the benefits of globalization, arguing that the spread of capitalism and the increased integration of the world economy will bring widespread benefits and prosperity. They believe that globalization offers the potential for living standards to rise with the spread of new technologies as the latter can, for example, increase productivity levels, alleviate health problems and allow innovation in education (UNDP, 1999). For developing countries this is seen as a positive process, bringing them into line with international trends and providing them with increased access to the 'fruits of progress'.

The global pessimists see globalization as a form of Westernization – or more specifically Americanization, with the extension of US hegemony (see Amin, 1990). They argue that multinational corporations, multilateral institutions and global markets have replaced the colonial empires and thus represent a new form of colonialism and imperialism. In this view globalization is an uneven process, where power and control remain in industrialized capitalist countries and in the hands of global elites. Thus from this perspective globalization has negative consequences for the poor and marginalized, who lack access to new technologies, experience unequal terms of trade in global markets and have limited opportunities to influence global decision making.

Global sceptics such as Hirst and Thompson (1999) agree that changes are taking place at the global level, but they are not convinced that what they refer to as growing internationalization is entirely unprecedented. For example Weiss (1998) suggests that the power of nation-states is underestimated in some discourses of globalization, and that the impact of external economic pressures cannot be predicted without exploring the ways in which the state mediates those effects. Thus in the view of the sceptics globalization has far from undermined the powers of the state, rather it has strengthened the state in several respects.

The third position is occupied by what Held calls the transformationalists (see Giddens, 1990). They occupy a middle ground between the globalists and the sceptics. They agree with the sceptics that the globalists' claims are often exaggerated, but they argue that something fundamental and unprecedented is happening in the world that is bringing about greater interconnectedness and transforming rather than reducing state power. However they make no predictions about the ultimate direction of these diverse and often conflictual trends. Unlike the other two camps, they are optimistic about the capacity of 'transnational civil society' to influence and shape globalization in the interests of social progress.

The following section begins with a clarification and critique of the economic interpretations of globalization, and then examines the politics of globalization.

The Political Economy of Globalization and its Implications for Development

Economic Issues in the Globalization Debate

Wiseman (1998, p. 1) suggests that 'globalization is the most slippery, dangerous and important word of the twentieth century'. Even economists are prone to use it as a relatively meaningless shorthand to refer to all types of international activity, and often seem to assume that the integrity of the concept is unproblematic. As indicated earlier, this is far from the case. It is evident that in the first place we need a clear understanding of what kinds of economic evidence and relationships have to be analyzed in order to test the presumption that the recent economic changes are of a different order and intensity than those experienced in earlier periods, and that we live and work in a global economy that is quite different in principle from the international economic relationships of the recent past. One way to approach this is to construct an 'ideal type' of economic globalization, setting out the conditions that such a model would have to satisfy. Hirst and Thompson (1992) offer such a typology, drawing a distinction between a *world-wide* international economy and a *globalized* international economy (Table 2.1).

Hirst and Thompson (1999) point out that in reality we are likely to find elements of both these models in a complex and messy coexistence, and that the relative relations between dominance and subordination are difficult to clarify and capture. Nonetheless, if we are to make a judgement about whether globalization is a reality or a myth, we need to consider trends in the international economy over defined periods of time, and to examine the extent to which there is an 'orthodoxy' of globalization. Hirst and Thompson (ibid., p. xii) set out this orthodoxy in a recent reformulation of their arguments and suggest that this view of globalization is an expression of what has emerged from analysis of the 'dominant economic discourse for the past decade'. This includes the ways in which distinct national economies have been dissolved into a global economy that is determined by global market forces as a result of the rapid intensification of flows of international trade and investment. The orthodox view sees economic liberalism as having clear benefits and supports the notion that public policy should continue to deregulate trade, investment and capital movements. According to this perspective (1) globalization benefits consumers by increasing the scale and allocative efficiency of markets for both goods and capital, (2) national

TABLE 2.1   *The characteristics of world-wide and globalized international economies*

World-wide international economy	Globalized international economy
• The principal entities are nation-states, which oversee the growing interconnectedness among national economies, and the increased integration of economic actors and nations into market relationships	• Distinct national economies are subsumed and rearticulated by essentially international processes and transactions
• Trade relations therefore take on the form of national specialization and division of labour; but the importance of trade is progressively replaced by the centrality of investment relations between nations	• The global economy 'raises ... nationally-based interactions to a new power ... as markets and production become truly global' (Hirst and Thompson, 1992, p. 361)
• Interactions are of the 'billiard ball' type: international events do not directly penetrate domestic economies, but are refracted through national policies and processes	• International forces become autonomous, and difficult for national regulators to control or resist
• International interactions (e.g. financial markets, trade in manufactures) function as opportunities or constraints for nationally located economic actors and their public regulators	• Nationally based multinationals are transformed into transnational corporations, a form of 'footloose capital', without specific national identity or location, but operating globally in global markets, and dominating or bypassing both national and international regulators
• Multinational firms operate in an international economy but from a distinct national base	• The economic bargaining power of labour is weak, and multinational firms often locate or relocate where labour costs are lowest
• Domestically based labour power is relatively strong in responsive national systems	

Source: Adapted from Hirst and Thompson (1992).

regulation is futile and (3) concern for welfare and labour rights within a national economy will damage international competitiveness and drive out foreign investment. Finally, the orthodox view assumes that developing countries and regions can only benefit from being integrated into this global economy.

While Hirst and Thompson do not seek to deny the existence of 'a growing and deepening international interconnectedness in trade and investment, an open world economy of interlinked trading nations' (ibid., p. xii), they express a strong antagonism to the orthodoxy set out above:

> This economic liberal view is pernicious: both because it is founded on a largely erroneous series of factual claims, and because it demands policies that result in established entitlements being sacrificed in favour of market-based increases in growth that will prove illusory (ibid., pp. xii–xiii).

How are we to assess the relative merits of the competing positions here? One approach to the problem of considering the economic evidence is provided by Thompson (2000), who puts forward a rigorous analysis of trends in trade and financial flows over the twentieth century. His main concern is to demonstrate that while there has been a clear and substantial expansion of trade and output in general terms, the measurement and comparison of trends over long time periods is highly problematic. Nonetheless trade flows can be used as a proxy measure for interdependency in the world economy, but using the ratio of merchandise trade to GDP at current prices as the most reliable indicator proves only that the openness of trade has remained steady since the First World War.

Capital flows, largely measured by direct foreign investment (DFI), can be used to measure integration in the world economy. DFI only contributed just over 5 per cent of world investment in 1995, and the ratios of total capital flows to GDP seem to indicate a higher degree of globalization in the pre-First World War period than at the present time.

A further element in the case for the existence of globalization is the position of developing economies (or the 'South') and their relations with the developed economies (the 'North'), since part of the presumption of the globalization orthodoxy of positivist globalists is that much of the expansion in international interdependency has been between North and South; that developed economies need to maintain the competitiveness of their economies in the face of the competitive advantages enjoyed by Southern economies with lower labour costs; and that Southern economies are bound to benefit from these changing relationships.

Perhaps the first step is to ask how the evidence has been treated from different sides of the argument. We begin by setting out the approach of development economists, drawing on Cook and Kirkpatrick (1997), who present recent data on the strengthening of cross-border economic relations, and the increasing integration of the world economy. They suggest that the analysis lends some support to the view that convergence is taking place between developed and developing economies (though they also indicate deleterious or 'divergent' effects).

Cook and Kirkpatrick propose that the vital indicators relate to world-wide direct foreign investment (DFI); to the growth of multi-national firms (they do not use the distinction made earlier between multinational and transnational corporations); to the growth of intrafirm trade, a major indicator of the fragmentation and distribution of the various parts of the production process to a variety of global locations; and to financial flows between developed and developing economies. They show that during the period 1986–90, DFI increased by 24 per cent per annum in developed economies and by 17 per cent per annum in developing economies giving rise to some of the earliest formulations of the globalization thesis. Furthermore DFI is substantially greater than domestic investment in both types of economy, and international trade in manufacturing has increased steadily since the 1970s. Multinationals are now estimated to account for at least a third of global output, and intrafirm trade (a major indicator of global production) now accounts for 40 per cent of global trade. They demonstrate that in both trade and foreign investment, services are the fastest growing component, accounting for a quarter of world trade and three fifths of DFI flows, and that the assets of international banks as a share of GDP increased from 6 per cent in 1970 to more than 30 per cent by 1990.

In relation to developing countries, trade and financial liberalizations imposed by the World Bank and the IMF have helped to produce outward-looking development strategies that have increased the integration of these countries into the international economy. But it is multinational cross-border trade that is providing the major impetus for genuine globalization.

According to trade theory these changes should produce gains for all participants. But Cook and Kirkpatrick show that the distribution of benefits has been very unequal, with an increased disparity between the richest and poorest 20 per cent of the world's population (from 11:1 in 1960 to 17:1 in 1989). There are also clear regional disparities, with the economies of East and South East Asia growing much faster than other regions, and sub-Saharan Africa being at a particular disadvantage. The response of the proponents of liberalization and globalization is to acknowledge the uneven distribution of benefits but to blame the poorly performing countries for their inability to take advantage of the opportunities available. It is argued that where administrative, institutional and organizational structures are weak, the capacity to manage globalization is undermined.

Both Held (2000) and Hirst and Thompson (1999) note that the orthodox debate on globalization tends to ignore regional biases in the international economy. The 'triad' (Europe, North America and Japan) account for between two thirds and three quarters of all economic activity, so that '85 per cent of the world's population are almost written out of any economic globalization process' (Thompson, 2000, p. 117). This is a reminder that 'the absence of the developing countries from the global economy is the result of the still very low levels of interaction between the North and the South in terms of . . . trade flows (ibid., p. 119). Held also notes that empirical studies conclude that North–South trade and migration account for no more than 10–20 per cent of 'lost' wages and employment in Northern economies, with most of this decline deriving from technological developments *within* Northern economies. This 'undermines the often repeated claim that somehow the living standards of the Northern working class are adversely affected by the forces of trade globalization' (ibid., p. 120).

Held considers that the arguments for economic globalization are highly exaggerated. Hirst and Thompson (1999) are even more sceptical. They rest their view that globalization is 'a myth that exaggerates the degree of helplessness in the face of contemporary economic forces' (ibid., p. 6) on the following propositions:

- The internationalization of the economy is in no way new, and has been proceeding since the mid nineteenth century.
- An open international economy is still fundamentally characterized by exchange between relatively distinct national economies, and factors such as the competitive performance of firms and sectors are substantially determined by processes occurring at the national level.

- Genuine transnational corporations are rare; most international firms trade multinationally but the location of assets, production and sales is predominantly national.
- The overwhelming proportion of flows of trade, investment and finance is concentrated in the triad regions of North America, Europe and Japan.
- The increase in trade, output and capital flows is not producing a significant shift in investment from developed to developing economies.

Hirst and Thompson consider, as does Held, that the debate on globalization is in part an ideological one and requires a political analysis, to which we now turn.

The Politics of Globalization

The thrust of the discussion on the political implications of globalization is captured in a quotation from Mittelman (2000, p. 4): 'globalization is not a single unified phenomenon, but a syndrome of processes and activities [that] ... has become normalized as a dominant set of ideas and a policy framework, while ... also being contested as a false universalism'. This neatly encapsulates the elements of ideology, policy and practice that constitute the essentials of any political anatomy.

The issue of ideology is strongly enunciated by Gray (1998), who is at pains to distinguish long-standing forces of economic and social transformation and modernization from the recent and specific project of neoliberalism to create a single world market.

> A global single market is very much a late twentieth century political project ... this political project is far more transient than the globalization of economic and cultural life that began in Europe in the early modern period ... technology-driven modernization of the world's economic life will go ahead regardless of the fate of a world-wide free market (ibid., p. 23).

Gray regards this attempt to create and impose a global free market as unlikely to promote stability or democracy because

> it does not meet the needs of a time in which Western institutions and values are no longer authoritative. ... A reform of the world economy is needed that accepts a diversity of cultures, regimes and market economies as a permanent reality (ibid., p. 20).

This resonates with the part of the globalization literature which is convinced that the neoliberal project is, in economic terms, well established. Mittelman (2000) suggests that we are experiencing a new intensity of economic competition, a sort of hypercompetition, in which decisions taken in one part of the world bear directly on decisions made elsewhere. He writes that the 'underlying dynamic is the ascendancy of the structural power of capital to discipline the state' (ibid., p. 235). This process is not resisted, but sustained by what Cerny (1990) calls 'the competition state', whose chief functions are to play an enabling role and prevent market failure. From this perspective, globalization has so reduced the autonomy and regulatory powers of the state that we can no longer refer in any meaningful way to the independence of nation-states, nor to an interstate system of international relations. The former is regarded as having ceded authority and control at a variety of internal and external levels to a plethora of public, private and hybrid institutions (this has been described as a new form of mediaevalism). At the extreme of this argument, nation-states are perceived as having become the 'local authorities' of the global system, unable independently to affect the levels of economic activity or employment within their territories, since these are now determined by the choices of internationally mobile capital (see for example Ohmae, 1990).

The schematic representation by Held (2000) suggests that this model is embraced by 'globalists', who are persuaded of the victory of globalizing forces in the global political economy. But that case is rejected by 'sceptics', who believe that the nation-state is actively thriving on the new demands and opportunities created by rapid changes in the international economy, and in principle is much the same type of state as in the past, and still in control. Finally, Held categorizes 'transformationalists' as supporters of continued autonomy for the nation-state, who nonetheless accept that the rapidity and intensity of recent economic and social changes require a considerable adaptation to changed roles, a reconfiguration of state powers. Held also suggests that another new dimension is the emerging constitution of elements of regional and global governance, which holds out the promise of recovery by the old nation states of the political powers lost to globalizing capital. There seems to be some contradiction here with Held's scepticism (referred to above) about the actuality of economic globalization – arguably any political version of globalization depends on the prior establishment of an economic version. However the multiplicity of versions in the literature, and the conflicting interpretations of both the data and the historical accounts used to support particular versions, is in danger of making 'confusion worse confounded'.

In this situation 'strong' versions, whether for or against globalization, have a certain appeal, though it may well be that 'third way' versions, while intellectually less coherent, correspond better to the complex realities. Hirst and Thompson (1992, 1999) fall into the former category, for they are strongly committed to the defence of the existing nation-state against what they see as the 'political rhetoric of globalization' (1999, p. 261). The undoubted fact of rapidly changing economic, political and social realities is for them a clarion call to clarify and redefine the position of the nation-state: 'the policies and practices of states in distributing power upwards to the international level and downwards to subnational agencies are the ties that will hold the system of governance together' (ibid., p. 270).

They do not see the logic of those who are equally anxious to reestablish the nation-state and advocate 'localizing the global' or urge that 'democracy must be reterritorialised' (Mittelman, 2000, p. 246), for they do not accept the premise of an ascendant global capitalism with untrammelled powers. Ultimately, they argue, the nation-state will retain a significant centrality because of its relation to territory and population, even if concessions will inevitably be made to new forms of regional and global governance.

A very different 'strong' version is provided by radical left theorists, whose work may reasonably be seen as represented by Hoogvelt (1997). She posits three models of political economy for the analysis of globalization. The *realist* model focuses on the autonomy of the nation-state, interstate competition and the organization of international relations, with an emphasis on concerns such as order, stability, hegemony and the international balance of power (this approach is broadly taken by Hirst and Thompson). The *institutionalist* model is based on liberal values of economic interdependence and cooperation, attachment to the market, support for viable governance institutions, and a plural world order tending towards global governance. The *structuralist* model rejects the other two as masking or enabling the operation of global capitalism, which structures global economic and political relations in terms of a dominant core and a subordinate periphery. The structuralist approach seeks to redefine the international political economy as a stable world order.

Hoogvelt (1997) accepts that comparisons with earlier periods of the twentieth century do not indicate any great changes in cross-border flows, or any serious reduction in the inequalities between developed and developing parts of the world. But she argues that there has been a major shift in spatial and temporal relations and this has produced a significant deepening of capitalist integration. She contends that there are three key domains to examine:

- *Changes in relations between state and capital* amount to an 'internationalization of the state' and 'emerging institutional forms of "elite interaction" between members of the international business class, state bureaucrats and members of international organizations' (ibid., p. 135). The state is expected to deliver a neoliberal policy agenda, and privatization is cited as an example of how an international agenda is forced on states by multilateral donors.
- *Changes in relations between labour and capital* involve deindustrialization and job reductions in developed economies and the relocation of jobs from the 'core' to the 'periphery'. Meanwhile the advent of the information society is responsible for producing the phenomenon of 'contingent' (or insecure) employment.
- *Changes in core–periphery relations* have been produced by restructured production chains that create forms of global networking, and a 'new social core–periphery hierarchy' (ibid., p. 145), resulting in the creation of advantaged elites and insecure middle groups while entirely excluding some 60 per cent of developing country populations from the benefits of capitalist expansion.

The combination of these trends and the unevenness of the distribution of the benefits of globalization creates and/or reinforces social exclusion amongst individuals and groups in the South as well as the North. Significantly, Hoogvelt detects varied responses to globalization in the principal developing regions, which suggests that however uniform the causes of globalization might be, the effects are mediated by local, national and regional differences.

The Developing State: 'Stepping Stone or Stumbling Block?'

This counterposition, suggested by Melo and Panagariya (1993), is adapted here to consider the pressures on nation states in developing countries, and the likely outcomes. One strand in the discussion must be the substantial efforts of aid donors to extend to governments in developing countries the 'new public management' reforms already applied in several developed systems. Their emphasis is on a reshaping of state boundaries and internal structures that blurs the distinction between the public and private domains, transfers some functions to the private market, and purports to convert traditional bureaucrats into entrepreneurial managers. But this should not be taken as firm evidence of globalization; the record of effective 'policy transfers' of this type has been patchy and even the 'flagship' of privatization is somewhat becalmed (Minogue, 2001). Moreover these changes can scarcely be compared with the major political, social and economic transformations achieved during much earlier periods of colonization.

A second dimension is the use by major aid donors of mechanisms of political conditionality to underwrite the imposition on developing countries of Western pluralist systems of democracy. This entails a process of homogenization by incorporating the claim of universalism of human rights (Stokke, 1995a; and see also Chapter 7 of this volume). This claim is not only disputed by social theorists, but also by political leaders in developing and transitional economies who seek to counterpose local political and cultural values to the globalizing tendencies of Western culture. While this has largely taken the form of a debate on 'Asian values' it is a theme that also resonates in Africa, the Middle East and the new states that have emerged from the detritus of the collapsed Soviet Union. It takes sharpest definition in marketizing socialist economies such as China and Vietnam, which wish to belong to the international capitalist economy but are determined to resist the political aspects of the package. Such societies are undoubtedly experiencing rapid and substantial change, and it has been suggested that closer attention is required to the new forms of regionalism being employed as a defence mechanism by states in the developing world as they adapt to globalizing pressures. We would agree with the assertion by Richards and Kirkpatrick (1999, p. 687) that 'there is a growing sense that posing the debate in terms of "global" versus "national" is yielding an impoverished understanding of important transformative processes'.

Globalization and its Implications for Development

The above discussion shows clearly that whatever the perspective taken in the globalization debate, the key issue is the extent to which global processes impact positively or negatively on developing countries, and more specifically on the poor and marginalized within these societies. Again there are different perspectives on the implications of globalization for Third World countries: 'In a relatively short career, the concept of globalization has accumulated a remarkable string of both positive and negative connotations without having achieved a particularly clear denotation' (Tomlinson, 1996, p. 22).

As we have seen, some are of the view that economic openness will stimulate growth and the resulting economic affluence will be accompanied by the gradual erosion of North–South differences and the 'end of the Third World'. Others argue, however, that rapid capital flows and trade liberalization lead to financial crisis and destabilization, and that Third World countries are the 'losers' of globalization as they continue to be exploited but in new ways by multinational capital. The benefits of globalization are highly unequally distributed, and with the possibility that the state will have less control over social policies it is likely that the poorer sections of the population will be further impoverished. There is also the concern that as globalization threatens local cultures and societies there is often a strong cultural and social backlash, which can be detrimental to people's freedom and quality of life.

Whatever the perspective, however, when we begin to explore the potentialities of globalization for poverty alleviation most agree that, if indeed globalization is taking place, the central challenge for development is how it can be managed in such a way that the benefits are more equally distributed. The recent UK White Paper on International Development, *Eliminating World Poverty: Making Globalization Work for the Poor* (DFID, 2000a) makes clear that globalization is creating unprecedented new opportunities and risks, and that these require further analysis in order to present an agenda for managing the process of globalization so that it works in the interests of the poor and, more specifically, creates the necessary conditions for faster progress towards the international development targets.

3
Feminist and Postcolonial Challenges to Development

UMA KOTHARI

According to some theorists, development studies had reached an impasse by the mid 1980s (see Schuurman, 1993, 2000; Booth, 1994). This impasse emerged partly because the dominant discourses, intellectual traditions and development practices were subjected to critique. The crisis in development was broadly conceived in two ways. First, it was argued that the exacerbation of poverty and inequality during the 1980s – labelled by some as the 'lost decade' – revealed a profound failure in development planning. Second, the ways in which orthodox development knowledge and practice had been shaped by a Western and masculinist bias were identified by postcolonial and feminist scholars as a process that claimed universality but instead derived from particular interests and understandings. The 1990s then saw both a proliferation of critiques of development that questioned the belief in modernization and the quest for progress that had underpinned so much development theory and practice since the 1950s, and numerous articles offering alternative visions and approaches (see Korten, 1990; Rahman, 1993; Escobar, 1995; Carmen, 1996).

Amongst other approaches, postcolonialium and feminism have challenged conventional meanings and ideas of development and questioned the process by which development knowledge was produced and gained legitimacy. These challenges, levelled at the masculinist and Western conceptions articulated within orthodox development, are the focus of this chapter, which begins by demonstrating how mainstream development theory and practice has perpetuated a Eurocentric and male bias.

The following section highlights the attempts that have been made to confront the Eurocentrism in development discourse and to integrate gender issues into all aspects of development, and explores how development studies can move beyond its complicity with Western and masculinist theorizing. The chapter goes on to acknowledge and examine the links between gender and colonialism, and investigates the advantages and problems of the, albeit partial, convergence of feminism and postcolonialism. Colonialist and masculinist discourses are invariably intertwined. Unfortunately, however, many critical feminist and postcolonial approaches have reinforced the theoretical divide between them. For instance much Western feminist debate deals only marginally with issues of race and racism, whilst feminist concerns are often absent in literature that challenges orientalist and Eurocentric discourses.

The conclusion discusses the ways in which these challenges have differently affected policies, theory and practices. I suggest that development studies needs to engage much more rigorously with feminist and postcolonial literature to challenge the cultural racism and gender blindness prevalent in development thought and practice, saturated as it is by Western and masculinist forms of knowledge and representation.

Development and its Colonial Legacy

The relationship between Britain and its former colonies after independence finds expression in contemporary discourses of Third World development. The transition from colonized subject to aid recipient, and from colonial administrator to development practitioner, can highlight the ways in which development theory and practice have been shaped and influenced by colonialism.

It is now generally recognized that the current economic, social and political situation of developing countries cannot be properly understood without an adequate understanding of their historical background (see Chandra, 1992). It is argued here that these historical relationships have to be analyzed in order to examine why development has evolved in the way in which it has, and to provide a historical context in which to evaluate the potential of future development strategies (see Amin, 1989; Chandra, 1992).

However Miege (1980) suggests that the very notion of a 'colonial past' may be misleading. He says that 'it leads one to imagine a clear distinction between the "before" of colonialism and the "after" of independence, seen as two sharply contrasted periods separated by the moment of decolonization. ... Nor must it be imagined that colonization always meant a complete break with the pre-colonial period' (ibid., p. 35–6). Thus, as Crush (1995) contends, the transition from the colonial moment to the development process signalled a shift in emphasis rather than the end of one project and the beginning of another. It may be asked whether, and to what extent, political sovereignty and national independence brought about a break in cultural and economic relations (see Miege, 1980). However it seems indisputable that colonial relations have influenced the postcolonial period politically, economically and culturally (see Dhaouadi, 1994). For instance Chandra (1992, p. 23) has identified psychological influences that colonialism engendered in the colonized populations: 'a sense of inferiority in themselves and their own people and a sense of confidence in European people and things'.

The origins of the field of development studies, and the resulting Eurocentric forms of knowledge that it produces, can be partly situated in the colonial moment, and thus the technologies and the approaches embodied in and articulated by development emerge from specific times and places. In turn these disciplinary effects must be located within a larger ensemble of the after-effects of colonization, which have been aptly summarized by Said (1989, p. 207):

> To have been colonized was a fate with lasting, indeed grotesquely unfair results, especially after national independence had been achieved. Poverty, dependency, underdevelopment, various pathologies of power and corruption, plus of course notable achievements in war, literacy, economic development: this mix of characteristics designated the colonized people who had freed themselves on one level but who had remained victims of their past on another.

Moreover Smith (1994, p. 268) warns that 'it would be a mistake to conclude that ... de-colonization marked the end of empire. It did effectively signal an end to colonialism as a specific form of empire, but imperial interest and global reach continue to the present'. Thus political sovereignty and national independence did not bring an end to all forms of colonialism; indeed neocolonialism and the process of recolonization are sustaining economic, political and social control by the West over 'the rest'.

There is a growing body of literature about the way knowledge is constructed and reproduced that emphasizes its Eurocentric genealogy and how knowledge itself is deeply rooted in a Western mindset that marginalizes other knowledges (Said, 1979; Barker *et al.*, 1994;

Shohat and Stam, 1994; Crush, 1995; Moore-Gilbert, 1997). David Slater (1995, p. 383) explores the spatiality of power this expresses and challenges, suggesting that notions of development and modernization portray the West as superior and permanently central, both philosophically and culturally.

> The power over other societies is not only a phenomenon connected to violent incursions, military invasions, colonial conquests and externally administered governance; it also expresses a relation of knowledge that posits a Western superiority over the non-West (ibid., p. 324).

Unlike anthropology and geography, in which crucial forms of knowledge have been 'produced by, indeed born of, colonial rule' (Mohanty, 1991, p. 31), development studies may have its origins in colonialism but it is better conceived as a postcolonial discipline, in the sense that its emergence as an academic discipline after the Second World War coincided with the onset of the decline of colonial rule. However, much of the theory and practice within the discipline suggests that it is also a neocolonial subject since it reconfigures and (re)presents unequal power relations between the First and Third Worlds, embodying the continuity of particular relations of power over time (colonial to postcolonial) and space (geographical West and Third World) (ibid.; see also Trinh, 1989).

As a neocolonial discipline, then, the authoritative discourse of development reproduces unequal relations by assuming the power to label groups of people. For example in development we construct an entity called the 'Third World' (see Toye, 1993) and then proceed to depict it as an objective reality to its inhabitants. Furthermore, the power to represent others is assumed in the portrayal of ways in which people live their lives, in articulating their experiences – and on this basis, in shaping the processes of change. This can be seen in the unquestioned notions of progress and modernity that continue to underlie much development thinking, and in the use of techniques such as participatory approaches (see Cooke and Kothari, 2001).

This form of neocolonialism is being played out not only in development theory but also in the policies and practices espoused by development workers who are interpellated by these ideas and reifications. Dominant strands within development theory and practice are constructed in the West and implemented in the Third World, with Western policy makers influencing which projects should be funded and where aid should be spent and withdrawn. Thus the boundaries and distinctions that formerly marked the power relations between colonizers and the colonized continue to be played out, and are reinscribed in the relationship between development administrators and recipients of aid. Maintaining this relationship often requires development planners and practitioners to dismiss as unimportant the voices of the individuals whose impoverishment and marginality they seek to address. By not recognizing their attempts at self-representation through various forms of struggle, they continue to view them as victims rather than participants and directors of their own independence and development (see Fanon, 1963; hooks, 1989). Attempts by postcolonial critiques to decentre this authority are now explored.

Postcolonial Critiques

Postcolonial critiques have problematized the construction of Western knowledge and its intellectual traditions, and expressed deep suspicion of the totalizing theories, grand projects and truth claims of Enlightenment thinking in which the non-West becomes reinscribed into a history not of its own making (Pieterse and Parekh, 1995; Seth *et al.*, 1998, p. 8). There are ongoing debates on the meaning of 'postcolonialism' (see Bhabha, 1984; Young, 1990; Shohat, 1992; Ahmad, 1995; McClintock, 1995; Hall, 1996), but certain common themes have emerged. Postcolonial theory is most often used as an umbrella term for diverse critical approaches that deconstruct Western thought, and the term refers not to a simple periodisation but rather to a methodological revisionism that enables a wholesale critique of Western structures of knowledge and power (McClintock, 1994). Bhabha reminds us of the issue of representation in this critique of history when he writes that:

> the term postcolonial is increasingly used to describe that form of social criticism that bears witness to those unequal and uneven processes of representation by which the historical experience of the once-colonized third world comes to be framed in the West (quoted in Mongia, 1996, p. 1).

Although postcolonial theory has been most influential in the disciplines of history, literary studies, cultural studies and increasingly within geography and other social science disciplines (see Pratt, 1992; Godlewska and Smith, 1994; Driver, 1995; see also Said, 1992), it was not until recently that a small minority of development studies scholars and practitioners began to reflect on the imperial origins of their discipline in anything like a critical manner. A discursive analysis of development began in the 1980s, together with the emergence of 'alternative' approaches and analyses of the language of development (see Ferguson, 1990; Sachs, 1992). Nevertheless the desire to reveal the many embedded, tenacious strands of colonial forms of knowing and representing is gaining momentum and is exemplified in the approaches of, for example, Crush (1995) and Escobar (1995), who illustrate the ways in which development ideology is (re)produced to valorize particular forms of (Western) knowledge and to maintain the economic and intellectual superiority of the West. Escobar (1995) focuses on the professionalization of development knowledge and the institutionalization of development practices. He argues against searching for grand alternative models or strategies, and proposes 'the investigation of alternative representations and practices in concrete local settings, particularly as they exist in contexts of hybridization, collective action and political mobilization' (ibid., p. 19).

Others have focused less on issues of representation and more on criticizing the Eurocentrism in development theory in general (Mabogunje, 1989; Hettne, 1990) and in economic theories in particular (Mehmet, 1995). Schuurman (2000, p. 8) attributes the impasse, or what he calls 'the paradigmatic disorientation within development studies', partly to the mounting critique of the essentializing and homogenizing of the so-called Third World and its people in postwar development paradigms. Others have attributed the failure of development to different forms of inequality such as gender inequality, and these considerations further question the perception that other people from other places are part of an undifferentiated mass. The following sections demonstrate the ways in which development discourse is not only Eurocentric but also highly gendered, and discuss attempts to ensure greater gender equity through the formulation of gender-aware policies and practices.

Development: a Masculinist Discourse

Until the 1970s women were virtually invisible to development planners and policy makers. When they were considered, assumptions were made about men's and women's roles in society in which women's economic activities were largely ignored. Much of women's work was unpaid and undervalued compared with men's labour. And even when women did carry out remunerative work, their contribution was rarely reflected in national accounting systems. In addition women were absent from planning and decision-making processes in donor agencies, in NGOs, at the national and community levels and often within the household. Women have also been marginalized in respect of political and legal rights and access to education. Since development was primarily concerned with economic growth, this exclusion of women from development was considered justifiable since women were not seen as economic actors and therefore need not be considered within the framework of what constituted development.

There were essentially two conceptual and empirical assumptions that made women invisible to planners. First, there was little information on what women's roles and needs were in society. Because national economic and social statistics did not disaggregate data by sex, many policies and plans were based on the experiences and lives of men but generalized to all people (see Evans, 1992). Thus the interests and needs of men were taken to reflect and represent society as a whole. This masked the extent of women's participation in the economy and society, and the status of women in terms of, for example, income, health and education were not generally known. Second, there was the assumption that men were the breadwinners, and women and children their dependents. The dominant view held that women's participation in development was outside the economic mainstream: women's activities were stereotypically seen as consigned to the spheres of family and childcare, and therefore as domestic and not economic. Overwhelmingly, development planners and policy makers tended to rely on narrow definitions of activities and assumed that the conventional conceptual categories of 'work' or 'productive activity', for example, held the same meaning for all people.

Diane Elson emphasizes how apparently gender-neutral terms and concepts have obscured this male bias in development. She argues that:

> Rather than talking about women and men, and sons and daughters, use is made of abstract concepts like the economy, the formal sector, the informal sector, the labour force, the household. Or the argument is conducted in terms of socio-economic categories which on the face of it include both women and men, such as 'farmer' and 'worker'. It is only on closer analysis that it becomes apparent that

these supposedly neutral terms are in fact imbued with male bias, presenting a view of the world that both obscures and legitimates ill-founded gender asymmetry, in which to be male is normal but to be female is deviant (Elson, 1995, p. 9).

In much development theory, planning and practice, two key concepts were rarely considered, and when they were, preconceptions about their form and implications hindered further analysis. These were the 'gender division of labour' and the 'household'.

As far as the gender division of labour is concerned, a variety of demarcations segment the work carried out in any society. Although these change over time they display some common features, including the somewhat reified dichotomy between paid and unpaid, formal and informal, skilled and unskilled, and mental and manual. Gender is typically mapped onto these dualisms to produce 'women's work' and 'men's work' – where men are thought to be primarily engaged in productive work and women in reproductive work. However in most definitions and classifications 'work' is synonymous with paid employment. Such thinking not only tends to discount or trivialize women's paid employment, but also ignores the gender division of labour in societies where it is women who are primarily responsible for domestic and (daily and generational) reproductive activities within and for the household. A consequence of this is that the contribution that unpaid forms of work make to economic productivity goes largely unacknowledged. Production outside the market is excluded in some census and national income accounting methodologies, and since women predominate in, for example, the informal sector it is often women's production that is undervalued and discounted. For example in the Peruvian Peasant Survey of 1976 only 38 per cent of women were recorded as being engaged in agricultural production, but once non-market production was measured almost 86 per cent were recorded as being actively involved in agricultural work. Moreover the work that is carried out within or for the household is neither valued nor considered to be productive since it does not directly generate income. Again, since women largely carry out these activities their work remains invisible.

The second misconception is that of the household, which forms the basic unit/site in which people live and is the most commonly used unit of analysis in development planning. Many development policies are household-focused, which means that they identify problems at the level of the household and implement policies at that level.

However there are many inaccuracies and common assumptions about the composition and constitution of the household, the nature of relations within the household, the range of activities carried out by different members, the functions of the household, and the idea that the household head is a man. The mythical household, then, is made up of those who live under one roof, coresidents around a hearth, members related through kinship and a married couple and their children.

Until the emergence of the 'women and development' approach in the 1970s women were seen as having had little impact on, and were not considered active participants in, the development process. More worryingly, they were thought to have been unaffected by development strategies, or when they were the impact on them was invariably considered to be positive. However in recent years there has been increasing awareness and evidence that the processes of development have affected men and women differently. The advantages of development have consistently by-passed women, or they have been disadvantaged by the ideological, conceptual and methodological inadequacies within the development process.

Feminist Critiques

In their introduction to *Feminist Visions of Development* (1998), Cecile Jackson and Ruth Pearson alert us to the tension between 'the essentially modernist project of development, and the subversive deconstructing tendencies of feminist analysis' (ibid., p. 13). This section adopts a deconstructive approach that focuses on feminist challenges to key concepts within development, rather than rehearse the history of the emergence and relative contributions by and limitations of the 'women in development', 'women and development' and 'gender and development' approaches, which have been explored effectively elsewhere (see Moser, 1989; Rathgeber, 1990; Visvanathan, 1997).

It is necessary briefly to summarize the meanings of gender, gender relations and gender differences in order to provide the conceptual tools that form the framework of gender analysis and the gender and development approach. While 'sex' is a natural category that reflects biological difference, 'gender', although often based on biological sex, is a social construction: individuals are born either male or female but over time they acquire a gender identity, that is, what it means to be male or female (Elson, 1995). Because gender is constructed through our social experiences in particular contexts, what it means to be a boy or a girl, a man or a woman varies from one environment to another and changes over time. Gender has been used to refer to the difference between men's and women's roles, interests and needs, and gender relations to the particular power relations embodied in those differences, that is, the inequalities between men and women. The main focus of the gender and development approach is not women *per se* but the socially constructed relations between men and women. Importantly it recognizes that men and women are positioned differently in society, and that not all women or all men share the same experiences. That is, there are other forms of differentiation in society that mediate an individual's position in society and their experiences, such as age, religion, class, race, caste, sexuality, disability and tribe.

The gender and development approach is a mode of intervention in a particular hegemonic development narrative (Mohanty, 1991), in that it demands a reexamination of the development process with an awareness that it has affected men and women differently, with women being increasing marginalized (see Kabeer, 1994; Elson, 1995). The very notion of gender is an assault on the idea that societies are a homogeneous mass of undifferentiated individuals, because its basic assumption is that women and men have different experiences. Prior to this, little distinction was overtly made, and male experiences were tacitly assumed as universal.

The gender and development approach required a shift in thinking about, amongst other issues, the two misconceptions identified above, that is, the sexual division of labour and the household. In order to make women's work visible it was imperative to broaden definitions of 'work' and 'productive activity'. Some suggested that the issue was more about measuring women's activities, and that methodologies of data collection needed to be adapted or devised anew in order to gain insight into the form and extent of women's work. One approach emphasized time-use studies, which captured in sequence all the activities engaged in by an individual over a given period of time.

The gender and development approach also challenged the notion that the household was a homogeneous unit within which resources were shared equally and the behaviour of the members was uniform (Kabeer, 1994). Young (1992) identified a general lack of knowledge and understanding of the dynamics of household resource management, the failure of household-focused policies to deliver the intended benefits to all household members, particularly women and children, and evidence that women were chronically underresourced relative to men, particularly in poor households. This emphasized that the household was difficult to conceptualize theoretically, for although concrete examples could be described, relations within households were partly structured by gender and seniority, and household members did not always operate collectively, have equal rights and obligations, or carry out similar activities. These critiques had important implications for development policy by stressing the need for more types of information, and to anticipate the differential effect on men and women of development interventions.

A gender perspective emphasized that it was important for men and women to benefit equally from processes of change, and for the inequalities between men and women to be reduced, particularly in terms of access to and control over resources and decision making, an ideal that is now widely recognized by large donor agencies, multi-national and bilateral organizations and NGOs. Strategies have been adopted to integrate gender into mainstream development policies, projects and practices, with varying degrees of commitment and success (see Goetz, 1997).

Gender analyses of power relations, both at the micro level of the individual and the household and at the macro level of the state and international agencies, have been important in reshaping development approaches and exposing the ways in which theories, concepts and methodologies within development are masculinist. While these critiques have taken many forms, there is evidence of greater gender awareness in mainstream development planning.

However it is not only at the level of policy and practice that a male bias has been made evident. More fundamentally perhaps, these interventions have challenged masculinist forms of knowledge (see Marchand and Parpart, 1995) in an attempt to make both the ways of knowing and the things known more representative of men's and women's experiences (Gandhi, 1998).

Postcolonial Feminism and the Politics of Representation

Gender and development approaches and postcolonial theory have attempted to decentre the universalizing of particular forms of masculinist/colonialist knowledge and focus on the study of those who have been represented as the marginalized in prevalent dichotomies of women and men, black and white, colonized and colonizer, in the process deconstructing the prevailing hierarchies of gender and race.

However, while it may be theoretically and strategically valid to separate the discourses of feminism and postcolonialism – in that they enunciate particular historical relationships, and are interested in deconstructing specific hierarchies and constructing particular forms of knowledge and politics – this analytical division simplifies the ways in which power is articulated and experienced in society.

Disparate strands of postcolonial feminist theory have emerged out of the social sciences and now constitute a growing and complex body of work that explores the interrelationships between identity, knowledge and power. Postcolonial feminists have stressed that the primary concern of postcolonialism is to decentre Western knowledge and the primary concern of feminism is to decentre masculinist knowledge. Accordingly they emphasize that it is imperative for postcolonialism to consider issues of gender, and point out that (Western) feminism has engaged only marginally and recently with issues of race and imperialism.

Postcolonial feminists have challenged these divisive approaches by developing theoretical frameworks for establishing and understanding the interconnection between gender, race and imperialism, by gendering postcolonial discourse and racializing feminist discourses. They raise the question, for example, of whether it is possible to frame discussions of colonialism without making any connection to gender relations. Postcolonial feminist theory offers a critique that is relevant to development studies since it demands a rethinking of how other places and people are constructed and problematized, while at the same time challenging common understandings of the concepts and representations within gender and development.

Postcolonial feminists such as bell hooks (1992, 1994), Lata Mani (1989), Trinh Minh-Ha (1987, 1989), Chandra Mohanty (1991, 1992) and Gayatri Spivak (1988, 1993) have engaged directly with issues of representation by exploring the ways in which Third World people are presented. Spivak (quoted in Lazarus, 1994, p. 206) argues that those involved in the representation of others often decontextualize cultural practices and mask their own position and agency. While these discussions have been taking place primarily in the field of literary criticism they have particular relevance to the study and practice of development. They have recently entered debates in development through, for example, discourses on participation, alternative development and postdevelopment (see Pieterse, 1998). The role of development 'experts' has been challenged, and attempts have been made to consider the importance of local knowledge and 'grassroots' movements (see Oakley, 1991; Chambers, 1992, 1997). These issues are most clearly seen with the emergence of participatory approaches to development, or more specifically the tools and techniques of participatory rural appraisal (PRA). Broadly,

> the aim of participatory development came is to increase the involvement of socially and economically marginalised people in decision-making over their own lives. The assumption is that participatory approaches empower local people with the skills and confidence to analyze their situation, reach consensus, make decisions and take action, so as to improve their circumstances. The ultimate goal is more equitable and sustainable development (Guijt and Shah, 1998, p. 1).

Whilst participatory approaches are considered an alternative approach to development, encouraging 'learning reversals', critics suggest that they have become yet another authoritative discourse that is often practiced in ways that conceal the agency of the 'outsider' or 'expert' and reinforce unequal power relations (Mosse, 1997; Stirrat, 1997; Cooke and Kothari, 2001).

These problems are more generally addressed by Gayatri Spivak, who writes that the marginalized are often silenced by the conventions and modes of representation that characterize contemporary academic writing, and that the very act of inscription by the 'saviours of marginality' robs them of their voice. The implications of this for development is that the processes and experiences of marginalization become another object for investigation (Spivak, 1990); 'we congratulate ourselves on our specialist knowledge of them' and in this way become experts on other people's lives (Spivak, 1988).

Within development studies, Robert Chambers (1997) has written about the problematic role of the 'insider' and 'outsider' but continues to ignore the historical and cultural location of the 'expert', who cannot shake off this status by adopting a few participatory techniques, and has been criticized for ignoring political power relations (Brown, 1998). Jane Parpart's (1995) interpretation of the development expert reminds us of the close connection between control over knowledge and assertions of power. She writes:

> Western scientific knowledge was presented as universally valid and consequently applicable to all, but not everyone qualified as an expert. Increasingly, only the 'properly' initiated could claim this title, and it is these 'experts' who came to play a pivotal role in the

process of collecting, controlling and transferring scientific knowledge between North and South (ibid., p. 223).

Issues of representation have frequently had recourse to discourses of 'race' and its intersection with gender. In their seminal account, Valerie Amos and Pratibha Parmar (1984) challenged many of the theoretical conceptualizations and descriptions of black and Third World women that existed in what they called 'white feminist literature'. These critiques were extended by Kum-Kum Bhavnani and Margaret Coulson in *Feminist Review* (1986; see also Mirza, 1997). Their arguments focus on the inability of Western feminist theory to speak about the experiences of black women in any meaningful way. They write that the failure of many white feminists to acknowledge the differences between themselves and black and Third World women has contributed to the predominantly Eurocentric and ethnocentric theories of women's oppression. They go on to identify different experiences between black and white women around conceptualizations of the family, household and sexuality.

A number of Third World feminists have furthered this argument by suggesting that even in these critiques there is a tendency to construct Third World women as an undifferentiated group, and in this way they 'colonize the material and historical heterogeneities of the lives of women in the third world, thereby producing/re-presenting a composite, singular "third world woman"' (Mohanty, 1991, p. 53). Development studies is replete with texts that present as homogeneous diverse groups of people and practices, such as books on agriculture in South Asia or gender relations in Sub-Saharan Africa.

To return to the earlier discussion, we are again reminded of how particular power relations and forms of knowledge prevalent in colonial times are apparent in strands of contemporary development discourse, including gendered and racial distinctions:

> in drawing racial, sexual and class boundaries in terms of social, spatial and symbolic distance, and actually formulating these as integral to the maintenance of colonial rule, the British defined authority and legitimacy through the difference rather than commonality of rulers and 'native' (ibid., p. 10).

The process by which colonial rule was legitimized was grounded in the construction of colonized 'others', utilizing a discourse of race and gender whereby colonized people were defined as incapable of self-government (ibid.), inherently predisposed to wantonness and irresponsibility, and possessing childlike characteristics. Colonized men were emasculated yet conceived of as wild, and women were eroticized but also imagined as dangerous (Kabbani, 1986). These absurd boundaries and distinctions, marking the power relations between colonizer and colonized, continue to be played out and reinscribed across academic disciplines, including development, where postcolonial gendered assumptions are often more subtle and nuanced, but no less pernicious.

The gender and development approach is far from immune to highly racialized preconceptions (see Kothari, 1997). While the necessity to challenge dominant development approaches from a gender perspective is unquestionable, the way in which much of the gender and development discourse is formulated and the way in which Third World people, particularly women are represented is problematic; a thread of power and domination emerges in the very discourse it seeks to challenge by being conscripted into the language it disclaims. The experiences and struggles of Third World women are often appropriated and fitted into Western conceptual frameworks, and interpreted according to Western benchmarks. Moreover the tendency to construct a singular category – 'woman' – to suggest a commonality of oppression fails to distinguish between the varied histories and imbalances of power among women. Furthermore it is difficult to speak of women's agency and empowerment when some development writers present Third World women as 'benighted, overburdened beasts, helplessly entangled in the tentacles of regressive "Third World" patriarchy' (Parpart, 1989). As Crush (1995, p. 21) says, this (gendered and orientalist) imaginary of poverty, powerlessness and vulnerability is readily captured in development discourse.

Despite the prevalence of highly racialized and gendered discourses within development there has been an ongoing challenge to these representations. Miranda Miles and Jonathan Crush (1993) have tried to show how life histories or personal narratives have methodological potential 'as a way of recovering hidden histories, contesting academic androcentrism, and reinstating the marginalised and disposed as makers of their own past'. Others have engaged with the critiques presented by postcolonialism by presenting the voices of the marginalized in specialized texts (Townsend *et al.*, 1995) or through discussions that challenge the centrality of particular forms of (white, masculinist) knowledge (Radcliffe, 1994). However, as Sara Suleri

(1993) reminds us, we need to be alert to the dangers of romanticizing the marginalized in our critique of forms of representation. Suleri is wary of the 'coalition between postcolonial and feminist theories, in which each term serves to reify the potential pietism of the other' (ibid., p. 274). She resents the 'Third World woman' being invested with an iconicity that is almost 'too good to be true'. This reminds us that while many writings on race, gender and colonialism provide a challenge to dominant (masculinist and racialized) views, they are in danger of reproducing the very notions and practices they aim to critique.

Rethinking Interpretations and Representations in Development

Those articulating a gender and development discourse have had some success in challenging the construction and presentation of masculinist knowledge and the sorts of power relations that are constituted through it, while others have successfully challenged the colonial constructions of knowledge and the Eurocentric bias in development. There remains, however, a need to bring together the discourses of feminism and postcolonialism that remain partial (Gandhi, 1998). It is further recognized that what is required is an extension of the inquiry into the discursive possibilities presented by the intersection of race, gender and imperialism, and a strategic engagement between feminist and postcolonialist thought that will transcend both perspectives rather than simply seek an alliance between them. This has important implications in that the different but interconnected strands of critique can come together to challenge more rigorously the male and Western orthodoxy within development.

It is increasingly clear that while development studies does have roots in a colonial past, the discipline now contains diverse political strands that constitute 'conflicting intellectual currents' (Crush, 1995, p. 8). Despite the continuing hegemony of the principles of modernization theory, there is now a growing body of intellectual resources, debate and people within the discipline with the potential to decentre masculinist and colonial thinking. These critiques interrogate and disrupt the assumptions made about knowledge, power and practice within development. This concerns not only the construction and universalization of particular forms of knowledge but also the processes by which this knowledge should be translated, interpreted and disseminated. However, while it may be increasingly unacceptable to allow the authority of colonial and masculinist discourses to go unchallenged, the production of other kinds of knowledge requires a more rigorous engagement with the ideas and workings of power, given that the production of knowledge is inseparable from the exercise of power.

The implications of the more theoretical critiques identified above on development policy and practice have been various. Some of the issues raised here have become part of the mainstream within development and in the process have lost the sharp edge of their radical origins. For example participatory or bottom-up approaches to development in which local knowledge is recognized and valorized, and through which people can become empowered, have been widely adopted in the development aid industry in much the same way as approaches to gender were incorporated in an apparent attempt to reduce gender inequalities. The problem here is that the ways in which these ideas are interpreted and the form in which they are integrated often, somewhat paradoxically, reduce the potential power that their marginality afforded them, in much the same way as other critical discourses became watered down when they were co-opted into the mainstream. The ideas are transformed and disseminated through policy and practice in ways that often make their radical origins unrecognizable, and they are implemented in ways that reinforce rather than challenge the orthodoxy. Furthermore the target of the critique has to be the persistent dominance of masculinist and Eurocentric notions, constructions and forms of knowledge, and not just the tinkering around with methodological tools and techniques, since unpacking these discourses constitutes a fundamental point of departure for questioning the categories and assumptions of male and Western thought.

Development theory and practice have not yet seriously engaged with the arguments of many feminist and postcolonial scholars. Part of the reason for this may be that those engaged in the implementation of development see themselves primarily as practitioners, and therefore have little use for (meta) theory. At the same time the emphasis on case studies and micro-level social relations and social differentiation makes each case unique and too complex to permit generalization or the construction of concepts of broader applicability. Thus we do not yet know what a decolonized, demasculinized development will actually look like (see Crush in Smith, 1994).

4

Social Development: Issues and Approaches

MAIA GREEN

Introducing Social Development

This chapter explores the evolution and preliminary impact of social development as an evolving field within development discourse and practice. Understanding and assessing the social impacts of development policies and programmes requires the combination of sound analytical skills with an awareness of the complex causal factors that drive development outcomes and social change in various settings. Social development as a discipline is emerging to meet this need, and its profile is increasing as agencies conventionally associated with economistic conceptions of development have publicly come to acknowledge the importance of a people-centred approach to poverty reduction. The World Bank now accepts that many of the key approaches to development pursued since the 1950s have failed. Its Comprehensive Development Framework recognizes the importance of social institutions and processes in meeting human needs (World Bank, 2000, pp. 1–21), and the World Development report for 2001 takes the idea of the social as the starting point from which to 'attack' poverty (World Bank, 2000).

But what is social development? During the 1990s the term shifted away from a narrowly welfarist conception of social policy for basic needs and came to refer to three related aspects of development policy and practice. Firstly, in general terms social development conventionally refers to planned development outcomes that prioritize social impacts, often through the social sectors of health and education. This conception of social development informs the setting of targets for social impact, focusing on such indicators as levels of maternal mortality and participation in primary education. Social development in another sense has come to refer to what amounts to an emerging professional discipline within development practice.[1] As a professional discipline social development claims to have the analytical capacities and tools to inform development policy, planning and implementation across all sectors in order to enhance social impacts. Consequently social development as a development specialization is not confined to social sectors or social policy concerns. The starting point for a socially aware approach to development is explicit recognition that *all* policies and programmes have social dimensions and implications across *all* sectors (Eyben, 1998). Finally, social development can also refer to an evolving interdisciplinary academic specialization that aims to combine an analytical understanding of development processes with a postmodern reflexivity in order critically to reflect on practice and contribute to its evolution and impact.

The Social Development Paradigm

In line with current policies that prioritize poverty elimination and the meeting of international development targets (OECD, 1996), the current aim of social development input to development planning and implementation is to ensure that poor and vulnerable groups either benefit directly from development interventions or – where interventions are not targeted specifically at the poor – are not disadvantaged and made poorer as a result of their engagement with development processes.[2]

Derived from an eclectic mix of social anthropology, social policy and development studies, with some adapted versions of development administration and management tools thrown in for good measure, social development currently stands ambiguously between classification as a discipline and classification as professional practice. Social development is a professional rather than academic discipline in the sense that it exists primarily within the professional world of development organizations. Although taught and recognized within academic settings, social development specialists tend to be practitioners too and work within institutes, such as the UK's Institute of Development Studies or Norway's Christien Michelsen Institute, which are heavily engaged in providing services to development agencies. Despite claims to international relevance, the centres of excellence and innovation in social development are currently situated in the West, as with other specialisms in development studies, although core aspects

---

Box 4.1   *Themes in the UK Department for International Development's Social Development Work*

1. Directing assistance to poor and vulnerable people for greater livelihood security.
2. Promoting the achievement of equality between women and men in partner countries by mainstreaming work to achieve equality between women and men in all development cooperation efforts, and supporting specific and focused initiatives to enhance women's empowerment.
3. Supporting very poor and marginalized individuals through appropriate safety net provisions that promote social and economic reestablishment and reintegration.
4. Protecting and strengthening social capital in order to ɪɴ reduce desirable developmental outcomes.
5. Strengthening policy reform by addressing the needs and interests of poor and vulnerable groups.
6. Promoting and protecting the human rights of women, children, ethnic minorities and vulnerable groups such as the elderly or those with disabilities.
7. Promoting social responsibility in business by supporting civil society movements (such as ethical consumerism) and private sector initiatives to improve practice.

Source: Eyben (1998, p. 2)

---

of social development practice are carried out in other countries under the auspices of social sector and gender programming.

While there is general consensus across agencies and academic institutions about what social development practitioners might do in terms of the assessment of social processes and key areas of interest, including poverty, social exclusion and gender, there are no accepted theories or bodies of empirical research that provide the foundation for social development practice. Current key approaches in social development are little more than policy statements about desired outcomes, and the assertions of causality at the heart of social processes are little more than speculation. Much of what is presented as social development knowledge, for example the purported relation between social capital and development or between participation and project impact,[3] is neither derived from specific studies nor based on evidence. Where examples are cited to justify certain approaches in the social development literature and agency documents they are often based on very localized case studies that rely on qualitative perceptions of situations, often articulated through the words of specific local individuals.

While such techniques can give voice and authenticity to the views of local informants, the reader must take it on trust that the individuals cited are somehow representative of those on whose behalf it is claimed they speak. Such representational devices also mask the absence of thoroughgoing social and economic research. The credibility accorded the comparative desk study as a significant contribution to social development research is explained by the role of agencies in commissioning both the studies themselves and the documents on which they are based, rather than an indication of their potential contribution to an evidence-based social policy.

Like other aspects of development discourse, much of social development thinking is in actuality specifically – if implicitly – ideological, presenting a particular view of what constitutes 'development' and of the kinds of social institution and process that may facilitate or hinder its achievement (c.f. Ferguson, 1990; Hobart, 1993; Escobar, 1995). This lack of both theoretical sophistication and a tried and tested body of knowledge on which to base effective practice enables social development to universalize hypothetical processes, and to work from the premise that certain kinds of social outcome are globally achievable through what are represented as universally implementable inputs, for example fostering participation or strengthening civil society. The analytical weakness of the current social development approaches has serious implications for the effectiveness of social development interventions and of the analyses that inform them. Some of the limitations of the current social development paradigm are explored more fully in this chapter.

Institutional Contexts

Social development as a discipline is still evolving and has yet to solidify in terms of content or analytic approach. Given the importance of policy environments in determining its focus and orientation, it is likely to remain an essentially adaptive discipline, or at least in the short term, developing tools and approaches in response to changing policy concerns. Social development as a professional practice is equally dynamic, although longer established in different institutional forms within key agencies, such as UK's Department for International Development (DFID), the Swedish International Development Agency (SIDA) and the World Bank.

The recruitment of social development specialists by bilateral and multilateral agencies has grown exponentially since the mid 1990s from what was essentially a limited position overseeing issues such as gender and marginality to a more mainstream role of providing advice on social impacts across a broad spectrum of agency activity. Agencies such as the DFID have taken the lead in redefining the scope and role of social development both within and outside the agency. Within the DFID social development advisers are involved in all programming, irrespective of sector, as well as managing their own programmes that are directly concerned with what the agency defines as specifically social development objectives.

Between 1990 and 2000 the number of social development advisers employed by the agency increased from around 12 to 60 (Gardner and Lewis, 2000, p. 24; Stirrat, 2000). Social development professionals are regularly employed as both long- and short-term consultants. As part of an ongoing drive to foster the consolidation of social development capacity in partner organizations the DFID has either seconded or directly recruited social development staff for UN bodies, including the ILO and UNDP. It is also providing funding to institutions in developing countries for the promotion of social development research and capacity building. The social development specialists at the DFID are institutionally equivalent to members of the other professional advisory groups that are represented on project management teams, and what are known internally as 'cross-cutting' advisers are involved in the appraisal of all programmes, along with economists and specialists in institutional development.

Other agencies have yet fully to integrate social development staff into project administration and management. However most bilateral agencies, including USAID, now employ specialists to analyze social and cultural issues cross-sectorally. SIDA is currently considering ways to increase the effectiveness and impact of its social development capacity by means of possible transformations in institutional structure. And although NGOs are less likely to have specialists dealing specifically with social development issues, the clear orientation of many NGOs towards what are currently defined as social development objectives means that NGO staff may be more likely in practice to perceive the social dimensions of development as integral to their work, irrespective of sector, than staff in bilateral and multilateral organizations.

This recent history of expansion suggests that social development as a professional category within development is here to stay. Whether this will have a significant impact on development outcomes remains open to question. Various factors currently constrain the potential impact of social development within development at all levels, the most critical being the absence in agencies and partner countries alike of a clear commitment to the achievement of particular kinds of social outcome, not merely as a means to economic improvement, but as ends in themselves (c.f. Thin *et al.*, 1998).

Despite the formal acknowledgement of the social, the economistic paradigm remains dominant in development (Eyben, 2000; Stirrat, 2000). It is likely to remain so as long as the actual processes – social, political and economic – that drive development-oriented change are so little understood. As long as social development continues to be associated with specific social categories and issues it is likely to remain marginalized within agency structures and within the content of policy. A recent comparative study of social development across key European agencies concluded that:

> In all agencies reviewed, 'social policy' and 'social development' advisory work and the policies and guidelines associated with them are concerned primarily with basic needs provision, with poverty, safety nets, 'social sectors', and specific categories of disadvantaged people. ... This means that both the discussion of social development and its specialists and policies are negatively associated with needs and costs rather than capacities and benefits (Thin *et al.*, 1998, p. 10).

If social development is to fulfil its potential as a key to understanding and achieving socially beneficial transformation it must refine its analytical tools and adopt a more holistic approach to the interpretation of social processes. Moreover social development professionals must be prepared to climb out of the poverty trap associated with a narrow emphasis on social categories and stake a claim to the central institutional space from which a contribution to broader policy outcomes can be made. This entails diversification on the part of social development practitioners and greater attention to economic and institutional issues, as well as macro policy concerns.

Development with a Human Face?

Although the evolution of social development as a specialization within development practice is a product of the past two decades, social development as a particular kind of expertise has a longer history in development planning and implementation. British colonial administrators charged with local level development in Asia and Africa studied social science subjects, including anthropology, as part of their basic training. In the US, what came to be known as applied anthropology became a recognized field allied to the development of social policies for marginal and indigenous groups as early as the 1930s (Gardner and Lewis, 1996, p. 31). Sociologists, demographers and anthropologists have provided input to the UK's official programme of development assistance on a contractual basis in both the colonial and postcolonial periods.

Early social analytical work and background studies were oriented towards the identification of specifically local or cultural factors that it was thought could constitute risks to the achievement of particular project objectives (Gardner and Lewis, 1996). Social outcomes were neither prioritized in development planning nor identified through social analysis, but were expected to occur as a consequence of project implementation. Development was held to lead to improved wealth and reduced poverty. It was thought that the benefits of modernization would eventually 'trickle down' and ensure that the excluded achieved what modernist-influenced developers believed to be a better kind of life (Escobar, 1995). The growing inequalities of the 1970s and the evident failure of the paradigm of progress led to a gradual, if delayed, reevaluation of development policy and practice by multilateral and bilateral agencies, together with the realization that the social implications of economic policies were not necessarily beneficial, particularly for the poorest. Economic growth did not automatically lead to poverty reduction. Adjustment, and economics, had a human face (Hill, 1986; Cornia *et al.*, 1987; Killick, 1995).

The human face of development was formally recognized in the new set of development indicators first released by the UNDP in 1990. Rather than focusing on the familiar econometric indicators of gross national product and national debt, the human development indicators aimed to provide qualitative proxies for human wellbeing, as well as a range of more instrumental proxies for participation in the development process. These included levels of maternal mortality and literacy rates. The achievement of what was defined as human development was not coterminous with economic growth but was seen to depend on the kinds of policy choice pursued by developing country governments. Poor countries that ensured that the bulk of the population had access to basic services in education and health, or human rights, could score relatively highly on the index. Better-off countries whose public spending was skewed towards the rich or which had a poor record in human rights could not.

Putting Poverty on the Agenda

By 1990, despite the successes claimed for adjustment in many countries, addressing poverty was the stated priority of multilateral and bilateral agencies and the unifying theme of that year's *World Development Report* (World Bank, 1990). Now perceived as the multifaceted and complex outcome of a range of variables depending on context, defining poverty was problematic. New insights derived not from formal social science but from the techniques of participatory rural appraisal, emphasized the importance of the qualitative dimensions of poverty for the vulnerable (Chambers, 1983). What was defined as the 'New Poverty Agenda' started from the recognition that social exclusion and disempowerment were as much a part of being poor in some areas as living below the poverty line, and in many cases had a more deleterious impact. The poor were not a homogeneous group in any context. Differential access to resources amongst the poor characterized social relations even at the household level, where gender and age constituted axes along which inequality was enacted and maintained (IDS, 1996a).

The evident failure of economistic models of development along with increasing awareness of the complexities of effecting the kind of social transformations conducive, as opposed to deleterious, to human development contributed to the creation of an environment in which social development both as a discipline and as a practice could flourish. However the institutional location of social development and its initial policy-determined concerns, while innovative at first, may have limited its potential to challenge development orthodoxies and inform development outcomes.

Social Development Assumptions and Approaches

Social development as a specific kind of development input was initially concerned with quite narrowly defined issues relating to poverty and marginality, involved specific social categories of people.[4] The perceived association between women's lower status and poverty made gender relations a legitimate focal point for social development concerns, along with what were categorized as vulnerable groups. The 'vulnerable' category in development discourse has been expanded to include various groups whose apparent plight has become, through UN conventions, a focus of international attention, such as children, minorities (including indigenous peoples) and the disabled (see Box 4.1 above).

The initial focus on specific groups that were perceived as vulnerable has encouraged an emphasis on strategies for including the poorest in the benefits of development, although much of this is confined to the level of policy analysis rather than practical intervention. Paradoxically it has also contributed to the institutional marginalization of social development within development agencies and discourse. Despite the best intentions of mainstreaming, as long as poverty and marginality are viewed both as minority issues and as the preserve of specialists, the chance of their being addressed through appropriate policy and interventions is slight. Furthermore some of the tools and approaches promoted by social development may foster a kind of social analysis that is so divorced from the broader political and economic processes that it is too limited to capture the complexity of the social constraints and motivations that one way or another affect development outcomes.

Part of this stems from the need in development to provide a range of simple and straightforward methodologies that are accessible to specialists and non-specialists alike. However there are risks to such an approach. Simple tools may oversimplify the complex range of factors that influence social processes and social actors. They may also foster the impression that specifically 'developmental' social outcomes are easily programmable through development interventions as long as developers are equipped with the right tools. In reality, of course, this is not the case. Social change of any sort is rarely attributable to single factors. It is highly unlikely to be caused directly by development interventions, particularly at the project level (c.f. Thin *et al.*, 1998, p. 13).

While different agencies have slightly different conceptions of what constitutes social development and the uses to which it is put, a clear consensus about the kinds of approach it promotes and the issues these approaches can address is evident in the agency literature. Current social development *issues* encompass poverty, equity and gender. Current *approaches* include participatory techniques for planning, appraisal and impact assessment, stakeholder analysis and the identification of local institutions through which the disadvantaged can achieve what they have defined as their own development objectives.

Toolkits and Techniques

Key approaches within the current social development paradigm are aimed at analyzing and building on apparent relations of causality between particular social processes and particular social categories. Not surprisingly, given the policy-determined content of social development approaches, they are neither objective nor value free. Current approaches centre on an implicit hypothesis on human development in which poverty is viewed in qualitative as well as quantitative terms, encompassing factors such as empowerment and rights. Eliminating poverty therefore depends not merely on the achievement of basic livelihood security and reducing the vulnerability of the poorest of the poor, but on securing access to human rights and empowering the poor to participate in development.[5]

Social development approaches in general constitute a commitment to specific techniques for the analysis and transformation of social relations among target groups, rather than general social analytical tools that could situate a target category within a wider socioeconomic context. But because social development takes as its starting point particular social categories, rather than society in general, and because it privileges certain kinds of social process as potentially leading to development outcomes, the current approaches tend to promote analyses that purport to universalize the social dimensions of development, obscuring the actual context-specific processes through which particular development outcomes may or may not occur.

Specific social contexts are not necessarily determined at the local level but by the socioeconomic environment in its totality. Accurate and effective social analysis of any local situation must take into account the impact of policy contexts and macro-level influences, as well as the meso-level institutional structures through which they are operationalized at various intermediary levels (Green, 2000). Moreover, despite the prioritization on the social, because social development tends to focus on a single group or category in isolation, actual relationships between social groups and categories are underplayed in practice, leading to a simplified understanding of the dynamics of relationships between different categories of people, for example between rich and poor, or men and women.

Different kinds of asset and capital contribute to the livelihoods of different people in different proportions in different places. Securing a livelihood may entail building up capital reserves, or investing in the necessary social and human capital to enable poor communities and individuals within them to transform their own lives and livelihoods. While the importance of wider macro policy and enabling environments is recognized, the burden of getting out of poverty and changing lives falls firmly on the poor, albeit through the intermediary structures of development agencies, NGOs and interventions. Much of this kind of paradigm is centred on a vision of the poor in developing countries as rural and village based, although this view is changing as urban poverty becomes a key priority for the World Bank and other agencies that are keen to legitimate the global decentralization agenda. However the enduring image of the poor is of tight-knit, culturally bound rural communities in which women are marginalized and people have a natural propensity to act collectively in a bid to seek solutions to local development problems. As we shall see below when we discuss social capital, communities that challenge this representation of themselves are considered to lack what is viewed as a key asset needed for development to occur, as having the wrong kind of social relations and institutions.

Engendering Change

In this conception of poverty, gender looms large as a key target for development outcomes and interventions. The recent effort to acknowledge the relational dynamic of gender as a relation between men and women that changes with age and status has informed the policy transition from a 'women in development' (WID) approach to a 'gender and development' (GAD) approach across key agencies (Goetz, 1997). In practice social development approaches to gender, mediated through the conservative structures of developing-country governments and activist women's lobby groups, remain woman-focused and static. Gender continues to be perceived as essentially a women's issue, contributing to women's disempowerment and poverty, despite the fact that in some instances only certain categories of women are disempowered relative to men, or are even truly poor (Cornwall, 1997; Jackson, 1996, 1997).

What is referred to as 'gender analysis' tends to be limited to a deconstruction of what men and women do in society, rather than a more sophisticated exploration of the axes of inequality and exclusion, including such factors as class, caste, age, education, ownership of resources and, significantly, individual agency and the willingness (or otherwise) to conform. Overemphasis on women distorts the social and political realities facing men and women alike as they struggle, often together, to maintain their livelihoods and secure a future for their children. While intrahousehold inequality and domestic violence are serious problems in many countries and communities, changing women's lives for the better depends as much on changing the attitudes of women towards women and girls as it does on changing men's perceptions and behaviour. A classic example of this can be found in northern India, where unconscious discrimination against girl children by their female kin and carers results in substantially higher rates of infant mortality for girls than for their male siblings (Jackson, 1996). Developers' perceptions of men also need challenging. The standard assumption that men in rural Africa do little work and live off the labour of women is not as straightforward as the literature suggests, and may in fact be downright misleading (Whitehead and Lockwood, 1999a).

As with debates and policies based on the assumed positive relation between democratization and economic growth, policies that assume that getting women into positions of power will lead to the kind of policy making that benefits poorer women may be hopelessly misguided. Studies undertaken in Kenya, for example, seem to suggest that the promotion of already elite women to positions of power in governmental and civil organizations does not automatically have an impact on gender relations. Indeed elite women are likely to pursue their own interests, which may not be related to gender, while continuing to provide the kind of low-paid, often exploitative employment opportunities for poor women in the domestic sector with which they have long been associated (Aubrey, 1998). Similarly while the distinction between practical and strategic gender 'needs', as proposed by Moser (1989, 1993), has been an asset to policy makers and planners, enabling them to differentiate between interventions that assist women immediately but that will not transform gender relations and interventions aimed at the latter, much gender programming still homogenizes women as a category associated with the domestic, irrespective of life cycle and aspirations, and assumes unrealistically that the transformation of formal sector institutions is the way to achieve gender equality (Goetz, 1997).

Projects and Process

Part of the limitation of social development approaches to gender has been a lack of attention to the contexts in which the processes of transformation are expected to occur, as opposed to the kinds of desired transformation that the intervention is expected to promote. This means that planners and policy makers are often unaware of key factors that may or may not contribute to changing gender relations in specific contexts, and they have little understanding of the broader processes of social change in which development interventions come to be embedded. Similar difficulties are faced by social development approaches in general, which tend to focus on desired or projected change from a snapshot, present-bound analysis of social relations, rather than an historically informed understanding of specific social and economic histories and cultural trends.

The historicism of this approach is partly the consequence of a project mentality in development that *projects* outcomes from an assumed base, and partly the consequence of a tendency to privilege what are seen as technical and universally applicable skills in social development over country- or region-specific knowledge and expertise. The consequence is an impoverished understanding of the social processes involved in change outside the narrow confines of a project at the abstract level, and – despite the new emphasis on development as a 'process' – the confinement in practice of the recognition of process not merely to the analytical boundaries of a 'project' or programme, but to externally initiated interventions.

Stakeholder Analysis or Social Transformation?

The problem of static representation of social relations is exemplified by one of the key project tools of social development, routinely used by some agencies as part of social assessment at various stages of the project cycle. The perhaps optimistically labelled 'stakeholder analysis' is a technique that aims to make explicit the relations between the various social categories and institutions that will be affected, either positively or negatively, by a project. Based on explicit recognition that a wide range of people and institutions have much to lose or gain from particular projects and have a legitimate stake in their future direction, stakeholder analysis seeks to differentiate between different categories of stakeholder in relation to project outcomes and impacts. Primary stakeholders are those whom a project seeks to benefit, either directly or indirectly. Secondary stakeholders are those – primarily agencies and institutions – with a specific role in project implementation (ODA, 1995b).

Stakeholder analysis usually takes the form of a diagrammatic representation of stakeholder groups in relation to the project, as opposed to each other, at a fixed moment in time. Generally conducted as part of an appraisal at the beginning of the project cycle, the analysis identifies key groups with an interest in the project and assesses the extent to which the individual groups might jeopardize or contribute to the project's success. Different categories of stakeholder may be classified as important or influential. In the words of the DFID's former chief social development adviser:

Influential stakeholders are those who can make a significant impact on project outcomes. These may for example, include government officials, local community leaders and the donor agency. Important stakeholders are those whose rights, interests and needs are central to project goals, for example poor women, or out-of-school children. *Stakeholder analysis can be the first step to identifying ways of helping important stakeholders become more influential* (Eyben, 1998, p. 4, emphasis added).

Although stakeholder analysis should in theory be accompanied by a narrative account of the interrelationship between the stakeholders and the proposed project, it often degenerates into a checklist of social categories and institutions whose interests may or may not conflict with the developers' intentions. In analyzing stakeholder relationships in relation to the project, rather than to each other, it fails to capture the social context of which the project will become part, overemphasizing the significance of the project on social relations while excluding consideration of other factors that are equally or more likely to promote changes during the same period. These factors will remain obscure as long as stakeholder analysis ignores the processes that have contributed to the relative positions of stake-holder groups *vis-à-vis* each other. And although stakeholder analysis could theoretically permit the identification of strategies to help important stakeholders to become more influential, it is hard to see how this could occur without the transformation of relations between the stakeholders themselves – rather than between the stakeholders and the project – being a key project output.

Despite the analytical limitations of stakeholder analysis, social development approaches do recognize that the relationships between different social categories are fundamental to the constitution of the specific kinds of social relations they seek to address. More nuanced understandings of poverty as a social relation, rather than an absolute condition, are informing work on social exclusion and inclusion (de Haan, 1999), leading towards the design of specific policy instruments that will prioritize social transformation as a desirable developmental goal. The Social Development Summit held in Copenhagen in 1995 explicitly situated the achievement of social inclusion within a rights-based framework with the assertion that 'The right to development defines the right of all people to inclusion in economic, social, cultural and political development' (OECD, 1996).

Social transformation is beginning to be viewed, mainly within NGOs and civil organizations, as a social development end in itself. This perspective is highly contested and most agencies continue to regard such an outcome as either complementary or instrumental to the achievement of sustainable economic growth (see Narayan, 1997; World Bank, 2000). As is so often the case, relationships between means and ends and imputations of causality are not necessarily what they are represented as being. Transforming social relations through project interventions or policy prescriptions is not particularly straightforward. As with stakeholder analysis, any approach that ignores wider contexts and flows of influence is risking failure in its own terms, although unintended outcomes may have significant effects on social relations, some of which are beneficial. Indeed studies such as Ferguson's (1990) account of the unanticipated out-comes of a development project in Lesotho suggests that closer examination of unintended impacts is likely to yield greater insights into what constitute, in particular contexts, the diverse drivers of change than the assessment of planned outputs alone. This factor should be given greater attention in assessments of development impact than is currently the case (Thin *et al.*, 1998).[6]

Participating in Development

The most obvious example of this kind of transition in the perception of social relations from a means to utilizing them as an end is the changing understanding of participation as both a project tool and a key outcome of the wider processes of social and political transformation (Rahnema, 1992; Narayan and Srinivasan, 1994). Emerging out of the populist action research approaches of the 1980s through successive incarnations of PRA (Green, 2000), 'participation' as an essential component of project planning and implementation became widely institutionalized during the 1990s. Increasingly professionalized by a self-regulating cadre of experts in the facilitation of participatory planning, research and evaluation, participation at the project level is now part of the standard toolkit of development planning and implementation for governmental and non-governmental organizations alike (Cornwall and Fleming, 1995).

The limitations of project-level participation through agency structures are being increasingly recognized (see Chapter 6). Imported structures for participation, including PRA, may in practice replicate existing social divisions, be appropriated by the elite and the articulate, and exclude poorer and marginalized groups, including women (Mosse, 1994) The fact that participation does not equate to representation has implications for the quality of social analyses that use participatory techniques (Mosse *et al.*, 1995; Richards, 1995), whether at the community level or, as in the case of the more ambitious participatory poverty assessments, at the national level. Perhaps more significantly, there is a risk that participatory development at the project level, divorced from local structures of political representation and process, will foster the creation of parallel structures for participation that – in a travesty of formal agencies' commitment to transparency and accountability as the essence of good governance – will serve to depoliticize development interventions and remove them from public scrutiny at the local level (Green, 2000).

Capitalizing on Society?

Although participatory approaches remain a key component of development implementation, the shift away from a narrow project focus towards wider policy instruments combined with the post-democratization legacy of liberalization has created opportunities for the exploration of new avenues for participation. Current social development policies prioritize the strengthening of civil society as a means for the poor to participate in development, particularly at the local level, despite the fact that the key assumptions about civil society and development, as with the earlier debate on democratization, remain untried. There are a number of obvious problems with the current civil society approaches, most of which stem from the fact that civil society is not a universal category, and does not exist in the same institutional forms or have the same political potential at the global level (see for example Girling, 1996; Sampson, 1996; Tripp, 1998).

The problem of identifying civil society and grasping its potential or otherwise as a vehicle for the representation of the poor should lead to an eventual rethinking and refinement of current policy priorities. There is no doubt that the emphasis on civil society, understood in practice as comprising community-based organizations and NGOs (Clayton, 1996), fits well with the social development tradition of working with specific social categories: the marginal, the rural and the communitarian. In actuality, in many countries not only is the identification of civil society difficult, but the more formal organizations with which donors can work often represent the better off and have strong, albeit informal ties to the government (van Rooy, 1998). More representative local level groups and institutions are likely to be *ad hoc* and informal, facilitating inclusivity while avoiding co-option by the bureaucratized elites. Such institutions may well contribute to local social capital, which is increasingly seen as a precondition for sustainable development. They are also likely to be difficult for planners to co-opt through development interventions, a characteristic that accounts for the recent multiplication of projects aimed at building the capacity of local organizations through what amount to attempts to facilitate their formalization.

Indeed, while strong local institutions and relationships may provide safety nets for the very poor and foster the trust needed for economic cooperation in high-risk environments, social capital in itself cannot have an impact on development unless other preconditions are met, including the existence of appropriate enabling environments, adequate transport networks and sufficient incentives for the poor to produce for the market. While the social capital ideology places part of the responsibility for development firmly on poor people's institutions and relationships, in a discourse that could be seen as a contemporary reiteration of the culture of poverty debates, governments can and should play a key role in ensuring that the necessary preconditions for achieving local development are met at the macro- and meso-levels. Finally, the options for consolidating social capital at the community level will be restricted as long as this form of asset remains invisible and unacknowledged by the poor themselves (Booth *et al.*, 1998). The fact that social capital as an asset is visible only to outside experts who are keen to place an economic value on social institutions must render its potential and reality open to question. And in situations where local institutions are strong, local power hierarchies are likely to be equally resilient. A recent study of the role of local organizations and networks in two slum improvement projects in India and Pakistan concluded that 'it is clear that the social capital concept ignores structural issues and obscures the issue of collective power, both at the macro- and micro-levels' (Beale, 1997, pp. 959–60).

Conclusion: Rescuing the Social from the Poverty Trap?[7]

This chapter has provided a brief overview of current issues and approaches in social development. While social development has the potential to contribute to improved development outcomes, its effectiveness is limited by weak analytical tools and institutional marginality within agency settings. Moreover the absence of obvious institutions with which to work at the operational level, apart from community organizations and NGOs associated with marginal social categories, renders social development an essentially analytic discipline, rather than being a driving force in development programming. With the current move away from projects towards sector programmes and macro policy environments, this analytic orientation need not be a disadvantage. Good policy will depend on a proper understanding of the context in which it is implemented as well as on a consideration of relevant evidence on policy performance and poverty. The future effectiveness and impact of social development will depend to an extent on its ability to transcend the narrow institutional location of its origins and become truly cross-sectoral. This will in turn depend on the institutional location of social development capacity within development agencies and on the willingness of practitioners to recognize that the prioritization of social issues and institutions transcends the boundaries of social sectors and of conventionally defined target groups.

Notes

1. For a recent welfarist definition of social development see Midgley (1995). Although he recognizes the holistic aspects of social development, Midgley's definition of development prioritises top-down and state-directed efforts. Development is 'planned social change ... in conjunction with a dynamic process of economic development' (ibid., p. 25).
2. See for example the ODA's (1995a) *Guide to Social Analysis for Projects in Developing Countries*.
3. See below.
4. On the issue of how specific social groups are represented as development categories see Pigg (1992) and Shrestha (1995). On children as a specific target see Hecht (1998) and Nieuwenhuys (1999).
5. See for example the UK government's recent white paper on international development.
6. Bearing in mind the fact that attributing causality, even at project level, is not straightforward and that the perceptions of assessment teams are likely to influence the interpretation of a project's impact. See Phillips and Edwards (2000).
7. The title of this section is taken from Jackson (1996). Much of Jackson's argument concerning the marginalization of gender and gender analysis applies equally to social development and social analysis.

5

Social Capital, Civil Society and Social Exclusion

PAUL FRANCIS

From the 1980s onwards, the limitations of conventional capital and state-led then market-led approaches to development became more apparent, and attention moved to the hitherto 'missing dimension' of development: its 'human' or 'social' side.

This shift led to a search for concepts through which the social and institutional dimensions of development could be understood, measured and ultimately manipulated through their application to policy. This chapter considers three terms that have acquired particular prominence in development discourse since the early 1990s: civil society, social exclusion and social capital. The speed and enthusiasm with which these concepts have been taken up and entered policy-speak has been interpreted in some quarters as a sign that a new, broader 'paradigm' of development has been born. Others have seen their sudden rise to currency as merely a symptom of the intellectual fashion that is often said to afflict the development industry. Undeniably though, these concepts are associated with new and sometimes far-reaching thinking on a wide range of questions, including the non-economic dimensions of poverty, the role of civil associations in governance, and the importance of social networks and values in economic life. At the same time, as will become apparent, vagueness and inconsistency in definition and usage have in all three cases accompanied their absorption into development discourse.

This chapter provides an overview of these three related concepts by reviewing their definitions and origins, and critically assessing both their conceptual coherence and their utility as operational and policy tools. Because social capital is the broadest of the three concepts, has been vested with the grandest explanatory claims and has generated the greatest theoretical and policy interest, this chapter gives prominence to that concept. The next two sections deal in more summary fashion with civil society and social exclusion.

Civil Society

The term civil society generally refers to the institutions that exist between the individual on the one hand and the state and economy on the other. The term embraces both a social space and the institutions that occupy that space (sometimes known as civil society organizations). Civil society thus includes political parties, the media, trade unions and professional associations, as well as informal associations based on common interests, activities or hobbies, such as the boy scouts, environmental lobby groups or bridge clubs.

The concept of civil society has its origins in the Enlightenment of the late seventeenth and early eighteenth centuries, and is associated in particular with the thinking of Locke, Hobbes and Kant. It is thought of as a multilayered, associational sphere that is at once private and simultaneously founded in public notions of equality before the law and the right to free association (Carr, 1998).

The revival of interest in civil society in the late twentieth century can be traced to the failure of earlier development decades, to global political events in the 1990s, and to the domestic concerns of industrialized countries.

Thus conventional development efforts' limited impact on poverty reduction led development thinking towards the 'third sector' of civil associations. Non-governmental organizations were seen as more effective deliverers of development goods and services, especially to populations that were socially, politically or spatially marginal. In the 1990s the transition to capitalism in the countries of the former Soviet Union and Eastern Europe, alongside the move towards democratization in Latin America and Africa, focused attention on the role of civic engagement as a counterweight to an overweening state, if not a means to topple unaccountable governments and fill the vacuum left by their demise. Thirdly, seeing the construction of civil society as an essential component of development policy might also be viewed as a response to domestic anxiety in industrialized societies, where civic engagement was declining at the very time that the rolling back of the state meant it was being looked to to play a greater role.

Hence the development of a 'healthy, vibrant civil society', as it is often called, has come to be seen – along with elections, the rule of law and good governance – as an essential component of the agenda for governance and democratization (see Chapter 7). The development of civil society was the object of substantial bilateral assistance in the 1990s. This was particularly marked in the case of the US development industry. One of the aims of UK assistance has been to 'spread the values of civil liberties and democracy, rule of law and good governance, and foster the growth of a vibrant and secure civil society.' (Department for International Development, 1997, paragraph 3.50)

Multilaterals, too, have in recent years begun to work more closely with groups in civil society. For example NGOs, churches and trades unions have been increasingly consulted at some stage in the formulation of the World Bank's country strategies and programmes. In addition, NGO/civil society liaison officers have been appointed to many of the World Bank's country offices over the last few years. Interviewed in advance of the 2000 annual meeting, the World Bank's vice president for the environment noted: 'now in nearly every country we have somebody whose sole job it is to work with local groups'. The private sector's way of engaging campaigning groups is increasingly seen by the Bank as providing a model for its own relations with critics. According to the vice president, 'the best companies in the next 20 to 30 years will be those that not only know how to manage their finances, but know how to relate to the societies in which they work' (*Financial Times*, 22 September 2000).

The notion of civil society has served as a useful construct for orienting and advancing a range of policies and operational initiatives, ranging from increased public consultation to the contracting of voluntary organizations for service delivery. However its usage also gives rise to a number of conceptual and operational difficulties. Three of these will be discussed here: the breadth of the concept, its occidental origins, and the potentially distorting role of external support.

The most fundamental problem is the very latitude of the notion of civil society. It is difficult to generalize about or develop a coherent strategy for a sphere that includes trade associations, political parties, burial societies, sports clubs and much more. Furthermore the contribution of some of its constituent groups to the public interest may be doubtful. Civil society is not only a heterogeneous field, but also a fragmented and conflictual one. As Fowler (1997, p. 7) explains, the implications of support in these circumstances are that '[i]n the short run, strengthening civil society is as likely to increase social tensions as to reduce them because more voices are better able to stake their claim to public resources and policies.'

The second concern is the cultural specificity of the concept of civil society. It is arguable that the notion is specific to the developed world, or even the Atlantic rim in the modern period. If this is so, making the development of civil society a core development objective risks, at best, inappropriateness and, at worst, imposing a form of cultural imperialism.

In practice development agencies have been selective in their support for civil society organizations, tending to sponsor urban-based organizations that are able to articulate aspirations that echo the agencies' own conceptions of progressive social change. On the basis of an extensive review of aid to civil society in South Africa, Ghana and Uganda, for example, Hearn (1999, p. 4) argues that:

> Foreign support to civil society in all three African countries is not about the breadth and depth of actually existing, largely rural-based civil society. Donors are not funding the popular sectors of society, but are strengthening a new African elite committed to the promotion of a limited form of procedural democracy and structural-adjustment-type economic policies in partnership with the West.

Even accepting the case that an active civil society is an essential precondition for development this tells us little about how the appropriate range of institutions that make up this sector can be nurtured. In particular there is a danger that external funding, far from contributing to the health of civil society, may create dependency among local partners and undermine institutional sustainability. As assessments of the impact of development assistance on NGOs have revealed, external resources and influence have their dark side in the distortion and domestication of more radical agendas, as accountability to the external sponsor expands at the expense of responsiveness to the grass roots (Hulme and Edwards, 1997). It could be argued that such a process is close to the reverse of the local rootedness and accountability that make civil society a positive force for development.

Social Exclusion

Social exclusion has been defined as 'the process through which individuals or groups are wholly or partially excluded from full participation in the society within which they live' (European Foundation, 1995, p. 4, quoted in de Haan, 1998).

This concept emerged in policy discourse in France in the mid-1970s, was adopted by the European Union in the late 1980s as a key concept in social policy, and has been influential in the social policy of the UK government elected in 1997. Social exclusion has been applied to developing countries, most notably in a series of studies undertaken by the ILO's International Institute for Labour Studies (IILS) under the rubric 'patterns and causes of social exclusion and the design of policies to promote integration' (Gore and Figueiredo, 1997).

Three questions are important when assessing the concept of social exclusion. First, how does it differ from that of 'poverty'? Second, what does it add to our understanding of deprivation? Third, does it increase our capacity to address such social ills? In distinction to poverty, which has primarily been thought about in economic terms, social exclusion encompasses deprivation in a number of spheres, of which low income is but one. Insecurity of employment, lack of access to health care, lack of social networks and inability to gain access to judicial fora are recognized as equally debilitating. The encapsulation of the multifaceted character of social deprivation, especially its institutional and cultural aspects, is one of the main strengths of social exclusion as a concept. The concept also suggests the way in which these levels of deprivation interlock as economic, spatial, cultural and psychological factors reinforce each other in causing poverty and making it so difficult to escape.

It has been argued that the application of social exclusion to Southern societies is indicative of a convergence of social policy between North and South as a result of globalization and international migration (Maxwell, 1998). Poverty and deprivation in industrialized countries is increasing as the poor and marginalized in every country come to constitute an emerging 'Fourth World' (Castells, 1998).

The spatial analogy of inclusion and exclusion is compelling, yet the apparent simplicity of its dualism can be misleading. As Silver (1995) has argued, the meaning of social exclusion depends on the nature of the society, or the dominant model of that society, from which exclusion occurs. The French paradigm of society, in the context of which the concept first evolved, is one of solidarity around a core of shared values and rights: a conception of society as a moral community. That of the Anglo-Saxon world, in contrast, is one of specialization, with individual producers and consumers, each with their own preferences and capabilities, linked by a market and enlightened self-interest. Exclusion from such a system implies the inability to function in the markets for labour and consumption goods. Other models exist: more closed societies may, for example, be viewed as monopolies, with resources being controlled by hierarchical and exclusive networks. Such differing conceptions of the nature of society clearly carry quite different conceptions of what constitutes inclusion and exclusion, and thus of the desirability and appropriate means of promoting social inclusion.

Even at the level of a single society, the concept, by presenting forms of social differentiation in terms of a single descriptor, implies that the various groups that make up the 'excluded' may have more in common than is in fact the case. The mechanisms that create and perpetuate disadvantage among, for example, the disabled, women, scheduled castes, pastoralists, the landless, the Roma and the industrial unemployed are very different. Whatever the superficial attraction of a common schema, placing these groups in a single category may do little to aid the understanding of the specific difficulties that any of them face, or to help to resolve these (on gender, for example, see Jackson, 1999). Furthermore inclusion and exclusion are inseparable sides of the same coin: the strength of intragroup ties and of the identity that forges them is inseparable from a community's definition of itself as distinctive. And if inclusion implies, as it may, incorporation into exploitative or violent relationships, exclusion may not always be a bad thing. More important is the ability of individuals and groups to control the terms under which they are included.

Hence the notion of social exclusion, while carrying a number of pointers for a broader and less income-focused conception of generation, is not a very precise or nuanced one. Indeed one may suspect with Atkinson (1998, p. 13) that it has gained such wide currency partly *because* it means all things to all people.

Social Capital

How do the poor, recent immigrants or others lacking access to formal financial institutions obtain credit? Are levels of civic activism related to levels of trust in society, and do these affect the quality of government? How do political stability and access to justice affect economic growth? How do ethnicity and family background affect school performance? Answers to these important but complex questions have increasingly been given in terms of the endowment and deployment of social capital.

Social capital is sometimes thought of as the metaphorical glue that holds groups and societies together and enables them to get things done. Few people would need to be told that values, ties and networks are essential to the accomplishment of all human activities, including economic ones. The social sciences – including economics, at least in its earlier forms – have long taken such bonds and institutions as their core subject matter. However the idea that this combination of networks, organizations and values should be considered as a form of capital is a relatively new one.

The rapidity of social capital's rise to currency in both academic and policy discourse is not simply a reflection of a new appreciation of the importance of social and institutional factors to economic performance. The strategic location of the concept on the boundaries between the economic and the non-economic social sciences (in particular sociology, political science and social anthropology) has given it a special role in the brokering of interdisciplinarity. Some have read this renegotiation of academic frontiers as an attempt by economics to colonize its sister disciplines. Certainly the implications of tangibility, comparability and quantifiability that social capital carries appear to be integral to its wide appeal, an appeal that also reflects a period of history in which the ends of human existence are increasingly expressed and evaluated solely in monetary terms.

Social Capital as a Form of Capital

Physical, natural, and human capital have long been conventional economic categories. Recognition that the predictability and coopera-tion lent by trust, convention and social organization are equally essential to production and exchange underlies the concept of social capital, which includes both normative and organizational elements.

The four kinds of capital are now conceived of as complementary inputs to economic development, though they may to some degree substitute for one another. Social capital (if we accept for the time being the validity of the analogy) is thought of as sharing certain properties with other forms of capital, yet being distinctive in respect of others.

A distinguishing feature of social capital is that it inheres in relationships rather than in individuals or objects. However, while this property makes social capital less tangible than other forms of capital, like them it nevertheless needs to be created and maintained, and this requires resources (in particular, time or labour). Hence social capital is not only an input, but also an output of economic and social activity. Social capital, in contrast to physical capital, is not usually created through conscious endeavour: more frequently it is a by-product of activities directed at economic or other ends. Like other capitals, it can be destroyed as well as created (indeed destruction may sometimes be easier than generation). It is built through constructive use, and decays through desuetude or misuse. Social capital has some of the characteristics of a public good (it produces benefits to society as a whole that cannot be captured by those who create it) and for this reason is likely to be underproduced.

The concept has now been applied in many fields. Woolcock (1998) groups these into seven: social theory and economic development; families and youth behaviour; schooling and education; community life; work and organizations; democracy and governance; and more general collective action problems.

Origins and Definitions

Woolcock (1998) attributes the first use of social capital in its contemporary guise to Jacobs (1961), although scattered use of the term can be traced back as far as 1920 (in Hanifan, 1920). The concept has been used by social scientists since the 1960s, particularly in the study of migration, ethnic enterprise and urban development. Bourdieu developed systematic thinking around the subject, drawing on the Marxist tradition. His work relates social capital to the structuring of class in society, and the ways in which networks and connections can be mobilized to draw on the economic, cultural or symbolic capital of others (Bourdieu, 1980). However Bourdieu's conception of social capital has had a limited influence on the evolution of the concept, at least in the English-speaking world, where it has been eclipsed by the work of Coleman and Putnam in the disciplines of political science and sociology respectively. It is to these that we now turn.

For Coleman (1990, p. 598):

> Social capital is defined by its function. It is not a single entity, but a variety of different entities having two elements in common: that all consist of some aspect of social structure, and they facilitate certain actions of individuals – whether persons or corporate actors – who are within the structure.

According to this definition, all aspects of social structure that contribute to the solution of public action problems, whether networks, firms, norms or links of patronage, count as social capital. In addition to this broad definition we may also note that, while invoking social links, social capital is a property or endowment of individuals rather than of groups.

Putnam (1993a, p. 167), who attached the concept of social capital to his comparative study of local governance in Italy, describes social capital as 'features of social organization, such as trust, norms and networks that can improve the efficiency of society by facilitating co-ordinated action'. In this study, which rapidly became a classic, Putnam and his colleagues seek to explain the differences in institutional performance and economic development between northern and southern Italy. They trace these to differences in patterns of civic engagement that extend back to the early Middle Ages. The study argues that institutional performance in any region, as assessed against 12 indicators, is related to the degree of 'civic community' that exists there. 'Civic community' itself is measured in terms of voting patterns (absence of clientelism and turnout for referenda), newspaper readership and the prevalence of sports and cultural associations in the region. Present-day patterns of civic engagement are related to those going back to the nineteenth century, and are traced by the authors to the emergence in the early Middle Ages of communal republicanism in the central and northern parts of Italy, in contrast to the Norman feudalism in the southern regions.

Putnam sees horizontal networks as more effective than the vertical ones of patronage because they increase the costs of defection, create norms of reciprocity and improve the flow of information and communication (ibid., pp. 174–5). Subsequently he applied the concept to the US where in Putnam's view social capital has become depleted as horizontal associations – a remarked-upon feature of the American social landscape since at least the time of de Tocqueville – have become decreasingly common (Putnam, 1993b, 1995). The main culprit, according to Putnam, is television.

For Putnam, as for Coleman, social capital provides a solution to collective action problems, but for him it is a property of societies rather than of individuals. Furthermore he restricts the kinds of relationship or group that count as social capital. Social capital is a set of 'horizontal associations' between people, or 'networks of civil engagement' and associated norms that enable things to get done.

Putman's thesis has been quite severely criticized on historical, methodological and conceptual grounds (see Goldberg, 1996; Skocpol, 1996). However his work has stimulated wide debate on the relationship between civic engagement, governance and economic growth. One reason for this may already be apparent: Putnam's notion of social capital, unlike other formulations, is very much consistent with the notions of civil society discussed above. A second reason is Putnam's subsequent attempts to turn the lens of social capital onto his own (American) society. Perhaps the greater part of the literature on social capital in development has been concerned with the exploration of his thesis and its application to other contexts.

While the formulations by Coleman and Putnam have been the most influential, some authors have argued for a still wider conception of social capital that encompasses the broad social and political environment within which social structures and norms develop and function (for example Grootaert, 1997). This definition adds the formal structures and norms to the informal social institutions included in the first two definitions: government, the rule of law, courts, and civil and political liberties. Such a notion of social capital is consistent with work of North (1990) and Olson (1982) on institutions.

The breadth and variability of the term social capital will already be clear from this brief overview of definitions. Several authors have attempted to clarify the concept by classifying and mapping the different forms of social capital that are present in a society. Some of these accounts have further argued that the process of development consists in the transformation of one kind of social capital to another.

A number of these authors draw on a distinction between the dense ties that are considered to characterize traditional communities and the wider but more generalized networks of more developed economies and societies. Granovetter's (1973) article on 'the strength of weak ties' is an influential formulation of this idea, which can be traced back to classical sociology, for example to Durkheim's distinction between organic and mechanical solidarity.

Portes and Sensenbrenner (1992), who have explored immigration, ethnic entrepreneurship and poverty through the lens of social capital, use such a distinction to move towards a systematic understanding of its different sources. They distinguish four mechanisms affecting economic and other goal-seeking behaviour, or sources of social capital. First, socialization prompts individuals to behave in ways that are other than purely selfish ('values introjection'). The second mechanism is the reciprocity that governs the myriad transactions of goods, favours and information that characterize social life. The third is bounded solidarity: mutual support born of awareness of common interests. The fourth and final mechanism is enforceable trust, through which the expectation of gaining long-term advantages and avoiding group sanctions induces conformity to norms. Portes and Sensenbrenner argue that social ties that are helpful in some circumstances may be constraining in others, a point to which we shall return when we consider the possibility that social capital may have negative as well as positive effects.

Woolcock's (1998) classification of social capital is also consistent with the distinction between 'strong' and 'weak' ties, in this case arranged across a social space extending between macro- and micro-institutional poles. He portrays social capital as a balance between 'embeddedness' (a concept originally attributable to Polanyi, but introduced into more recent debate by Granovetter, 1985), and 'autonomy' (the need for links to complement or cut across these primary ties), at both the macro and the micro level. Hence, as we have already seen from Portes and Sensenbrenner, the organic solidarity of community ('integration' for Woolcock) needs to be balanced by connections made beyond the local group to the broader economy and society ('linkage'). In an analogous way, at the macro level state structures need to have organizational autonomy ('integrity') that ensures that procedures are predictable, fair and objective. At the same time macro institutions should be guided and constrained by external ties to clients and constituents that ensure accountability to the public and a 'synergy' between the actions of the state and other social actors. Woolcock's schema thus generates four dimensions of social capital, which may be combined, and interact, in various ways.

Narayan (1999) builds an analytical framework from similar blocks, highlighting the interaction between two key dimensions: cross-cutting ties and state functioning. Cross-cutting ties (equivalent to Granovetter's 'weak ties' or Woolcock's 'autonomy' at the micro level) connect disparate groups with access to information, resources and opportunities, and also build a kind of generalized social solidarity based on respect for diversity. Meanwhile the state provides the overall governance environment, which fosters the rule of law, citizens' rights and freedom of association. It is also the source of the competence, authority and accountability of government organizations.

Development, in these models, is frequently seen as a transition from one kind of social capital to another, as traditional societies consisting of small communities where interactions are restricted, face-to-face and multipurpose give way to modern societies where transactions are more likely to be impersonal and single-purpose. This is resonant of a whole lineage of distinctions between the traditional and the modern, including those made by Maine, Tonnies and Durkheim, and, as Coleman notes, of Gluckman's (1967) distinction between simplex and multiplex relations. During this process, formal and market institutions take over the functions of community and social networks; and the nature of trust moves from trust based on individual reputation to a more generalized form across society, supported by third-party sanctions.

The final classification of social capital considered here, that of Harriss and De Renzio, is rather different in that it combines both structural and functional dimensions. Though quite critical of the concept, these authors argue that it can be analytically serviceable if different usages and forms are distinguished. They offer a sixfold classification of social capital: family and kinship connections, associational life, cross-sectional linkages ('networks of networks'), political capital, institutional and policy framework, and social norms and values (Harriss and De Renzio, 1997, pp. 932–3).

Drawing together what has been said in this selective review of the definition and typology of social capital, we can find no consensus on a single definition. However the differing conceptions considered do have certain features in common: all are concerned with the way in which the social sphere conditions the economic, and in particular with the positive externalities of social phenomena. These may include elements of organization, groups, social networks, social structure, values and predispositions such as trust. As we have seen, one way of dealing with the breadth and inconsistency of the definition of social capital is to classify it into types. A number of schema have been proposed, distinguishing between dense family and local ties on the one hand and generalized, 'weak' links going beyond communities on the other; between horizontal, 'civic' links and vertical ties of patronage; between informal micro- and formal macro-level institutions; or between institutions and social norms. These classifications often embody, at least by implication, an account of the process of development: either as the balancing of differing kinds of tie, or as the development of one form of social capital at the expense of another. We shall postpone consideration of the overall coherence of these concepts until we have examined the functions of social capital and the contribution that the concept may make to development policy and practice.

The Functions of Social Capital

Both Coleman's and Putnam's conceptions of social capital are functionalist. Indeed for Coleman social capital is defined by its function – it is what enables individuals to get things done. Putnam's formulation of the concept – as a property of societies rather than individuals – posits social capital as an ingredient that provides societies with more effective governance and a dynamic economy. These functions of social capital, whether conceived of from the point of view of the individual or of society, are frequently described in the language of neoclassical economics as ways of overcoming informational asymmetries, problems of collective action and other forms of 'market failure'.

Norms, values and institutions are thus seen as ways of sharing and obtaining information, coordinating action and making collective decisions (Grootaert, 1998, p. 7). Social interaction through networks and organizations provides information to economic actors about the reliability and creditworthiness of others and the costs of default. It also affords opportunities for the activities of other parties to be monitored. This informational role of social capital is so universal as to be generally taken for granted, although mutual credit groups, where the group guarantees the conformity of its individual members, illustrate its importance in a development context.

At the level of action, social capital can provide a kind of infrastructure for reaching decisions, coordinating their implementation and preventing free-riding. This function of social capital is common, for example, among irrigation-water user groups and community-forest user groups, where coordinated action and the restriction of opportunism are critical. Combining the information and action aspects of social capital, immigration studies have shown how social networks function for recent immigrants in providing access to employment, credit and other opportunities (for example Portes and Sensenbrenner, 1992).

Macro-level organizations such as a society's political, administrative and judicial systems may also be considered part of an endowment of social capital. Consistent and reliable decision making in these spheres is certainly a precondition for meaningful development. The scarcity of social capital at this level in the former Soviet Union led to what Rose (1998) describes as an 'hourglass society', where the trust of citizens in formal institutions was minimal, and links were fragile and arbitrary.

Negative Social Capital

Most discussions of the term tend to celebrate social capital as a good thing. But like other forms of capital, social capital can have both positive and negative implications for society. While social capital facilitates collaboration to achieve virtuous ends, it also enables conspiracy against the public by cartels, cronies and criminals. We can identify four circumstances in which the overall social impact of social capital is likely to be negative. In the most obvious case, organizations with criminal or antisocial objectives do not make a positive contribution to the broader society: drug cartels and the Ku Klux Klan are frequently cited examples. Second, Olson (1965) argues, interest groups that capture political influence that is disproportionate to their size can distort policy in favour of particular interests, with the result that overall welfare and efficiency is reduced. Third, social groups and networks that perform positive functions for most of their members most of the time, may in other circumstances work against some of their own members by restricting opportunities. Portes and Sensenbrenner (1992), for example, discuss how obligations to kin may erode potential capital from enterprises. Similarly a solidary culture based on low expectations of advancement into the 'mainstream' can restrict individuals' opportunities and inhibit their motivation to succeed in the terms of the broader society. Fourth, if we accept Putnam's thesis, then some types of organization (that is, horizontal associations) are good for governance and the economy while others (hierarchical institutions – though Putman himself might not classify these as social capital) are not.

The consideration that social capital is not always a force for good is perhaps a commonplace one. However attempting to assign value to social capital along a unidimensional scale brings us face to face with a critical weakness at the heart of the concept, unmasking its apparently neutral and apolitical nature. For who defines social capital as positive or negative, and according to what criteria? As the examples above reveal, institutions and practices that are good for many may simultaneously be bad for some. Likewise those which damage society as a whole may still work to the favour of a minority, perhaps even a substantial one. The concept of social capital as a benefit analogous to other forms of capital obscures the fact that attributing economic value to social norms and relations is problematic in the extreme. The dualism of 'good' and 'bad' capital does nothing to resolve this difficulty as attribution to either category is itself open to contestation. As a concept, social capital tends to technify and homogenize the social dimension: it has little to say about the differences of interest or power that underlie its accumulation, use and definition.

Social Capital as a Policy and Operational Tool

We have seen that the concept of social capital has been used to analyze and explain a whole array of social phenomena, and the ways in which these condition economic and political life. What contribution can the concept make to the formulation of social and economic policies and programmes? More particularly, does it have a contribution to make towards the development of more effective ways of addressing poverty and marginality?

The term social capital is increasingly used to describe a wide range of development interventions. The World Bank identifies five ways in which it can increase the extent to which social relationships and local and national networks are taken into account, and these might serve as a starting point. They are: 'do your homework, do no harm'; using local-level social capital to deliver projects; creating enabling environments; investing in social capital; and promoting research and learning (Grootaert, 1997).

Social capital is often used in haphazard if not opportunistic ways. For illustrative purposes, four of the most common usages are considered here: in monitoring social change; in describing community-based development; in the 'sustainable livelihoods' approach to rural development policy; and in work on conflict and post-conflict situations.

Sudarsky and Bogota (1998) have developed a 'barometer' of social capital, consisting of ten main dimensions (including civic participation, social control and institutional trust), each of which in turn consists of a series of variables. This is being used to track social changes in Columbia. Similarly, in the countries of the former Soviet bloc the 'new democracies barometer' involves the conducting of regular sample surveys to compile basic economic, political and social indicators covering freedom, attitudes towards democracy, earnings, destitution, and coping strategies (see for example Rose, 1999). In a comparative study of four deprived urban locations, Moser (1996) tracks the responses of urban households to adjustment, illustrating the ways in which social capital can be eroded by continual economic crises, resulting in increased violence and criminality.

Community-based development activities are increasingly described as 'building social capital'. The term is particularly used to justify the existence of social funds (autonomous institutions established to fund small community-level initiatives in response to local demand), which are a growing part of the poverty-alleviation portfolio of international aid. Their contribution to the building of community institutions is sometimes seen as secondary to the material benefits that flow through these vehicles. Narayan and Ebbe (1997, p. 45), for example, describe social funds as 'instruments for contributing to community well-being and social cohesion among the poor, through the engagement of community groups in the creation and management of local infrastructure, basic services and natural resources'.

However, lacking even the limited concreteness of 'institutional capacity', the credibility of the concept of social capital sometimes seems to be stretched in these circumstances. It is often far from clear (nor is it regarded as necessary to specify) what abilities are created by participating in such programmes, as the skills acquired during project negotiation and coordination are unlikely to be those needed for long-term, self-reliant development.

Our third example of the operational use of the concept is the sustainable livelihoods (SL) approach to rural development, an analytical framework that has become influential in some development-assistance quarters (including the UK Department for International Development, DFID). This framework, which has its origins in the work of Robert Chambers and others in the 1980s, offers a way of thinking about the livelihoods of poor people in terms of their access to five kinds of capital: human, social, natural, physical and financial (DFID, 1999). Social capital is defined as 'the social resources upon which people draw in pursuit of their livelihood objectives', and these may include networks and 'connectedness', membership of more formalized groups, and relationships of trust, reciprocity and exchange (DFID, 1999, S. 2.3.2).

The strength of the sustainable livelihood approach is that it focuses on people and their existing strengths and constraints, including their social assets, rather than on what they do not have. The framework encourages a holistic view of the poor and their livelihood strategies, including those not directly related to natural resources such as urban migration. Change and diversification, and the relationship between the macro and micro levels (for example the local impact of national policy changes) may thus be better understood and explained.

A more accommodating and cohesive social environment for sustainable livelihoods can be promoted through direct support for the accumulation of social assets, for example by improving the leadership and management of groups or their external connections. Social assets can also be built by indirect means, such as promoting a more open and predictable policy environment or supporting a consultative stance on the part of implementing organizations. Success in improving livelihoods may lead to a virtuous circle of asset accumulation in the social sphere reinforcing bonds of collaboration that have been successful and generating resources that permit greater levels of interaction (DFID, 1999). Critics of the SL approach consider it excessively micro-focused and complex, and question whether it carries either explanatory weight or clear operational implications (Farrington *et al.*, 1999).

The fourth context to be considered here is conflict resolution. Conflict can be seen as both a result and a cause of the depletion of social capital. Rutazibwa *et al.* (1998) have analyzed the recent history of Rwanda in terms of the destruction and restoration of social capital. The study looks back to the precolonial period to identify an 'authentic Rwandan social capital' and the indicators that characterize it. Appreciation of these characteristics will, the authors hope, enable the necessary elements of social and economic reconstruction to be identified.

As the above examples of social funds and the livelihoods approach illustrate, building social capital is often promoted as a new key to poverty alleviation. The underlying assumption is that the poor are more able to benefit from increased social capital than the non-poor. Grootaert (1999), for example, argues that the poor have to rely on social capital (their kin or patrons) more than groups who can afford to purchase insurance or services. This is undeniable, but while the poor may not have many other assets (though their human capital, in the form of indigenous knowledge and practical knowledge of livelihood and coping strategies, may be considerable) it would be misleading to view social capital as the province of the marginalized. As noted in the discussion on social exclusion, and articulated by the poor themselves, poverty is often a poverty of connections. The better-off are typically better organized, and are frequently able to sway formal or informal processes to their advantage. Indeed as Olson has made clear, social capital is a vehicle for the maintenance of privilege as much as for the survival of the poor.

In general the application of the concept of social capital to development policy has probably contributed to the broadening of its agenda beyond the narrowly economic, allowing increased recognition of the importance of social and institutional factors. The five modes of social intervention identified by the World Bank seem eminently sound. For the most part they are consistent with the call for a better understanding of local institutions, their potential roles and their need for support, long since advocated by non-governmental organizations and other critics of conventional development models. Indeed it might be asked whether use of the term 'capital' adds anything to either diagnosis or prescription. In any case, different definitions of social capital inevitably imply different strategies for building it. Furthermore the idea of 'investing in social capital', though compatible with concepts such as building institutional capacity or community participation, carries the implication that the transmutation of financial capital into social capital is a relatively unproblematic process. But recognizing that building social relations and institutions requires time and resources falls far short of identifying reliable means by which sustainable and equitable institutions can be crafted in practice. Distinguishing cause from effect is problematic, and even if successful methods for institutional replication by external invervention were developed, which seems implausible, it remains equally unclear what their wider impact would be. The establishment of numerous choirs and football clubs and the abolition of television would not inevitably lead to civic engagement, efficient administration and a dynamic economy.

Measurement

One of the attractions of the concept of social capital is the promise – at times implicit, at others explicit – that, having distilled all social variables into a single essence, it will somehow be possible to count them. But of course definition must precede measurement, and we have already seen that this is problematic. Given the wide range of possible operational definitions of social capital, researchers typically face the dilemma that while narrow definitions are likely to generate indicators that are easy to measure, these will probably not be the most meaningful to social action.

However this has not prevented attempts to quantify social capital, as the example of the Columbian barometer for social capital indicates. In another frequently quoted study, a multiple regression of data on 750 households in 45 Tanzanian villages established that the level of social capital in a village, defined by membership of groups and networks, was a key contributor to household welfare, even after taking other factors into account. However household-level social capital appeared less significant (Narayan and Prichett, 1997).

There are relatively few studies that relate social capital to prosperity, perhaps because of the serious problems of methodology and interpretation that face attempts to explain income in terms of sociability. However a number of quantitative cross-country analyses have used variables relating to 'trust' (as assessed by respondents in the World Values Surveys) as a proxy for social capital. These have explored the contribution made by associational life to civic culture and development, as well as the contribution made by generalized trust to economic development – an argument paralleling that by Fukuyama (1995). Knack and Keefer's (1997) analysis of World Values Survey data failed to reveal any association between membership of formal groups on the one hand, and trust or improved economic performance on the other. However, higher levels of trust and civic norms were found to be associated with higher and more equal incomes, with institutions that constrain predatory activities by chief executives, and with better-educated and ethnically homogeneous populations.

Conclusions

The problems we have identified in respect of the conceptualization, measurement and operationalization of social capital are rooted in the breadth of the concept and its multiple meanings, and these are, in turn due to the multiplicity of traditions that have been mined in its formulation.

While condensing the entire terrain of social theory into a single variable does enable its users to argue for a kind of interdisciplinarity, it is one based on the lowest common denominator of concepts, or worse, the distortions resulting from the imposition of one discipline's categories onto another. This intellectual homogenization also predisposes the concept to become trapped in frequent circular reasoning: social capital is what social capital does. Social capital may be structure, value, process or outcome. It explains everything and nothing.

The methodological individualism of the concept, at least in the versions inspired by Coleman, make it asocial and ahistorical. It is a functionalist answer to a problem posed by economics: the dilemma of collective action. In doing so it reinforces a separation between the economic and the social that is itself of doubtful validity (Fine, 1999). The result is a totally chaotic concept that is unable to capture the dimensions of power and the political, or as Harriss and De Renzio (1997, p. 932) argue, the negative consequences that social capital may have for the powerless in particular: 'the idea of "social capital" as "community" is thoroughly conservative-populist'.

The breadth and vagueness of the other concepts treated in this chapter – civil society and social exclusion – although less serious, open them to similar criticisms in terms of both coherence and utility. All three terms have been used to map a new direction in social and economic policy, advance a kind of multidisciplinarity and allow some new directions to be taken in research. However the promise to unite and ground diverse social science disciplines on a common policy terrain has not been fulfilled. Despite, or perhaps because of this analytical weakness, demand for the intellectual capital to which they pretend has remained strong among policy makers and advisers. To conclude, I suggest that there are four, only partially compatible ways of interpreting the rise of social capital and its cognates.

The first is to welcome the attention now being given to the influence of social factors and institutions in economic change, and to the interdisciplinary approach that has accompanied it. This *technocratic* response has characteristically been made by development agencies, which have enthusiastically sought to realign, or at least to represent their policies as 'people-centred'. There is optimism that this new conceptual framework will provide a platform for a new generation of social policy tools that will allow key social variables to be measured, created and manipulated through a combination of social research, 'participation', financial investment and social engineering.

The second interpretation is a more radical one: that these concepts are the first glimmerings of a new paradigm, one that will free top-down development planning from its technocratic chains and enable it to respond to the social energy of the populace as the subjects rather than the objects of development. This *transformative* approach stresses that social capital differs from other forms of social capital in that, by and large, it cannot be bought and sold. For example Wilson (1997) argues that the social capital concept undermines mainstream economics by challenging two of its tenets. The fact that social capital is free opposes the assumption of scarcity. Second, social capital, in focusing on the individual-in-community, contests the tenet of individual self-interested rationality. Wilson concludes that social capital will not be built through social engineering by technical experts, but rather 'humbly in small increments by individuals stepping out of isolation, enjoying connectedness and taking responsibility for their public lives' (ibid., p. 756).

A third, more critical interpretation would focus on the breadth and inconsistency that these concepts share. This analytic and *sceptical* response would see social capital, despite the burgeoning literature for which it has been responsible, as 'an attempt to gain conviction from a bad analogy' (Solow, 1999, p. 6), a policy vehicle whose incoherent design would fate it ever to drive in circles.

The fourth and last interpretation represents a counterpart to the radical optimism of the transformationalists, one which could be called *communitarian*. The upsurge of interest in social capital happened only when it became clear that the degree of erosion of this asset was so serious as to be possibly irreversible. Changes associated with globalization have torn apart the bonds of community through increased geographical mobility, growing inequality, familial instability, violence and the increasing commercialization and monetization of societal goals. While the embrace of social capital by the development establishment creates an agenda for intervention, this is an illusory comfort. For the development process, now inseparable from that of globalization, is mining the very social bonds on which it depends, fuelled as it is by an irreversible consumption of social capital. As Arrow (1999, p. 5) notes: 'labour or supplier turnover in response to prices may destroy the willingness to offer trust, or more generally to invest in the future of the relation: this leads to an important and long-standing question: does the market ... destroy social links that have positive implications for efficiency?' Arrow expresses this in economic terms, but if this insight is correct, then not only will efficiency decline, but human well-being and security will decline too.

6

Participating in Development[1]

ROSEMARY McGEE

When people in developing countries do things for their own survival and advancement, they are living their lives and exercising human agency. The exercise of agency only becomes participation when the impetus or framework for a development activity is located outside people's life worlds. Although a truism, this fact needs to be borne in mind when documenting when and how participation became common currency in development discourse and practice, as noted by various observers:

> Historically, the issue of participation is intrinsic to *public* programs. This issue does not arise in the spontaneous development that is accomplished ... by the 'people themselves', through their regular activities, since this development happens precisely because the people initiate it, finance it, and carry it out without having to be called 'to participate'. Overall development is the composite result of myriads of such self-started activities and of the interactions and linkages between their social actors (Cernea, 1992, p. 2).

> People do not participate in external interventions; they live their lives. External interventions interfere in their lives and, therefore, the onus lies on external agencies, not people, to devise methods to participate (Bhatnagar and Williams, 1992, p. 181).

People have always been agents of their own development, sometimes working alone, sometimes through collective endeavour. Only since the 1980s have the terms of their agency in development interventions been a focus of attention.

This chapter describes the background and current status of participation as a central concept and operational approach in development. An account is given of the 'participation in projects' current of the 1980s, itself alternative and novel at the time; and of the emergence of a more radical alternative, here termed the 'participatory development' current. The challenges and critiques of various actors engaged in promoting participatory approaches are discussed against the fast-changing backdrop of development cooperation throughout the 1990s. A review of responses to these critiques reveals a convergence between the mainstream development agenda and the participation agenda. This, it is argued, is more a sign of the success of the transformative project of 'participatory development' than evidence of absorption of the alternative by the orthodoxy. By way of conclusion, connections are pointed out between the critics' main contentions and the frontiers at which participation advocates – academic, non-governmental and official agency staff – are working.

As a caveat, documenting the history of participation in development tends to play up the Northern development institutions' role in promoting it, and to play down the role of Southern grassroots organizations and actors in supporting the agency of the poor. This tendency arises partly because NGOs and Southern activists concentrate on doing development rather than on writing about it; and partly because paradigm shifts in development more often take the form of modifications to Northern donor and policy-maker perspectives, than of anything that happens in the South.

The Early Orthodoxy

In the beginning was the development project. There was the development agency, which conceived, designed, funded, managed, implemented and evaluated the project from somewhere outside its boundaries; and there were the project beneficiaries – undifferentiated, passive recipients of goods and services provided through project channels. People – whether in the agency or in the 'beneficiary population' – were scarcely acknowledged to be there. Created as a bureaucratic convenience, a manageable way of packaging assistance, the project model need not have been a problem in itself. However a tendency to reify 'the project' in development discourse and practice throughout the 1970s and 1980s contributed to a distorted and incomplete apprehension of the realities of poor people in developing countries, and the consequent privileging of development agencies' viewpoints and imperatives over these (see for example Harrold, 1995).

Beyond the domain of the major development agencies, since the 1970s the Latin American action research school, associated with Freire, has promoted a view of people as conscious agents in social and political life (see for example Freire, 1972). In the early 1980s two influential publications helped this notion to find its way into mainstream development. Chambers in *Rural Development: Putting People First* (1983) exposed the ignorance and arrogance that underpinned many rural development interventions. Exploding the myth that outsiders knew best, he attributed to the 'object' population subjectivity and expertise, and challenged development professionals to unlearn much of their training in order to put the last – the poor, physically weak, rural, isolated, vulnerable, powerless people – first. The arguments were pragmatic and also moral, stemming from a critical attitude towards a narrowly technical and discipline-specific approach to development, and from outrage at the persistence of widespread poverty despite decades of development interventions.

Soon after came Cernea's *Putting People First: Sociological Variables in Rural Development* (1985). This highlighted the neglect of sociological perspectives in comparison with the technical and financial aspects of rural development planning, despite the repeated failure of 'sociologically ill-informed programmes' (ibid., p. 3). Noting the limitations of 'the project as a framework for social endeavour', and in the absence of alternative frameworks, Cernea called for the identification and exploitation of sociological variables in development projects, entry-points and methods for the incorporation of sociological and anthropological knowledge in the project cycle, and the institutionalization of sociology as one among several legitimate disciplines in development planning (ibid., p. 17).

Despite the similarity of their slogans, Cernea's arguments are different from Chambers' in that they seek to enhance the success of 'financially induced change programs' by adding sociological knowledge, and to stress the role of development sociology in providing the methods needed to achieve this. Each of the two books made a distinctive mark on development practice. Both contributed to a wave of thinking about and debate on human agency in development,[2] which became loosely known as 'participation'.

Four factors fuelled the debate on participation in the 1980s, as noted by Nelson and Wright (1996). First, in Northern official development agencies, 'discussions began on why thirty years of conventional technocratic, top-down forms of development were not working. Initially the failure of many such public programmes was traced to the alienation of "beneficiaries" ' (ibid., p. 3). Second, in Southern former colonies, countries emerging from dictatorships and leftist academic circles there was growing disillusionment with the whole development endeavour, which was characterized as excessively paternalistic and driven by the nation-state or – for newly independent nations – the erstwhile colonial powers. Third, in the 1970s non-governmental development organizations (NGOs) in the North and South began to shift away from a welfarist approach towards one of self-sufficiency and empowerment. This entailed changes in their ways of working, away from centralized control and direct implementation of projects, towards decentralization, partnership and greater control by beneficiaries. Fourth, the 1980s saw the rise of monetarist economics, a global trend that manifested itself in debt-burdened developing countries as stabilization and structural adjustment programmes. Prescriptions for rolling back the state and tight restrictions on social sector spending made self-sufficiency a survival imperative rather than a high-sounding ideal for people in adjusting countries. The concept of participation was extended – some would say twisted – to cover cost-sharing policies and the levying of user charges in this context.

These four factors are of different orders. On the one hand there was a technical concern that the development project – at that time virtually the only vehicle for development cooperation – was not producing the results it should. On the other there were ideological concerns: one from the South, premised on a vision of development as releasing exploited peoples from oppression by the wealthy and powerful; one from the North seeking to extend the market ideology throughout the world; and one from the development NGOs – somewhere in between North and South – based on the pragmatic realization that bottom-up worked best, and on an ideology of client empowerment and self-reliance, pursued through capacity-building and accompaniment.[3] Predictably enough, the technical concern with project efficiency was influential in shaping the outcome of the early participation debate, being compatible with the dominant paradigm of efficiency-obsessed neoliberal economics and conducive to the extension of this paradigm into the sphere of development assistance.

By the late 1980s these strands of thought had coalesced into a proposition that might be paraphrased as 'people's participation in planning development projects is desirable because it makes projects more efficient, effective and sustainable'. To many development practitioners, especially those working with Southern organizations, the proposition must have seemed self-evident, and only relevant to the extent that Southern people's lives consisted of projects – which, of course, they only very partially did.[4]

From the early 1990s the 'participation in projects' proposition was tested, substantiated and refined through various initiatives of operational experimentation and research. Influential among these was the World Bank's cross-organizational Participation Learning Group, established in 1990 by committed World Bank staff after pressure by the World Bank NGO Working Group. Its mandate was to document the Bank's experience of participation in projects, catalyze learning within and outside the Bank, and identify internal modifications that would be needed for the Bank better to foster popular participation. Three key reports issued by this group document the development of the Bank's approach to participation: Bhatnagar and Williams (1992), World Bank (1994a) and World Bank (1995a).[5] Initially the emphasis was on the Bank's systems and the alterations needed therein to enable beneficiaries to participate at certain stages of the project cycle (Bhatnagar and Williams, 1992). World Bank (1994a), the final report of the Learning Group, gives the Bank's definition of participation: 'a process through which stakeholders influence and share control over development initiatives, decisions and resources which affect them'. It reports that since 1990 'low-intensity' forms of participation (information-sharing, consultation) have become routine in Bank lending operations and increasingly in economic and sector work,[6] but 'higher-intensity forms' (empowering mechanisms for joint decision making, and control by beneficiaries over initiatives) much less so (ibid., p. 10). In contrast to Bhatnagar and Williams (1992), where the framework for participation is clearly the *project*, World Bank (1994a) notes the need to work with governments to enhance stakeholder participation in *policy* analysis, design and implementation (ibid., p. 2), and the potential of participation as a tool to increase state responsiveness and accountability (ibid., p. 13). However, as in the earlier document, clear limits are set on the extent to which the Bank can pursue participatory approaches:

> the Bank's Articles of Agreement explicitly prohibit the Bank from becoming involved in a country's political affairs, [so] the specific issue of democratization is outside its mandate. ... Given the Bank's focus on economic development, its interest in participation is primarily one of improving the results of its investments (ibid., p. 19).

The *World Bank Participation Sourcebook* (1995a) unambiguously acknowledges the importance of participatory approaches in policy work, and at all stages of interventions, explaining that neglect of these aspects so far is due to the Bank's 'relatively recent ... institutional commitment to supporting participatory approaches' (ibid., p. 8). A more discerning analysis of who might participate and why, leads to a distinction being drawn between primary and secondary stakeholders[7] and the beginnings of a power-relations perspective on the contexts in which development takes place. Different methodological approaches are proposed for use with different stakeholders, in recognition of the need to relate differently to people with different stakes and levels of influence; and of the precondition that power differentials must be addressed before participatory approaches can work with a mix of stakeholders. Far-reaching implications of participatory development principles for individuals' and institutions' behaviour are suggested, and a clear preference is evident – at least at the rhetorical level – for more empowering forms of participation over less empowering ones. At the same time the limit imposed by the Bank's constitutional prohibition on political intervention is reviewed and eased somewhat.[8] These progressive trends notwithstanding, Narayan (1995), by presenting systematically gathered evidence from Bank projects, seems to claim for the Bank the last word on the 'added value' of participation, and narrowly focuses on projects to the total exclusion of non-project work, on beneficiary participation as opposed to the more nuanced stakeholder participation and on cost–benefit analysis rather than any empowerment framework.

Several bilateral donors, seeking to promote participatory approaches by the Bank, supported the Learning Group while also advocating participation within their own agencies.[9] Technical guidance notes issued by the UK's Overseas Development Administration[10] to its staff on enhancing stakeholder participation define this similarly to the Bank (ODA, 1995a, 1995b). Although mainly about the project cycle, these notes refer to 'aid activities' (including policy reform programmes) rather than to 'projects', and before stating the familiar objective of increased project efficiency, offer as a primary objective the full involvement of people in 'issues concerning themselves and the society in which they live' (ODA, 1995a, p. 4). The United Nations Development Programme's position on participation, on the other hand, stems not from a project-based view but from an analysis of the democratic transitions occurring in many developing countries, and of the role of civil society in shaping the new political and governance contexts that are emerging (UNDP, 1993).

As mentioned above, lobbying by NGOs provided one stimulus for the formation of the World Bank's Participation Learning Group. Clark's influential book on the voluntary sector's role in development shows that by then the 'participation in projects' orthodoxy was already outdated among NGOs (Clark, 1991). According to Clark participation, which he calls 'a favourite NGO term', 'should be seen as a two-way involvement of the poor in the project design and execution, but also participation of the funding or intermediary NGO in the poor's struggle for equity, human rights and democracy' (ibid., p. 58). NGOs were exhorted to recognize the importance of policy reform and to clamour for it. The traditional, service-delivery focus of NGOs was now perceived as dangerously disconnected from the broader context; and the confinement of the language of participation and empowerment to the project alone was viewed as a handicap to wider transformation: 'Broader effective participation in the decision making process by which both local and national development decisions are shaped is increasingly seen by NGOs as the key to future development progress' (ibid., p. 137).[11] The NGO ACORD's (1991, p. 47) review of its experience with participatory techniques was similarly ahead of contemporary official agency thinking in noting that the ultimate aim of participation should be to 'engender a real involvement of civil society in issues that surpass the micro level'.

Within the early orthodoxy, then, a range of institutional positions is detectable. In the case of the World Bank, there is evidence of a variety of understandings of participation, ranging from the 'participation in projects' view in early Bank documents, to a more open-ended exploratory attitude in some – but not all – later documents. In the case of the ODA/DFID, from the start participation was fostered for reasons of empowerment as well as efficiency, and ways were sought to promote it beyond the project framework. In the case of the UNDP, an unapologetically political analysis urged that civil society be empowered to take an active role in national development. The NGO perspectives reviewed above prove the point made by some official agencies that where participation is concerned '[their] best teachers have been the NGOs' (see for example Racelis, 1992), and render absurd the claim in a Bank publication that 'participatory approaches have been used by other institutions but not as extensively as by the World Bank' (Robb, 1999, p. 3). They also offer an early insight into a contrast summed up later by Chambers (1995, p. 30):

for some participation advocates the objective is that 'they' participate in 'our' project; for others it is that 'we' learn to participate in
'their' project.[12]

Methods of Promoting Participation, and Methods for Participatory Development

The years between the mid 1980s and the mid 1990s were marked by
prolific methodological innovations to promote the concept and
practice of participation (meaning a variety of things to different
proponents) in a wide range of development activities (from tightly
defined projects to broad policy reform programmes) and among just
as wide an assortment of development actors (from donor agency
staff to poor people in isolated communities). The methods adopted
or developed by different actors reveal much about the kind of human
agency each sought to promote, whatever its rhetoric might have
implied. Methods typically pioneered and promoted by official
agencies were stakeholder analysis, social analysis, beneficiary assessment and logical framework analysis. Essentially toolkits applied by
planners or implementors to the stakeholder population, these were
characterized either by promotion of participation by primary or
secondary stakeholders in preidentified initiatives, or by the performing of a 'market research' role, checking on the suitability of a
particular intervention for a particular target group.[13]

The other major body of participatory methods was fundamentally
different in orientation. It sought to enable people 'to share, enhance
and analyze their knowledge of life and conditions, to plan and to act'
(Chambers, 1994a, p. 953). The 'family' of approaches and methods
referred to as participatory rural appraisal (PRA) owed much to the
natural resources sector and agro-ecosystems analysis, to experimentation among Asian and African NGOs, and to the Latin American
action research school, dating from the 1970s (see Chambers,
1994a).[14] These methodological developments are well documented
elsewhere (see especially IIED, 1988; Chambers, 1994a, 1994b, 1994c;
Pretty, 1995) and are not the focus of this chapter, but a number of
observations will help to show how, in the methodological revolution,
a number of strands of participatory thought and practice coalesced
into an alternative to the early participation orthodoxy: the 'participatory development' school.

Rapid rural appraisal (RRA), the main precursor to PRA, had
emerged in answer to Cernea's (1985) cry for sociological methods

and Chambers' (1983) concerns about rural development tourism. PRA developed in recognition of the limited power of RRA and other methods to open up the fundamentals of development (its purpose and its nature) to scrutiny, critique and ownership by poor and relatively powerless people. RRA, and the agency tools mentioned above, were primarily for outsiders to learn about poor people's lives and priorities so as better to fit these people into outsiders' development initiatives: they were methods for *enhancing people's participation*. PRA, on the other hand, was intended to enable poor people to define what sort of development they aspired to, and to become empowered through the very methods and processes of PRA: these were methods for fostering a *participatory development process*. By extension it is appropriate to call the advocates of PRA the 'participatory development' school ('development' here being subject to definition and redefinition through myriad participatory processes), and to call those who sought to engender participation in a development process mapped out and led by the agencies, the 'participation in projects' school, this analysis still being dominated by a view of development as containable and manageable in discrete units, and mainly controlled by outsiders.

To understand the development of participatory approaches an analogy can be drawn with the WID (women in development) and GAD (gender and development) schools of thought, themselves often counted as branches of participatory development.[15] For the WID school the problem was that women had been left out of development processes. Hence it prescribed actions to bring them in and developed techniques to this end. The GAD school, conversely, subjected the whole development enterprise to a gendered analysis, and derived from it far-reaching critiques of the paradigm itself, prescribing a radical transformation of the social, economic, political and cultural institutions on which development was founded. In terms of methods, it offered not a toolkit for transforming the development paradigm (a formidable task, beyond the scope of any toolkit), but frameworks for analysis and awareness-raising that would be capable, over time, of convincing a critical mass of people of the need for transformation. Analogously, the 'participation in projects' orthodoxy generated methods to bring people (beneficiaries, stakeholders) into a development process conceived by others. The participatory development school, in contrast, proposed analytical and awareness-raising frameworks capable of mobilizing a critical mass of development actors, both those with influence and those with no influence but much at stake, in order radically to transform the development paradigm, making it more democratic, equitable and inclusive. The end to which the participatory development school aspired was to make the enhancement of poor, marginalized people's lives the central objective of development, to which all other objectives would be secondary.

The prominence and proliferation of associated methods contributed to the impression that 'participation in development' was chiefly about methods. It was not: it was about human agency, but whereas the early orthodoxy was about human agency in *projects*, the debate shifted to agency in *development* as a whole, with correspondingly broad and deep methodological implications. Whereas in the 'participation in projects' agenda methods were a set of tools through which stakeholders were enabled to interact with a predefined project, in the 'participatory development' agenda methodology was the key to how development was conceived and by whom, and what sort of development was promoted and how.

The methodological revolution of PRA, while perhaps occurring at the expense of more conceptual and theoretical work on participatory development, forced development practitioners and theorists to confront some fundamental differences between the two camps, and to distinguish the irreconcilable differences from the reconcilable ones. Among the reconcilables was the proposition that people's own analysis was to some extent valid as a form of knowledge; that it could even be relevant to, and influential in, the formulation and modulation of development policy; and that development interventions took place in a political context, shot through with power relations, wherein measures to empower some social groups were likely to encounter resistance because they implied the disempowerment of others. The irreconcilable differences included the call for profound changes in powerful institutions, among them the major development donors, and in the global economic, social, cultural and political status quo on which the primacy of these institutions rested.

The Changing Context of Development Cooperation in the 1990s

Beyond the participation debates, several major changes occurred in the development cooperation context throughout the 1990s, all interrelated and all relevant to the participation issue: reduced reliance on projects as the sole vehicle for development cooperation; the refocusing of aid programmes on poverty-reduction goals; a new emphasis on governance, human rights and partnership; and the ascendance to prominence of 'civil society'.

The shift from the project as the framework for development aid to the packaging of cooperation as sector-wide programmes was 'part of a wider shift in developing thinking which focuses on the importance of developing consistent and effective policy frameworks at the macro and sectoral level, as a prerequisite for sustainable poverty reduction' (Norton and Bird, 1998).

The reduction of poverty was firmly reinstated as the prime aim of development cooperation, marked in the UK context by the white paper on international development (HM Government, 1997). The forces behind this refocusing were several: diminishing aid budgets, necessitating a sharper focus and more convincing evidence of their impact on poverty; ethical concern about the confusion of aid objectives with donors' geopolitical and commercial interests; the poverty focus of the *World Development Report 1990* (World Bank, 1990) and the *World Development Report 2000/2001: Attacking Poverty* (World Bank, 2000b); UN conference commitments to poverty reduction and basic needs satisfaction, which were underwritten by Northern and Southern countries throughout the decade; and in 1996 the crystallization of these commitments in the International Development Targets of the donors' consortium (the Development Assistance Committee of the Organization for Economic Cooperation and Development).[16]

Governance emerged as a new theme in development cooperation, defined as 'both a broad reform strategy, and a particular set of initiatives to strengthen the institutions of civil society with the objective of making them more accountable, open and transparent, and more democratic' (Minogue, cited in Gaventa and Valderrama, 1999, p. 4). This brought together older concepts of stakeholders' rights and public accountability with newer interpretations of citizenship and polity; and echoed the principle of empowerment through participation that was found in the earlier participation discourse of NGOs:

> Raising standards of governance is central to the elimination of poverty. Making government more responsive to the needs and wishes of poor people can improve the quality of their lives. Accessible systems of justice help to address family and personal insecurity. Poor people, and especially poor women, are likely to be the last to enjoy these rights unless they receive support (HM Government, 1997, p. 10).

The translation of good government into better lives for the poor was expected to happen via the mediation of 'civil society'. Those 'organizations in society which fall outside government and which are not primarily motivated by profit' (DFID, 1998, p. 6) were the major new development actors of the 1990s. Demands for good government and poverty eradication, the theory went, stemmed from 'diverse and vibrant' civil society organizations, which stimulated community action, articulated the needs of the politically powerless and voiceless, reduced the poor's vulnerability to economic and environmental shocks, and generally contributed to socioeconomic stability and equity (ibid., 1998).

There was a marked convergence of the development agenda with the human rights agenda, prominent in the late 1990s with the fiftieth anniversary of the Universal Declaration of Human Rights (1998). Closely linked to governance debates and founded on the universal acceptability of norms endorsed under UN auspices by most governments, the 'human rights approach to development', still espoused by several major development agencies, was 'participatory, inclusive and pro-poor' (Hausermann, 1998, p. 35).

Horizontal relations of partnership, between Northern and Southern governments and between governments and civil society organizations, began to replace the traditional vertical relationships between donors and recipients. 'Partnership' was a concept long used by Northern NGOs to describe their relationships with developing country NGOs,[17] but was now being adopted by official agencies. The UK government's white paper (HM Government, 1997) illustrates this shift in approach, paraphrased by commentators thus:

> Put simply, the bargain on offer to developing countries is this: commit yourself to poverty reduction and good government, and in return you can expect a longer-term commitment from DFID, more money and greater flexibility in the use of resources. The philosophy underlying this ... pact is [that] development is about autonomy, self-determination and self-respect, as much as income growth. All these require an aid relationship founded on mutual respect and maximum feasible equality in political power (Maxwell and Riddell, 1998, p. 257).

As Maxwell and Riddell go on to show, it is infinitely complex to translate into practice the intention of 'putting the government and the people of developing countries in the driver's seat', the task to which donors are now turning.

Critical Views on Participatory Approaches[18]

Many have remarked that the word 'participation', like 'community', generates a warm feeling, a laudable ideal with which few would disagree (Nelson and Wright, 1995; Eyben and Ladbury, 1995; Cornerhouse, 1998). Yet others observe that PRA is 'either glorified or vilified' (Guijt and Cornwall, 1995, p. 3).

Even among its proponents, opinions diverge on the extent to which participation is appropriate or convenient, for whom and of what type; and on the political underpinnings or suspected hidden agendas of participation. Several typologies of participation have been devised. A distinction commonly made, as noted by Nelson and Wright (1995, p. 1), is between participation as a *means* (to accomplish the aims of a project more efficiently, effectively or cheaply) and participation as an *end* (where the community or group sets up a process to control its own development).

A refinement of the means/ends dichotomy is the distinction between participation for instrumental purposes and participation for transformative purposes, whereby getting people to buy into a donor's project (to share the costs and ensure commitment and project sustainability) is instrumentalist, and facilitating people to decide on their own priorities is transformative (ibid., p. 5; McGee and Timlin, 1999, p. 4). A third typology is that of levels or intensity of participation, often represented as a ladder or continuum (see ODA, 1995a, pp. 98–100; Narayan, 1995, pp. 7–9; Centre for Rural Development and Training, 1998). The continuum ranges from information-sharing through consulting and joint decision making to the initiation and control of action by the stakeholders themselves.[19] A more politically discerning analytical schema is suggested by White (1996, p. 7), who draws on fieldwork experiences to break down the concept into its various forms, the way it is perceived from the 'top down' (that is, by policy makers and donors) and from the 'bottom up' (by people or grassroots organizations), and the range of functions it serves.

None of these typologies is incontrovertible. Some rest on questionable assumptions about the divisibility of means and ends and about the ultimate aim of development. Some harbour implicit or explicit value-judgements. Some hint – disclaimers notwithstanding – that the latter category (or categories) is more truly participatory than the former and that the former is in some way exploitative of 'participants'. It would be easy – facile even – to label the early orthodoxy as participation as a means rather than an end, promoted by agencies seeking legitimization, for instrumental rather than transformative purposes and confined to the levels of information-sharing and consultation rather than espousing joint decision making or initiation and control by stakeholders. The alternative current shines by comparison, as participation as an end in itself, for transformative purposes, with a stress on empowerment through joint decision making, initiation and control by stakeholders. However, as with the WID and GAD discourses, the differentiating frameworks were devised with the benefit of hindsight. The later current would not have arisen in a vacuum but came as an improvement on the earlier one (which, it must be recognized, remains the dominant form in which participation policies are put into practice in development work around the world). Moreover where the 'participation in projects' orthodoxy can be accused of excessive pretensions of improving poor people's lot, given the insignificance of the project in their lives and the extent and complexity of the deprivations and structural discriminations they face, the 'participatory development' school is open to the criticism that its claims are excessive. We shall return to this point below.

Aside from these typologies and the criticisms implicit in them, there are two main bodies of critique of participatory approaches: one from within, and one from without.

'Self-critical epistemological awareness' (Chambers, 1997) is an integral, permanent aspect of PRA philosophy and practice, to be applied both in interpreting PRA outputs and in observing PRA dynamics and process. It generates not critiques in the normal sense of the term, but an ongoing dialogue between practitioners – and on the part of the individual practitioner – on the quality, validity and ethics of what they are doing, which guards against slipping standards, poor practice and the abuse or exploitation of the people involved. This self-critical epistemological awareness is increasingly articulated publicly, heightened by alarm at the speed with which PRA has spread, and at the possible consequences of such rapid spread for quality and integrity.

Welbourn (1991) and Mosse (1994), drawing on experience of PRA practice, question the simplistic notion of 'community' that under-pinned early PRA discourse, finding it naïve and simplistic. The image of communities as homogeneous, harmonious units whose members share common interests and priorities contrasts sharply with reality, and leaves RRA/PRA ill-equipped to deal with power differences between participants or discern the weaker voices among them. In particular the unquestioning treatment of 'community' has caused PRA practitioners to reproduce the gender biases that mark most real-life communities and – to a greater or lesser extent – the attitudes of most development and PRA practitioners. While increased gender equity is an implicit goal of the empowerment project of PRA, this is not the case with RRA, and being implicit has proved insufficient. Critical practitioners argue that, since experience shows clearly that PRA is not gender-sensitive, PRA training must focus trainees' and participants' attention on gender and other axes of social and economic difference (age, ethnicity, poverty) and explore, rather than evade, related tensions and disparities between people (for example Welbourn, 1991).

Other concerns centre on the social and physical context in which PRA is carried out (Mosse, 1994, 1995). In a self-critical reflection on experiences in India, Mosse (1994, p. 499) poses searching questions about the extent to which the successful use of PRA depends on established links between an agency and local communities; who does and does not participate in PRA sessions, especially those organized as very public events; and the problems posed by the existence of multiple kinds of knowledge, not all of which are equally suitable inputs for planning processes. The myth of representativity of views forthcoming in public PRA meetings, and of the kinds of knowledge disclosed and easily absorbed via PRA tools, is exploded, and the tendency of particular groups who conform to the PRA mould – never women – to capture proceedings and agendas is analyzed. Admitting culpability for these shortcomings in the project he describes, Mosse presents them as 'an indication of the continuing need for context-specific methodological adaptation', especially as PRA spreads ever wider. PRA techniques, he concludes:

> have contributed significantly to the promotion of participatory development. But, while they offer new opportunities for the articulation of local knowledge, including perspectives of women and other subordinate sections of communities, they may also expose projects to new risks by creating public contexts and a new idiom in which dominant interests can gain legitimacy. Perhaps the greatest danger is the promotion of PRA as a short-cut methodology of participation, rather than as a set of techniques or tools which have to be used in the context of project-specific strategies for participatory planning. ... Its advantages ... over

other tools of participatory development – its speed, the visibility of its outputs, its amenability to use on a large scale – may also turn out to be its greatest weaknesses (ibid., p. 522).

This is a rallying cry to all those seeking to improve the quality and credibility of participatory techniques, and it echoes many of the concerns raised in a special issue of *PLA Notes* dedicated to 'Critical Reflections from Practice' (Guijt and Cornwall, 1995). The editorial warns:

> We have come full circle. PRA started as a critical response to the inadequacy of existing research and planning processes. Yet many of the concerns discussed here focus precisely on the inadequacy of local participation in the process. .. By describing what we do, and not claiming to do what we do not or cannot do, much of the confusion can be avoided. By reflecting critically on what we do, we can learn from our mistakes and move forward (ibid., p. 7).

While participation advocates work to address these concerns, a tide of antiparticipation sentiment has arisen outside the camp, largely in development academia. The same sort of accusation that participatory development advocates have levelled at the project-bound participation orthodoxy is being directed at them: hubris with respect to the capacity of participatory approaches to effect beneficial change for poor people. Some go as far as to dub participation the 'new tyranny'.[20] The papers from a recent conference on this subject are a curious mixture of destructive and constructive. Space constraints preclude a detailed review here, but most of the contributions relate to two central concerns: the predominance of rhetoric over authentically participatory realities that justify the claims made for PRA and other participatory approaches; and a blindness to context, leading to mechanistic applications of participatory techniques and the neglect of power differentials within project communities.[21] Among the destructive critiques, many are only weakly grounded in practice (for example Henkel and Stirrat, 1999), or cite examples that are clearly cases of bad practice (for example Mosse, 1999; Biggs and Smith, 1998), and hence hardly justify writing off the entire approach. Instead of addressing the agencies and organizations that manage the bad-practice projects cited, in some cases the criticisms target the project model, and in others the target is the participatory development school associated with PRA – and even named individuals. Few of the destructive critiques offer any comparison of outcomes achieved via participatory techniques with outcomes achieved using other techniques; nor do most propose plausible alternatives. Moreover, as noted above, the two central concerns (and several of the peripheral ones) were identified long ago by participation advocates as areas needing corrective attention, and they have since received it.

Among the constructive academic critiques are several that make a real contribution to understanding what can happen in projects in the name of participation.[22] They offer two important reminders: that notwithstanding the general trend away from the project as the sole framework for development assistance, and the diverse agenda of the participatory development school, most ongoing attempts to promote participation on the ground are still of the 'participation in projects' kind; and that despite the recent resort to greater caution by the participatory development school, some proponents – in official development agencies, Southern government agencies, and NGOs – are still making claims for participation that are scarcely vindicated by the evidence from the grassroots. Areas for further work are identified to help donors and others promoting participation to consolidate and validate their approaches.

Nonetheless, even these constructive critiques do not isolate the problems of participatory approaches *per se* from the general problems intrinsic to official or bureaucratic development programmes: the rigidities of the project framework, the perversity of policy processes, obstacles to implementation, and the cumbersome and conservative nature of bureaucracies. Failure to distinguish between the very divergent strands that exist within the bundle of 'participatory approaches' leads to blanket generalizations that – given the differences highlighted above between the 'participation in projects' orthodoxy, PRA as a methodology and the broader, alternative, participatory development current – are hard to substantiate. As a whole the 'tyranny' school smacks of a reactive backlash against a new and fast-spreading phenomenon, rather than a measured and reasonable verdict – which is not to deny that it enjoins a serious response.

The official agencies have created opportunities for critical reflection on their own efforts. In December 1998 an international conference entitled 'Upscaling and Mainstreaming Participation of Primary Stakeholders: Lessons Learnt and Ways Forward' was held at the World Bank, organized by the NGO Working Group with support from the Bank and bilateral donors. The conference identified a need to move the focus from participation by the poor in projects, to a more complex vision of development as multiple stakeholders with multiple objectives. While 'islands of participation' could be achieved through donor interventions, the feeling was that efforts should instead focus on propelling long-term processes of change. A broader concept of 'participation' than the project-bound one was in evidence, encompassing issues of autonomy, agency, rights, governance and accountability (Andy Norton, DFID, personal comment).

The NGO Working Group put a series of recommendations to the World Bank, based on its monitoring of the Bank's participation policy from 1994 onwards. In essence they called for incentives to support institutional innovation in favour of primary stakeholder participation; and for an extension of norms of transparency and accountability downwards (to primary stakeholders) as well as upwards (to senior management and the Northern tax-paying public). The Bank was urged to promote participatory policy development systematically, building on the good examples that already existed (for example in the form of participatory poverty assessments and country assistance strategies).[23] To enhance partner countries' capacity for participatory approaches, it was recommended that flagship country partnerships be selected and efforts focused on building capacity there among civil society and government actors. To foster an enabling context for participation, the Bank was urged to link the participation concept to governance and human rights agendas in partner countries, and to strengthen participation advocates in their respective agencies or organizations by supporting networking activities and continuous learning (Tandon, 1999; Norton, personal comment). Accepting these recommendations, the Bank noted that since Bank projects were increasingly 'owned' by member governments within a framework of partnership, success in promoting participation was contingent on real commitment to participation among member governments.

The DFID commissioned research on the potential for increasing stakeholder participation in its country programmes. The ensuing recommendations relate to operational lessons (the need to develop staff skills and guidance available to them, and to learn from the DFID's and other agencies' experience); project cycle management (the need to make it more flexible, enhance commitment to stakeholder involvement in it, increase 'downwards accountability' in monitoring, and use the logframe more critically and discerningly);

and staff competencies and training needs in the area of participatory development. Most challenging are the recommendations on institutionalizing participation. The DFID has been encouraged to pursue more participatory outcomes through aid delivery models that involve closer partnerships with secondary stakeholders (Southern governments), longer-term partnerships, interdonor collaboration such as occurs in sectoral programmes, more active policy dialogue and advocacy with secondary stakeholders, and greater consensus and focus on achieving internal institutional change (INTRAC, 1998).

A Changing Participation Agenda

How have the orthodox agencies and the alternative school responded to these critiques? The striking aspect of current participation agendas, whether in NGOs, official development agencies or 'alternative' academic circles, is their apparent similarity.

As befits their learning philosophy, the self-critics of the participatory development school have taken measures to address their concerns about the theory and practice of participation. Definitional confusion between PRA and RRA is now routinely addressed via the setting of parameters – in terms of participation or empowerment – on exercises referred to as PRA/PLA. The tendency to neglect ethical, political and process dimensions is being redressed through a new emphasis on personal behaviour and attitudes and on the dynamics of institutional changes during training in participatory methods (for example that provided by the Institute of Development Studies in the UK, Actionaid in many countries, and Southern NGOs such as Outreach in south India) and in research agendas and publications (for example the 'Pathways to Participation' project at IDS – Garett Pratt, personal comment; Chambers, 1997). Links are being made upwards from the micro level to macro structures and processes through a growing focus on the policy process, and on influencing it via the use of participatory methods (IDS, 1996b; Holland and Blackburn, 1998). The criticism that early participation discourse lacked an explicit gender perspective has resulted in a concerted effort to imbue participatory practice with gender awareness, via methodological adaptations and explicit treatment of gendered power differences in field PRA processes or in organizations undergoing training; and to document the evidence and build theory on the links between participatory approaches and transformation in social relations (see for example Guijt and Shah, 1998). Methodological complementarity between participatory and other approaches was the theme of an issue of *PLA Notes* in 1997, and is a burgeoning area in development research, poverty assessment and planning (for example Carvalho and White, 1997; Booth *et al.*, 1998). The political aspects implicit in participatory approaches are finding articulation in new work on governance, decentralization, democratization and civil society (Gaventa and Valderrama, 1999).

Meanwhile, the major official institutions are grappling with the tensions inherent in promoting participatory approaches in their own and Southern government bureaucracies, while simultaneously advocating partnership and stronger local ownership. The World Bank has already introduced innovative forms of lending to accommodate the flexibility and slower pace demanded by participatory approaches, radically revised its information-dissemination policies and practices for greater transparency, and instituted stakeholder participation in much analytical and policy work. However according to the Bank the further-reaching questions are still outstanding: how it can create a demand for participatory approaches among partners; how participation can support the goals of governance, transparency and accountability; what systems can be devised for assessing change in processes and institutions; how the quality of participation can be improved; and how the critical masses can be empowered to influence policy and institutional change (Aycrigg, 1998).

The DFID is presented with similar challenges by the Participatory Approaches Learning Study (INTRAC, 1998), which finds evidence of progress in the areas of stakeholder consultation and adaptive use of the project cycle to increase the potential for participation, but concludes that:

> If DFID as a whole is to take forward the [government] White Paper's ideas on partnership it will have to achieve one of the more resonant senses of participation – viewing development partners as political equals. This is an enhanced sense of participation that goes well beyond the mechanics of project aid delivery (ibid., p. 1).

The introduction of Poverty Reduction Strategy Papers (PRSPs) by the World Bank and the International Monetary Fund (IMF) as the main prerequisite for development finance is perhaps the acid test of donors' and Southern governments' commitment to participation and ownership. From 2000, PRSPs have to be in place before debt relief or IMF concessional loans can be granted to highly indebted poor countries (HIPCs). With donors and governments espousing participatory processes for developing, implementing and monitoring national poverty reduction strategies, and in the same breath pushing for the rapid endorsement of PRSPs so that debt relief and aid flows can continue uninterrupted, it remains to be seen whether genuine participation by civil society can be fostered under these pressurized conditions, and how civil society actors will rate the 'participation' afforded to them.

Concluding Comments

To sum up, when participation pervaded development discourse and practice in the 1980s it was seen as a key to the greater effectiveness and sustainability of projects. In the 1990s the focus of the participation debate shifted to policy, governance and institutional concepts, and linkages with the newer concepts of civil society, citizenship and a rights-based approach to development. Concurrently, critiques on operational and methodological grounds surfaced both within the participation school and without, presenting several challenges to participation advocates, both in shoring up existing theory and practice and in breaking new ground.

The fact that the alternative participation school's current agenda reflects many of the critiques recently expressed should not be taken to indicate that it is in a defensive, reactive mode. Rather, numerous parallels can be observed between this agenda and the changes in the wider context of development cooperation in the 1990s, described above. Did the alternative participation current became absorbed into the tide of mainstream development, and take up the issues it encountered there? Or have the mainstream development cooperation agenda and the participatory development current converged, bringing into the mainstream a number of issues previously confined to the alternative agenda?

While the evolution of participation discourse and practice to some extent reveals the adoption of aspects of the radical alternative by the orthodoxy, this should be interpreted as a positive development for both the mainstream and the alternative current, rather than as a triumph of the former over the latter. For any transformative project, the convergence of the mainstream agenda with key tenets of its own is a sign of success. Most importantly, while working ever more closely with the institutions they seek to transform, a significant number of participatory development advocates in the North and South have succeeded in retaining their intellectual autonomy *vis-à-vis* these institutions while in many cases depending on them for funding, thanks in part to allies within the institutions themselves, who, recognizing the benefits of energetic advocacy by civil society – especially on the part of NGOs and academics – bolster it and use it strategically.

Returning to the question of who participates in whose project, at the level of practice the central challenges are marrying the participation agenda with the governance agendas of partner countries, facilitating change in bureaucratic institutions, and fortifying civil society to the point where it can effectively exploit new openings for participation in polity, society and development. At the level of rhetoric, the participation orthodoxy no longer finds it sufficient to permit 'them' to participate in 'our' projects, but recognizes that 'our' projects are not going to change their lives much, and seeks to find out what 'their' projects of life might be, and how we – practitioners, academics, NGOs, official agencies and partner governments – might most usefully participate in them. There is quite a distance between taking cognizance of this and actually altering time-honoured and institutionalized practices so as to privilege 'their' projects, but there are grounds for cautious optimism that steps are being taken, and that the alternative current, without compromising itself, can continue to prompt and steer the transformation of mainstream development.

Notes

1. I am grateful to Andy Norton (DFID), Martin Minogue (IDPM), Jennie Richmond (Christian Aid) and colleagues at the IDS for comments on earlier drafts of this chapter.
2. According to one definition, human agency 'attributes to the individual actor the capacity to process social experience and to devise ways of coping with life, even under the most extreme forms of coercion. Within the limits of information, uncertainty and the other constraints (for example physical, normative or politico-economic) that exist, social actors are "knowledgeable" and "capable". They attempt to solve problems, learn how to intervene in the flow of social events around them, and monitor continuously their own actions, observing how others react to their behaviour and taking note of the various contingent circumstances' (Giddens, cited in Long and Long, 1992, pp. 22–3).

3. An NGO term describing a particular approach to supporting partner organizations: 'A local accompanier is a skilled, experienced development worker who spends regular periods of time, mutually agreed by a local NGO and its funding partners, to help increase the local NGO's capacity to work with the local community to bring about development' (Hughes, 1998, p. 6).

4. Cleaver (1999, p. 15) cites Long and Long (1992): 'individuals are only ever partly enrolled in the projects of others'.

5. Other important World Bank documents, related to the Learning Group and its outcomes, include Cernea (1992), Narayan (1995) and Aycrigg (1998).

6. 'Economic and sector work' refers to World Bank analysis of the situation and prospects of a borrower country and the devising of a framework for lending and policy advice to reflect them. It is distinguished from 'lending operations', the actual allocation of funds in accordance with the framework devised.

7. As defined by the DFID and the World Bank, primary stakeholders are those who are directly affected by a planned activity (for example the inhabitants of a community that is to be provided with a well); secondary stakeholders are those who have an interest in it because they will be indirectly affected, or can influence the project, and whose participation is therefore vital to its success. Secondary stakeholders include local people, NGOs, other civil society and private sector organizations, different levels of government, and donors, including those supporting the project.

8. 'The Bank's General Counsel has explained that it is appropriate for the Bank (a) to advocate to member governments that they use participatory approaches and civil society consultation in the selection, design, implementation and evaluation of development programs, on the grounds that this enhances development effectiveness; and (b) to advise governments to allow and foster a strong civil society participating in public affairs' ('Prohibition of Political Activities in the Bank's work', legal opinion to the Bank's Board, 12 July 1995, cited on World Bank website in 'Guidelines and Good Practice for Civil Society Consultations', no date).

9. The Swedish International Development Authority (SIDA), the German GTZ, and the UK Overseas Development Administration (ODA, now the Department for International Development, DFID).

10. Now the Department for International Development (DFID).

11. Citing Lok Niti of the Asian NGO Coalition.

12. The contrast is noted early on by Bhatnagar and Williams (1992); but this important differentiation seemed to become submerged in the course of operationalizing the concept in the World Bank, resurfacing only recently.

13. For more details on these tools see World Bank (1995a), pp. 173–97. See Francis (1999) for comments on the differences between the rationales, methods and epistemologies of what he calls the 'client consultation approach' (beneficiary assessment) and the 'participatory development' approach (the school associated with PRA).

14. The popularization and dissemination of PRA was spearheaded by two UK institutions: the International Institute for Environment and Development (IIED) and the Institute of Development Studies (IDS) at the University of Sussex. That these activities have emanated mainly from the North reflects the greater opportunities for writing, publishing and disseminating enjoyed by members of Northern institutions, rather than the places of origin of the approaches, which lie in the South.

15. For a distinction between these see Moser (1993, pp. 2–4) and Canadian Council for International Cooperation (1991). White (1996, p. 14) also draws a comparison between the early participation orthodoxy and the WID approach, highlighting their shared focus on bringing in actors that were assumed – shortsightedly – to have been 'left out'.

16. Two major development happenings in 2000 were expected to heighten the renewed prominence of the poverty-reduction objective: the publication of the *World Development Report 2000* on poverty, and the granting of significant debt relief to highly indebted poor countries via the enhanced HIPC Initiative (HIPC II), conditional on countries having a viable national poverty-reduction strategy in place.

17. That is not to say that our partners always use the term to refer to 'us': the asymmetry with which they and we view our 'partnership' has been the topic of rich and revealing debates between partners and Christian Aid staff.

18. The term 'participatory approaches' is used here to cover all the approaches discussed, since there are critical views on all variations of participation.

19. Ladder or continuum diagrams usually carry the disclaimer that although they might appear to imply a preference for the latter-mentioned levels, no such hierarchy is intended, and the appropriate level or intensity of participation will vary from case to case.

20. 'Participation: the New Tyranny?' was the title of a conference held at the Institute for Development Policy and Management in November 1998. The papers are published in B. Cooke and U. Kothari (eds), *Participation: The New Tyranny?* (London: Zed Books, 2001). The dictionary definition of 'tyranny' is 'the cruel and arbitrary use of authority' (*Concise Oxford Dictionary*), which is out of proportion to the critiques actually made in the conference papers, even the most negative ones.

21. These two are the cross-cutting concerns that inform many of the conference papers, and indeed were strongly suggested by the conference organizers in the call for papers: 'We will consider the limitations of participation, and the extent to which phrases like "bottom up" and "empowerment" are delusions. Papers are sought which explore how participatory methodologies, far from reversing power relations merely reinstate and reinforce them in a different guise'. Other critical angles, some of them quite singular and based on dubious premises, are adopted by individual contributors. See Cooke and Kothari (2001).

22. Most notably, Cleaver (1999), Musch (1999) and Mohan (1999).

23. Participatory poverty assessments (PPAs) were initiated as a complement to the poverty assessments promoted by the World Bank, in which

conventional economic and social data-gathering approaches are used to describe poverty in largely economistic terms. In PPAs, participatory appraisal methods are used to enable poor people to describe and analyze their own realities and priorities, and to facilitate the incorporation of these into the design of national policy and official aid programmes. Country assistance strategies are the World Bank's 'main vehicle for designing its program to support sustainable development in a member country, taking into account the country's specific needs and conditions' (Aycrigg, 1998, p. 10).

7

Power to the People? Good Governance and the Reshaping of the State

MARTIN MINOGUE

Most political questions turn on controversial empirical claims and debatable speculation about right and wrong (Berkowitz, 2000).

A major development strategy in the past decade has been to reshape and improve 'governance', defined as the entire set of relationships between the state, the market and society. This has produced an active agenda to slim down the state, increase efficiency in the delivery of public services and extend the range of public–private working relationships. A major motivation behind all this has been the political reward expected for reducing public expenditure and related taxation (Manning, 1996).

These public sector reforms, mainly initiated in the UK, have steadily diffused to developing and transitional economies via multi-lateral and bilateral aid mechanisms (Common, 1998). A significant component of this increasingly global agenda has been the concern of aid donors to promote 'good governance' (democratization, the rule of law, human rights protection, transparency, participation and accountability), often by attaching what are in effect political conditions to development aid. 'Good governance' and 'new public management' are regarded as mutually supportive reforms, with greater political accountability contributing to more efficient government. This chapter will outline the 'good governance' orthodoxy and its mixed origins (partly in the classic Western political tradition, partly in neoliberal thought).

Critical analysis presents a 'contested' literature of governance, reflecting the ideological nature of the debate and its political origins in the so-called 'collapse of socialism', and the determination of aid donors to impose upon recipient countries their preferred economic strategies and development policies. The critique also focuses on the absence of empirical support for many of the assumptions about economic and political relationships that underlie the orthodoxy, and draws attention to the flawed application of the strategy due to uneven and inconsistent policy implementation.

The concluding section suggests the need for a learning process, leading to recognition of a varied set of cultural perspectives on what might constitute an acceptable model of good governance (Blunt, 1995), and a valid dialogue on human rights.

The Meanings of Governance

Rhodes (1997, pp. 52–3) declares that 'governance has too many meanings to be useful', but the concept can be rescued by stipulating one meaning and showing how it contributes to the analysis of change. His own stipulation centres on 'self-organizing, interorganizational networks', which consist of non-state as well as state actors and rest on relations of exchange and trust, rather than on formal institutional roles and boundaries. The state retains a role, but the primary characteristic of governance networks is their degree of autonomy from the state.

When we examine the debates on governance in the context of development, we find that different actors do stipulate their own meanings, but that these various definitions throw up similar ideas and similar terminologies, as the examination below of three main proponents – all major aid donors – demonstrates.

The United Nations Development Programme (UNDP)

The definition provided by the UNDP (1995), with the label of 'sound governance', sets out the following factors:

- Political legitimacy.
- Freedom of association and participation.
- A fair and reliable judicial system.
- Bureaucratic and financial accountability.
- Freedom of information.

- Efficient and effective public sector management.
- Cooperation with institutions of civil society.

It is clear that in comparison with the UK approach, similar principles are rehearsed but there are two significant differences of interpretation. First, less emphasis is placed on the assumed superiority of pluralist, multiparty, electorally oriented systems, recognizing that different forms of political authority might combine efficiency and accountability in different ways. Second, the UNDP document recognizes the problem of relative cultural values, accepting that systems of governance may vary in the weights attached to such ideas as participation, order and authority, and in the values placed on individual or collective economic, social and political relationships.

Since 1995 the UNDP after considerable internal debate has revised and extended its position on what constitutes sound governance. Its most recent policy document, *Governance for Sustainable Human Development* (UNDP, 1998a) emphasizes that the aim of governance is to ensure that the three key players – the state, the private sector and civil society – are equally represented and valued as partners in the affairs of a country; while 'good governance' (note the change of nomenclature, accepting what has become a standard label among aid donors) should focus on making government participatory, accountable and transparent, and especially on ensuring that the voices of the poorest and most vulnerable are heard. The UNDP's implementation strategy is largely to operate through country assistance programmes. An example of this is the UNDP's aid programme in Vietnam, where explicit links are made to major Vietnamese economic and administrative reforms, and the 'three partner' scenario is repeated:

> The State creates a conducive political and legal environment. The private sector generates jobs and income, and civil society facilitates political and social interaction ... a major objective of good governance is to promote a constructive partnership between all three, recognizing shared values, and the unique role that each plays (UNDP Vietnam, 1999).

What is notable here is that the interplay between state, market and society makes governance at once an inclusive and a vague concept, leaving considerable room for flexible interpretation in individual cases.

The World Bank

The World Bank's approach (1992a, 1994b) moves rather uneasily between the neutral term 'governance' and the trickier 'good governance', tricky for the World Bank because its articles of agreement explicitly prohibit political intervention and require it to take into account only economic considerations. Accordingly the World Bank avoids statements about preferred types of political system, or human rights, referring rather to 'the management of a country's economic and social resources for development' and to the need for 'a predictable and transparent framework of rules and institutions'. Yet in its references to the need for a participatory civil society, operating within the rule of law (World Bank, 1992a), it steps straight into unavoidably political territory. Moreover it reveals that the bulk of its governance lending in 1991–93 was to projects with clear political connotations (Table 7.1):

TABLE 7.1   *Content of World Bank governance lending, 1991–93*

Category	Number of projects
Decentralization, capacity-building	68
Economic management	49
State-owned enterprise reforms	33
Participation	30
Legal framework	6

Source: World Bank (1994b).

Of these categories, only 'economic management' can be said to be non-political, and even that operates (as do all state activities) within a political framework. Projects that promote state enterprise reforms (especially if this involves privatization) or decentralization are politically controversial in many developing and transitional economies, principally because they entail attacks on heavily institutionalized political patronage or on national ideology.

If we compare these definitions by major aid donors it is clear that governance strategies involve much more than the more efficient management of economic and social resources or the improved delivery of public services; it is also a strategy to strengthen the institutions of civil society, to make governments more open and accountable, and even to transform the political context (through democratization) of the developing and transitional economies.

The UK Government

The most overtly political definition was that produced by the UK aid ministry (then the Overseas Development Administration, ODA) in 1993 under the label 'good government' (ODA, 1993). This set out a policy that has been continued in modified form by the ODA's successor, the Department for International Development (DFID, 2000b), and has effectively been extended by association with the Foreign and Commonwealth Office's new commitment in 1997 to give more weight to an 'ethical dimension' in foreign policy. The founding document has four main components:

- *Legitimacy* implies that a system of government must operate with the consent of those governed. The latter must therefore have the means to give or withhold their consent. Subsequent ministerial interpretations made clear that such legitimacy was thought most likely to be guaranteed by pluralist, multiparty democracy.
- *Accountability* involves the existence of mechanisms to ensure that public officials and political leaders are answerable for their actions and use of public resources, and requires transparent government and a free media.
- *Competence* refers to the design and implementation of appropriate public policies and the efficient delivery of public services.
- *Respect for law and human rights* stresses the significance of providing protection for civil and political liberties, guaranteed by the establishment of the rule of law and independent judiciaries.

This policy was criticized for being too vague, for appearing to privilege Westminster-type democracy over other political systems and for introducing a new form of conditionality. However the responsible ministers, Lynda Chalker (overseas development) and Douglas Hurd (foreign secretary), between 1991 and 1995, while insisting that they did not seek to impose Westminster democracy on other countries, held firm to the objectives of promoting 'democratization', efficient government and market-oriented economic policies, if necessary by the attachment of political conditions to development aid (see Crawford, 1998, pp. 47–50).

The Origins of Good Governance

But where did these ideas and strategies come from, and how have they come to be so dominant in development discourse and the practical development agenda? The first point to make is that many of the component parts of this strategy are not new. The development administration movement of the 1960s was just as concerned with the building of efficient and capable institutions, and possibly even more convinced that economic modernization of Third World economies would bring in its train political modernization in the shape of Western-style liberal democracies (Heady, 1996). Decolonization in the 1950s and 1960s, in the British case at least, was predicated on the transfer of the institutional model of the metropolitan power, the so-called Westminster–Whitehall model (Goldsworthy, 1971), and this was initially assumed to include a parliamentary system, electoral competition, a neutral civil service, decentralization, the rule of Western-style law and the protection of civil and political rights. Even before this, in the 1920s colonial stewardship was committed to fostering 'development and good government' (Lee, 1967). So we can see that even the label 'good government' is not new.

What *is* new is the degree to which contemporary aid donors are speaking with one voice, and enunciating what begins to look like a strategy intended for universal application. Also new is the explicit intention to enforce this agenda through the attachment of political conditions to lending; what is termed 'political conditionality'. Political conditionality enshrines a definite shift of direction by aid donors, and must be distinguished from the economic conditionality that has always been a feature of traditional development aid (Cassen *et al.*, 1994; Burnell, 1997). Whereas aid has always supported latent political objectives, this link has rarely been expressed openly, and certainly has not amounted to a global strategy.

The shift in the early 1990s is not difficult to explain. Crawford (1998) identifies three explanatory factors, on the basis of existing literature.

Political-Economic Linkages

Major donors were unhappy with the ineffectiveness of aid pro-grammes, and the World Bank and IMF in particular ascribed the failure (or what they euphemistically called 'policy slippage') of several structural adjustment reforms to the weakness, incompetence and corruption of recipient governments. If economic conditionality was not working for political reasons, the obvious answer was to extend conditionality into the political sphere. Such thinking had emerged as early as 1989 in a World Bank report on structural adjustment programmes in Africa, and despite the political restric-tions on the Bank's mandate, this approach had rapidly gained ground (Nelson, 1992). Other commentators (for example Stokke, 1995a) have noted the emergence in the 1990s of the view that there was a positive relationship between democracy and economic success, and therefore a link needed to be created between economic liberalization reforms and democratization reforms.

The Collapse of Socialism

Most commentators agree that the end of the Cold War and the collapse of communist regimes in the former Soviet Union and Eastern Europe were highly significant (Gibbon, 1993; Burnell, 1994; Crawford, 1995; Robinson, 1995; Stokke, 1995a). These events seemed to produce a surge of triumphalism, one component of which was renewed confidence in the demonstratable power of the capitalist democracies. At the same time Western governments were released from the obligation to support authoritarian regimes on geopolitical grounds (Moore, 1993b), and were in a strong position to insist on economic and political liberalization in return for Western aid to former communist countries (Stokke, 1995a, p. 9; Uvin, 1993, p. 63). This stance by bilateral donors such as the UK and the US soon fed through into multilateral donors' aid programmes (World Bank, 1992a, 1994b, 1996).

Domestic Aid Constituencies

The governance literature identifies a third factor behind the policy shift in the 1990s: the pressure on donor governments to reduce public expenditure and the consequent need to justify the protection of aid budgets. Crawford (1998, p. 8) suggests that policies emphasizing democracy, human rights and good governance provided 'a new principle, unanimously agreed as desirable', while allowing donors to rationalize discrimination between 'worthy' and 'unworthy' recipients of aid, who would now be held more accountable for the use of donated funds.

The Critique of Good Governance: Disputed Concepts

The vagueness, breadth and all-inclusive nature of the concepts of governance was noted earlier. This section examines some of the questionable assumptions that seem to underlie donors' perceptions. These assumptions are treated in relation to economic–political linkages and universalist notions of human rights.

Political-Economic Linkages

The Processes of Economic and Political Change

Policymakers responsible for governance strategies and policies appear to work with oversimplified and superficial perceptions of the causal relationship between economic and political change, and of the (presumed) causal relationship between democratization and development. Yet this is a highly problematic area, because different theoretical positions on these relationships produce different chains of causation, leading to different prescriptive models. Nothing in the official literature on governance would lead one to suspect that these ambiguities exist, or that the precise relationship between economic and political change is a strongly contested one. There is a sometimes implicit and frequently explicit assumption that political reforms must precede, and will produce, economic reforms. Yet the whole history of Western development suggests the opposite, that economic change precedes and produces political change. The most impressive account in this respect is by Barrington (1969), whose study *The Social Origins of Dictatorship and Democracy* concludes that:

- The crucial features of modernization (industrialization, the commercialization of agriculture) do not invariably lead to democracy; they may equally lead to fascism (Germany, Japan) or totalitarianism (Russia).
- The most significant factor in achieving democracy may be the elimination of peasantry as a class and the convergence of old landed and new urban classes: no bourgeoisie, no democracy.
- The achievement of democratic change is not necessarily a peaceful process: revolutionary violence may contribute as much as peaceful reform to the establishment of a relatively free society.

Barrington emphasizes the long-term nature of economic and social interaction, and the political changes these interactions produce; the whole thrust of the analysis is that changing structures of economic and social relations produce political effects, not the other way round.

Democracy and Development

A related assumption in governance thought is that there is a clear relationship between democratic political systems and effective economic development. This assumption is disputed, with the orthodox modernization approach claiming that there is and should be a link, while a critical literature rejects such a view, which is seen as no more than a Western project to maintain the West's dominance in the post Cold War world (Barya, 1993; Leftwich, 1994). The prodemocracy literature is best exemplified by Diamond *et al.* (1990) who consider the following to be essential to democratization:

- Regime legitimacy.
- National political–cultural norms and values.
- The adaptation of political forms to socioeconomic change.
- Relative autonomy for pluralist groups.
- Autonomous decentralized structures.
- A developmental state.
- Political will.
- A capacity for consensus building.
- Enhancement of legal institutions.
- Protection of rights.

In this perspective, democracy is defined as a system that incorporates competition for political power, has a high level of participation in political activity and a high degree of civil and political liberty. This democratic system is contrasted with totalitarian and authoritarian regimes, both of which are regarded as state-dominated. Democratization (the desirable movement towards democracy) is defined as acquisition of the list of characteristics listed above. Little attempt is made to explain why different countries have taken different political routes, or why so few developing countries could tick off this list (even less is there any suggestion that the model may be imperfectly realized in developed industrial economies).

The radical critique of the type of model espoused by Diamond *et al.*, and put into practice by aid donors, centres on an alternative explanation of global political and economic relations and the history of development. It is argued that the political economy of these relations would incorporate the following elements:

- The colonial system and its legacies.
- Continued neocolonial domination of economic relationships.
- The perception of democracy as a facade to disguise the realities of dependent economic relations.

From this perspective, democratization as a political form of conditionality is viewed as a further expression of domination by the Western industrial economies (Gibbon *et al.*, 1992; Barya, 1993; Gills *et al.*, 1993; Leftwich, 1994).

A middle-of-the road view is offered by White (1994), who sets out four positions:

- *Optimistic*: liberal democracy is a powerful stimulus to development as it is more conducive to market-led development and offers the possibility of efficient and accountable government. It emphasizes the perceived benefits of an idealized model rather than actual operation in poor societies.
- *Pessimistic*: democracy is a luxury that poor countries cannot afford and is an active impediment to development, tending to smother the political system in demands it is unable to meet.
- *The don't expect anything school*: of democracy is a solution to the problem of tyranny, but not necessarily to anything else. Democratic regimes are legitimized by their procedures; authoritarian regimes by their performance. New democracies face a dilemma: lacking legitimacy, they cannot become effective; lacking effectiveness, they cannot develop legitimacy.
- *Regime neutral*: here the nature of the regime is much less important than capacity and good performance; an effective development state is all that counts.

White concludes that both democracy and development depend on the prior construction of an effective developmental state that is regulatory, competent and redistributive, and has the political authority to manage social and political conflicts.

Research Evidence

What evidence does research provide on the links between type of political regime and developmental effectiveness?

Relevant studies show how difficult it is to establish even clear correlations, let alone causal connections, between economic performance and type of political regime. An examination by the World Bank (1991) of the effectiveness of different political systems in meeting structural adjustment targets from 1950–80 demonstrates an almost identical performance by democracies and authoritarian regimes. A review by Moore (1995a) of 24 cross-national quantitative research studies found it impossible to establish any clear relationship between regime type and economic record.

Healey and Robinson (1992), while finding some correlation between authoritarian governments and poor economic performance in Africa, admitted that their extensive review of the comparative literature was inconclusive about the relationship between regime types, economic growth and income inequality. They concluded that 'there must remain considerable scepticism on the importance of regime types in relation to the timing and scope of economic change' (ibid., p. 12). Overall, then, the link assumed by good governance advocates between type of regime and level of economic performance is unproven. Quite simply, while some democratic states perform well, others perform badly, and exactly the same applies to authoritarian states.

A different argument is that democratic systems produce more accountable governance (Diamond *et al.*, 1990; Haggard and Kaufman, 1992; Hyden and Bratton, 1992). Critics of this view argue that developing countries exhibit alternative forms of accountability between state and civil society that differ from those of the Western pluralist model, suggesting that the definitions of democracy being used are too limiting (Chabal, 1986; Barya, 1993).

A comparative study of four relatively democratized systems (Botswana, Sri Lanka, Zambia and Jamaica) produced a qualified and somewhat lukewarm endorsement of the proposition that competitive democratic systems are more accountable to their civil societies (Healey and Tordoff, 1995). But in a chapter that considers the experience of single-party systems it is firmly concluded that in at least two cases (Taiwan and South Korea) 'competent public bureaucracies were created which had a major influence on the accountable management of public resources and subsequently stimulated successful economic performance' (ibid., p. 256). This appears to lend weight to the view that the creation of effective public bureaucracies and state management is just as likely to lead to successful economic performance as the construction of institutions of political accountability, though these 'authoritarian' successes do seem to require the construction of internal administrative accountability (by bureaucratic to political leaders) and a set of strongly internalized economic reform values (Wade, 1990). However Moore (1993a) believes that the lessons offered by successful East Asian experiences appear to have been ignored by the World Bank. Presumably the strong, interventionist, authoritarian state is, for the major donors, an unfashionable model of governance.

Human Rights

A concern for human rights is often at the forefront of statements about governance, for it is a rhetoric that is satisfying both to political leaders who are anxious to justify decisions about aid allocations, and to their political constituencies; it is also a constant rallying cry for non-governmental organizations dedicated to the extension to developing countries of civil and political rights that are the norm in developed countries. It would scarcely be possible to guess from all this that the theorization of human rights is a philosophical and moral minefield, raising issues on which there is a great deal of fascinating debate but little in the way of agreed principles. It is not possible to treat this extensive subject in depth here, so the discussion will be confined to questions of particular relevance to the debate on governance.

In the first place, it is useful in the human rights discourse to distinguish between national and international contexts (Penna and Campbell, 1997). In the national arena, human rights are defined in terms of specific laws (often constitutionally entrenched), and specific actions that give effect to these laws and indicate the extent to which rights can be genuinely claimed and enforced; this combination of law and practice will reveal the strength (or otherwise) in that particular society of human rights values. At the international level the discourse is mainly theoretical, in the sense that there is no agreed set of global laws that could be put into global practice, resting on global values. While the framework for such a global system exists in the United Nations Declaration of Human Rights (plus a number of subsidiary documents), to which the majority of nationstates are signatories, the mechanisms for enforcement are hopelessly weak. Many of the signatory countries are in serious breach of the provisions to which they have in principle signed up; but this type of criticism also applies to several national systems where legal provisions are honoured more in the breach than in the observance.

One defence advanced in the international sphere is that international human rights documents reflect a Western consensus (rather than a global consensus) that is ethnocentric in its overriding preoccupation with political rights, to the neglect of economic and social rights. The alternative proposition is that developing countries must put the achievement of economic development before political development; and that alternative social values exist in non-Western societies that offer an equally valid basis for development priorities and choices: the so-called 'Asian values' argument. This discussion also spills over into the debate on economic–political linkages referred to earlier. Dahrendorf (1996, p. 242) suggests that 'Asian values have become the new temptation, and political authoritarianism with them'.

While there is a danger that such positions may be used as an excuse for the suppression of political opposition and internal human rights movements, or at best to buttress resistance to the 'political' invasion now being practised by aid donors, it is interesting to discover that the theoretical literature is also preoccupied with these 'relativist' questions. This debate is neatly exemplified by the contributions in a special issue of the *European Journal of Development Research* in 1998, which in particular explored the apparent opposition of ideas of universality and relativism.

Universality refers to the notion that there is a universally applicable morality, valid for all humans, in all times and places; it is therefore possible, in principle, to lay out a universally valid set of criteria for human rights claims. This approach rests on two propositions (Lund, 1998):

- That all humans are worthy of equal respect, so their rights and entitlements must be formally equalized.
- That we need a set of universal moral standards, based on the fundamental idea of what it is to be human, and therefore superior to systems of rights that are culturally embedded and historically fixed.

Relativism supposes that there can be plural moralities, reflecting the different sets of values held by different societies. As Bauman (1998, p. 7) neatly puts it: 'you can be human in more than one way, and it is not evident which of those ways is preferable'.

The main criticism of universalism is that in practice human rights constitute a variable category that changes according to changing historical circumstances, so 'it is difficult to see how a fundamental principle can be attributed to rights which are historically relative' (Bobbio, quoted in Lund, 1998, p. 3). Acceptance of the socially and historically embedded nature of human rights leads most commentators to the perception that 'universal' human rights are in reality Western-based and represent Western values. The universal model itself represents a form of historical progress, a practice of extending Western modernity and domination until it becomes truly universal. Bauman (1998) proposes that universality is complemented by 'universalization', a process by which those who are powerful identify their own values as universal values, then seek to extend them.

Universality is not a prior set of absolutes, but the end product of a process of universalization; choosing the form of humanity for others is an exercise in power, not in morality.

The relativist position does not exclude consideration of what might constitute appropriate rights, but defends culture itself as 'the supreme ethical value' (Lund, 1998) and cultural relativism as a universal moral principle. Bauhn (1998) attempts to square the circle by distinguishing between *positive* rights, which are those actually recognized in a specific time and place, and *normative* rights, which are justified whether people recognize them or not. He sees the absence of recognition of universal human rights as no obstacle to the formulation of a normative set of universal human rights.

Gewirth (1978) tries to reconcile the conflict between universality and relativism by stressing the role of human agency: all actions express values, so while agents may have different goals they might agree on the necessity of primary conditions for success. The latter are freedom and wellbeing. *Wellbeing* covers the basic conditions of life and health: 'non-subtractive' rights that allow people to maintain their capacity for action, unhindered by harmful living or working conditions; and 'additive' rights that allow people to improve their capacity for action, for example through employment or education. In this 'generic' approach, if one agent can claim such rights then all must be able to do so, and the role of the state is to maintain a 'community of rights' in conditions of supportive mutuality. This implies a 'historical locatedness', a community with its own sense of history and identity, its own cultural narrative.

However Gewirth's second category, *freedom*, harks back to what has been criticized elsewhere as a Westernized notion, 'a system of civil liberties whereby each person is able if he chooses to discuss, criticize, and vote for or against the government and to work actively with other persons in groups ... to further his political objectives, including the redress of his socially based grievances' (ibid., pp. 308–9). But this is a reminder that 'the creation of rights accelerates with the transformation of society', which makes political claims and their transformation into recognized rights a particularly interesting process for developing societies (Lund, 1998, p. 3).

The Critique of Governance: Disputed Practice

For aid donors, both multilateral and bilateral, governance is a firm if broad strategy that is buttressed by specific initiatives to strengthen the institutions of civil society and make their related governments more accountable, open, transparent and democratic. First we shall examine the means by which this strategy is realized, and its effectiveness as an instrument of development policy. This leads to a discussion of the idea and practice of 'political conditionality', that is, the attachment of political conditions to development aid. Aid is thereby used as a system of rewards to and punishment of recipient countries based on the degree to which they satisfy or fail to satisfy these conditions. We have already noted the backward linkage to economic conditionality, and in seeking to evaluate the effectiveness and consistency of political conditionality it is worth reflecting on the findings of major evaluations on economic conditionality. A clear picture emerges of ineffectiveness and inconsistency. The structural adjustment programmes investigated were characterized by serious levels of non-compliance with the agreed conditions (anywhere between 40 per cent and 85 per cent), yet these 'slippages' largely went unpunished, or were inconsistently dealt with (Mosley *et al.*, 1991). Policy reversals were frequent, with only five out of 26 adjustment programmes being completed (Collier *et al.*, 1997). The most recent study concluded that 'conditionality-applying donors ... are often unable to put in place a system of rewards and punishments sufficient to overcome the frequent perceived conflicts of interest between themselves and recipient governments' (Killick, 1997, p. 483). The evidence indicated that 'implementation is poor when there is a clash between donor and government objectives', and that the 'objectives and interests of donor agencies and recipient governments rarely coincide' (Killick, 1997, p. 492).

Clearly this troubled relationship is likely to be exacerbated by a demand for governance reforms as the price of aid donation. Political conditionality has proved more controversial than economic conditionality, especially when it involves the use of sanctions (Barya, 1993; Gibbon, 1993; Baylies, 1995; Burnell, 1997). It can be seen as having twin objectives: the improvement of government competence, the lack of which is seen as a major obstacle to effective aid management; and the universalization of pluralist politics to make defective authoritarian states more responsive, accountable and efficient in the delivery of economic, especially market-based reforms. In addition human rights groups have pressed for aid to be linked to human rights performance in recipient countries (Stokke, 1995a). This two-pronged approach captures the dilemma that while the state is perceived to be a problem, it is also regarded as crucial to the successful implementation of economic reform programmes, especially where markets are imperfect and the institutions of civil society undeveloped (Wade, 1990; Sand-brook, 1993). Of course donor-driven economic and social reforms are intended to remedy these very deficiencies, so reducing dependence on the 'big state' (World Bank, 1996, 1997).

Analyses of donor practice are relatively sparse, and this is a field where research should be a priority. Stokke (1995a, pp. 42–5) sets out a framework of factors that might condition success or failure, including the relative domestic strength of the recipient government and its degree of aid-dependency, but suggests that there are not enough case studies to support confident conclusions. Others are more critical. Crawford's comparative survey of British, American, Swedish and European Union governance lending concludes that these donors have been ineffective in relation to the achievement of political reforms, and inconsistent and selective in policy application (Crawford, 1995, 1998). Robinson (1995) warns of the dangers of overloading non-governmental organizations in the attempt to reduce state activities, and of the risks involved in forcing the pace of political democratization (perhaps most directly illustrated by the perverse outcomes of donor policies in Kenya and Indonesia). Moore (1995b) is critical of the emphasis on institution building and capacity building, given the poor past record of such initiatives. The same point might be made in relation to the World Bank's continued espousal of decentralization reforms, despite past failures (Crook and Manor, 1995; World Bank, 1997).

Cook and Minogue (1993) draw attention to the inconsistent application of political conditionality even where serious human rights abuses have been acknowledged. The differential treatment accorded by Western aid donors to Myanmar (Burma) and China is a reminder that aid is as much the handmaiden of politics in donor countries as in recipient countries. Cook and Minogue also point out that while political conditionality rests on the assumption that political change will precede and produce economic change, the official donor position on China is 'economic change first, political change later'. Ostergaard (1993, p. 116) comments that most aid donors resumed relations with China within 18 months of the Tiananmen Square massacre, and that 'even today, concepts of participatory development and good governance are not being applied to China'. Ostergaard also notes that Japan, 'the world's largest aid donor, is torn between Asian and Western views of human rights, which is bound to influence the future efficiency of political conditionality' (ibid., p. 120).

Another issue that provokes divided views is corruption, hitherto much neglected both in the development literature and by aid donors but now emerging as a significant factor in public management reform (World Bank, 1997; Hondeghem, 1998; Langseth and Pope, 1998). Corruption and crime are recognized as major threats to effective reform in Russia and China (World Bank, 1996). Despite its being so pervasive and persistent, aid donors have found corruption difficult to target in the past because of its political context. Academic analysts of corruption have noted a complexity that derives from its location at the nexus of economic, social and political relationships. Little (1996) suggests that the root of corruption is the state's dominance over society and that reduced and more efficient government will reduce corruption; but that in the long term only substantive (rather than formal) democracy will secure its elimination. On the other hand it has been noted that in China and Vietnam, rapid transition to the market economy appears to have stimulated an increase in corruption (White, 1996; Kolko, 1997). This is explained in part by the continued strength of institutionalized patron–client relations in state bureaucracies, that were well placed to target the new rents being generated. Unlike most commentators, White points out that corruption can be necessary and beneficial in places where the administrative and economic mechanisms for resource allocation are defective. Political scientists have long accepted that patron–client relations may be a necessary stage in political development (Sandbrook, 1993), as they were for example in the political history of the UK and US.

Good Governance and New Public Management

The twentieth century saw the emergence of the activist and interventionist model of the state, based on the assumed superiority of the bureaucratic model of large-scale organization. This both helped to produce and was sanctioned by the post-1945 'Keynesian consensus', and the related expansion of state responsibilities into social provision – the 'welfare state'. Rapid postwar decolonization meant the emergence of new but poor states committed to economic and social betterment: the 'developmental' state.

The most important assumption underlying the activist model was that a crucial role of the state was to make good the deficiencies of the private market. But in the 1980s this perception was turned on its head, on the grounds that government failure was pervasive, and that the resultant deficiencies needed to be corrected by a return to the market. Rooted in neoliberal economic theory, the critique combined an attack on the inefficiency of public bureaucracies with strictures on the flawed nature of the activist state. The alternative proposed was a model of 'new public management' (NPM) (see Minogue, 2001, for an account of the origins of this model and its application in the UK). The defining characteristics of the model were its entrepreneurial dynamic, its reinstatement of the market as a potentially more efficient provider of public services than the state, and its proclaimed intention to transform managerial behaviour in the public sector. The practical realization of the model usually produced the following public sector reforms:

- Restructuring through privatization.
- The restructuring and reduction of central civil services.
- The introduction of competition, especially by contracting public services to the private sector.
- The improvement of public services by means of service charters and the conducting of performance audits and assessment.

While there has been substantial implementation of NPM reforms in developed economies, particularly in the UK (Dunleavy and Hood, 1994; Minogue, 2001), New Zealand (Boston *et al.*, 1996; Schick, 1996) and elsewhere (Kickert, 1997; Lane, 1997), the application in developing and transitional economies has been uneven. While aid donors are enthusiastic proponents of a reshaping of the Third World state in line with NPM principles (World Bank, 1996, 1997), critics point out the difficulty of making such 'policy transfers' across different political and bureaucratic cultures (Nunberg, 1995; Dolowitz and Marsh, 1998; Schick, 1998). Moreover a substantial body of research literature points to the failure of NPM reforms in developed economies to fulfil their promise (Minogue, 2001), and some even judge that these reforms have actively damaged both public services and desirable public service values (Lawton, 1998).

Conclusion

The main building blocks of governance are transformative conceptions of the purposes and nature of governance. The first is the 'new public management' model, which involves a major rethinking of the state and its relations with the market. The second is a clear redirection of aid policies to promote a particular model of state–society relations. The two conceptions are brought together through their derivation from a radical critique of the centralized, inefficient, unaccountable, overextended state, and through their global application. When integrated they provide a new exemplar of state–market relations, incorporating universalist political values. It is a reasonable assumption that the current trend to adapt and apply this new model on a global basis will continue in the foreseeable future.

But this chapter has indicated that these strategies are by no means uncontested in terms of their validity and effectiveness. Given the complex nature of the interaction of economic, social and political systems, and the varied cultural contexts this interaction produces, it is to be expected that at the very least problems of policy transfer and application will occur. At best, this might be seen as a process of flexible adaptation to local cultural conditions, a series of experiments that might constitute a valuable learning experience by countries anxious to secure the benefits of effective modernization. But those with a more pessimistic view regard governance strategy and political conditionality with grave suspicion, as a development 'which merely marks a new phase of surveillance and control on the part of international capital' (Baylies, 1995, p. 335). It is even argued that the free market is antagonistic to, rather than supportive of, democracy, and that both Marxism and neoliberalism are Western universalizing projects that have failed (Gray, 1998). On current evidence it seems likely that good governance will also fail as a universalizing project, representing as it does the attempted imposition of a Western model at a time when globalizing tendencies are producing a world in which the economic power of Western countries is increasingly under challenge, and their cultural values are increasingly at odds with those of other societies.

8

Development Policies and Environmental Agendas

PHILIP WOODHOUSE

Environmental Dimensions of Development Policy

At the start of the twenty-first century environmental issues affect virtually all aspects of development policy. In October 1999 the World Trade Organization, facing the prospect of environmentalist groups disrupting the Seattle round of negotiations on international trade, maintained that trade is not the root cause of environmental degradation but conceded that 'not all kinds of economic growth are equally benign to the environment' and '[e]nvironmental measures are sometimes defeated because of concerns about competitiveness, suggesting a need for improved international cooperation on environmental issues' (*Guardian*, 14 October 1999).

The same year environmental concerns generated major international debates on the impact of technological choices on future development. Worries about the ecological impact of genetically-modified (GM) crops brought into question the role of technological change in agricultural development. The social and environmental costs of the Narmada and Three Gorges dams (in India and China respectively) provided a focus for doubts about the overall benefits to be had from such large projects. Growing concern about the impact of industrialization on the global climate translated into increased urgency for an international agreement on measures to reduce the emission of greenhouse gases.

Environmental concerns also dominated policies to develop non-industrial economies. Rural poverty was identified with the failure to assure the productive use of renewable natural resources, such as land, water and forests. The rural poor were seen as both victims and agents of the degradation of these resources: victims because they were dependent upon such resources for their livelihoods; agents because poverty left them no alternative but to overexploit them and reduce their future productivity.

The permeation of environmental concerns throughout development policy was formally recognized first in a report by the United Nations Commission on Environment and Development (WCED, 1987) – the Brundtland Commission – and at the conference that followed in 1992, the Earth Summit in Rio de Janeiro. Together these produced an international consensus on the need to apply environmental criteria to development policies in order to ensure 'sustainable development', defined by the Brundtland Commission as 'development that meets the needs of the present without compromising the ability of future generations to meet their own needs'. Achievement of consensus that development needed to be sustainable marked a victory for movements and organizations that over the previous thirty years had sought to raise awareness of environmental issues among policy makers. It also marked a shift in the continuing debate on the role of environmental considerations in development policy. Whereas previously the debate had been about whether the environment was important in discussions of economic development, under the new consensus it centred on what was meant by sustainable development: 'Ambiguity runs through all of the most important discourses on economy and the environment today. ... Precisely this obscurity leads so many people so much of the time to talk and write about "sustainability": the word can be used to mean almost anything ... which is part of its appeal' (O'Connor, 1994, p. 152).

This chapter seeks to identify the reasons for this ambiguity, and the implications it has for the role played by environmental issues in development policy. First it is necessary to review what is meant by 'environment', and how environmental agendas have influenced development theory.

The Nature of the Environment

When trying to understand how environmental concerns affect perspectives on development we soon confront the paradox that while the roots of much environmentalist thinking can be traced back to ideas about development in the sense of human progress, many environmental agendas are not concerned with developmental goals. This is because there are two different views on what is meant by the term 'environment'. One identifies the environment as the natural world, while the second regards it as all human and non-human activities and entities external to a particular sphere of decision making and action (such as a development policy or project).

The Environment as Nature

The boundary between humanity and nature is a strong theme running through human consciousness, influenced by perceptions of the degree of human domination over or subordination to the 'forces of nature'. Early human societies commonly perceived nature as endowed with superhuman powers, codified in religious form as spirits or gods identified with land, water, forests, animals, seasons, fire and so on. The perceived subordination of humanity to nature was challenged by the Enlightenment movement in sixteenth- and seventeenth-century Europe, which proclaimed that 'the conquest of nature' was a necessary human mission to overcome the constraints of the natural or 'primitive' human condition. The Enlightenment was reinforced by, and possibly dependent on, technological progress, notably in firearms and navigation, which allowed Europeans to explore continents and subjugate peoples previously unknown to them. In this imperialist relationship the role of nature was entirely utilitarian, to be used for the achievement of happiness by humanity.

This perception of human domination over nature was further fuelled by the dramatic technological innovations of the industrial revolution in the eighteenth and nineteenth centuries, which transformed landscapes and societies. However the development of industrial society also prompted a questioning of the extent of humanity's understanding of the changes it was imposing on nature. In part this was a straightforward flight by the wealthy from the life-threatening squalor of urban life to an English landscape remodelled to meet the agricultural and recreational requirements of landowners. For such people, 'dark satanic mills' were counterposed to a newly arcadian rural order. For the Romantic poets (for example Wordsworth and Coleridge), rejection of the industrialists' utilitarian approach to nature was rooted in their perceptions of the power of the forces of nature they experienced in the wilder, mountainous areas of the UK which emphasized the limits to human domination of the wild. Mary Shelley's celebrated novel *Frankenstein* (1985, originally published 1818), a parable about the folly of humankind's presumption that it could control nature, foreshadowed by two hundred years the debates of the present biotechnology era which seek to define an appropriate relationship between humanity and nature, and between science and society.

Between industrial society's prevailing utilitarianism and the Romantic celebration of an indomitable and vengeful nature, was a third view in which humanity was perceived as 'above' nature but accountable to God for its management and conservation. O'Connor (1994) quotes a secular example of this 'stewardship' view from Karl Marx's *Capital*: 'Even society as a whole, a nation, or all existing societies put together, are not owners of the Earth. They are merely its occupants, its users; and like good caretakers, they must hand it down improved to subsequent generations.' This view was also associated with the growing conservation movement in Europe and North America, which pressed for areas of natural wilderness to be set aside and protected from the impact of human activity. As a result the latter part of the nineteenth century witnessed the designation of national parks as conservation areas, the largest of which was Yellowstone in the US.

In the growth of industrial society of the eighteenth and nineteenth centuries, therefore, can be found three principal views about the relationship of humanity to nature, and these continued to influence environmental debates in the twentieth century: utilitarianism (the domination of nature by humanity), romanticism (the subordination of humanity to nature) and stewardship ('accountable' management of nature by humanity).

The Environment as an 'Externality'

While the environment is commonly visualized in terms of the natural world, the practice of environmental regulation in industrial society has been driven by a much broader interpretation of the meaning of 'environment'. Specifically it has grown out of the recognition that developmental activities such as the construction and operation of industrial plants, agricultural expansion and mineral extraction incur costs and produce benefits that may be distributed unevenly in society. Of particular concern has been the recognition that while developers capture most of the benefits of such activities, significant costs are borne by the public, the workforce or other social groups who benefit far less or not at all. These external costs not borne by developers include unsafe working conditions, unhealthy living conditions due to air and water pollution, and diminution of the aesthetic or recreational quality of people's surroundings.

In nineteenth-century industrial society these costs were effectively externalized to the public majority, who paid in terms of poor health and high mortality, or to public authorities that took action to mitigate the burden, for example by constructing public sanitation infrastructure. By the mid-twentieth century the extension of the right to vote to all adults and the growth of organized labour had brought about political, economic and social change and society had become less willing to bear such costs. The establishment of public health provision in the UK translated the cost of poor health into increased government expenditure, providing an incentive to legislate to improve those environmental conditions that were a major cause of ill health, notably poor air quality, which was tackled by imposing emission standards on industry. In the US, growing concern about the hazards posed to public health by development projects such as the notorious 'Love Canal', where houses were built on an industrial waste-disposal site, put public authorities under pressure to ensure that all costs of development projects were identified and 'internalized' – a principle that has come to be known as 'the polluter pays'.

This approach was first institutionalized in 1969 in the US with the establishment of the Environmental Protection Agency (EPA), which was charged with ensuring that an environmental impact statement accompanied all major federal works. The approach has since been widely adopted by the governments of industrialized economies, and extended to include both private- and public-sector developments (Wood, 1995; Lee and George, 2000). The significance of the environmental impact assessment (EIA) to our interpretation of the environmental dimensions of development is that it concentrates on conflicts and natural resource constraints that could affect the viability of projects, examines how projects might harm people, their living environments, or their livelihoods, and identifies measures to minimize problems and improve project suitability.

In this perspective the environment includes not only nature but also those parts of human society that are external to a particular development project or activity. Assessment of the environmental impact of a hydroelectric dam or a forestry plantation would therefore include not only the effects on natural ecosystems in terms of habitat disruption or species loss, but also the displacement or impoverishment of people as a result of such developments. In this sense, therefore, the term environment addresses the conflicts of interest posed by the unequal distribution of costs and benefits – the 'externalities' – of development.

It is important to understand the two senses in which the term environment is used. The environment as nature is associated with an agenda of conservation that may be explicitly opposed to the exploitation of particular natural resources such as species and habitats in forests, rivers, wetlands and so on. The wider interpretation of the environment, which is used to assess the impact of development in terms of who bears the costs, may include the impact on nature but is predominantly applied from the utilitarian perspective of who owns, uses or manages the natural resources concerned. The overlap between the two interpretations explains the ability of the environmental agenda to unite a broad range of interests into a common programme of sustainable development, but also suggests there will be divergent and possibly conflicting approaches to its practical implementation. This aspect is discussed in the final section of this chapter; first we shall review how different theoretical perspectives on development have interpreted environmental concerns.

Perspectives on the Environment in Development Theory

Modernization Theory

As might be expected from a theoretical framework that takes industrialized European and North American society as the normative developmental model, modernization theory incorporates the utilitarian view of nature. Neither the capitalist nor the socialist variants of modernization in the 1950s and 1960s considered natural resources to constitute a limit on economic growth. The early postwar period was marked on both sides of the Iron Curtain by technological triumphalism, manifested in attempts to harness nature on an ever-larger scale, particularly in relation to the damming or diverting of rivers. The emphasis on large hydrological infrastructure was also a feature of development policy in newly independent (ex-colonial) territories in the 1950s and 1960s, such as the Kariba and Akasombo Dams in Zambia and Ghana respectively. At Indian independence, Nehru claimed that dams would be 'the temples of modern India' (Roy, 1999, p. 56). In the face of such major transformations of nature under modernization, conservation was to be achieved by designating reserves from which human activity was to be excluded, except in the form of scientific ecological study and management: nature was to be separated from development.

As in the nineteenth century, industrial society recognized no environmental limits to continued growth; and as before this cornucopian view was subject to challenge. For many people, or at least in the West (less so and with damaging consequences in the Soviet system), the achievements of postwar technology were offset by a growing sense of vulnerability to its destructive power. This was first articulated in the case of nuclear technology, not only because of the threat of nuclear war but also because of the less visible risks associated with the leakage of radiation into the environment. Similarly the evidence emerging in the 1960s of pesticide accumulation in food chains demonstrated the interconnection between humanity and nature through ecological processes that generated exponentially increasing harmful effects from initially imperceptible events.

Doubts about the capacity of industrial society to sustain the growth of production and consumption were further fuelled in the 1970s by studies predicting that depletion of the finite reserves of minerals on the planet would soon pose 'limits to growth' (Meadows *et al.*, 1972), echoing Thomas Malthus's concern in the eighteenth century that the rural population would increase faster than the increase in production of food from the land. As with Malthus's agricultural fear, the neo-Malthusian prediction for twentieth-century industry was largely invalidated by technological change, which resulted not in scarcity but in a surplus of supply and declining prices for primary commodities.

In 1985, however, the environmental impact of industrial society was forced onto the international political agenda when it was confirmed that a hole in the ozone layer was forming over Antarctica. This indicated that the overall stratospheric ozone layer, which shields the earth's surface from ultraviolet (UV) radiation, was becoming depleted. The significance of the discovery was threefold. First, the depletion was blamed on the release into the atmosphere of chlorofluorocarbons (CFCs), chemical compounds that do not occur naturally and had been manufactured since the 1930s as refrigerant gases and aerosol propellants. Second, the phenomenon was on global scale and could have potentially catastrophic effects in terms of the genetic damage that UV exposure would inflict on all forms of life. Third, the dynamics of ozone depletion had not been predicted by the existing models of atmospheric chemistry, demonstrating the limitation of science's understanding of nature. For all these reasons the discovery marked a turning point, after which the technologically optimistic approach to development was tempered by fear about the consequences of industrialization throughout the world, and a concern to subject newly industrializing countries to global regulation. The emerging consensus in favour of sustainable development represented a victory for the environmentalist movements of the 1960s and 1970s, but set the scene for a new struggle between neoliberalism and its opponents.

Neoliberal Perspectives: Environmental Economics

By the 1980s, when the environmental threat posed by the continued growth of production and consumption had become widely acknowledged, neoliberalism had become the dominant development paradigm. This addresses environmental concerns through neoclassical environmental economics, which seeks to rationalize the use and management of the environment by converting it into commodities governed by market price mechanisms (Pearce *et al.*, 1990) It is an explicitly utilitarian approach that identifies the 'services' provided by nature: raw materials for production (land, minerals, energy), essential life support (air, water), waste disposal and recreational and aesthetic provisions (landscape). The capacity of the environment to supply such services is considered to constitute a form of natural capital that can be accumulated or depleted, or used to generate other forms of capital: financial, physical (for example productive capacity) and human (for example education). The central argument of environmental economics is that the depletion of natural capital (degradation of the capacity to supply services) results from overuse of a resource whose scarcity is not reflected in its price: increasing scarcity should be reflected in increasing price, and consequently in reduced demand, leading to conservation of the resource. A central concern of environmental economics, therefore, is that the price of environmental services should reflect their scarcity. The conversion of environmental concerns into monetary values has played an important part in the incorporation of environmental considerations into the mainstream development debate, particularly in relation to the international efforts to manage the global environment, as exemplified by the Kyoto Protocol (discussed below).

As with all neoclassical economics, the approach assumes that competitive markets will tend towards equilibrium when allocation is optimal. It deals with aggregate demand and does not address the distribution of that demand (that is, those to whom environmental services are available), except in terms of purchasing power (effective demand). The extremely unequal distribution of purchasing power internationally and within national economies has profound implications for the operation of environmental management in practice (this is discussed further in the final section) and highlights the cardinal importance of the distribution of ownership of natural capital. Property rights, and institutional questions of access to and use of natural resources more generally, are critically important to environmental management because economically rational (utility-maximizing) individuals' use of a resource must often be shared with others (that is, exclusive individual use is not possible) so use is 'subtractable', that is, the amount used by any individual subtracts from that available to the others.

Such a situation is relatively common in both local and international development contexts (Keohane and Ostrom, 1995) and has attracted attention to the importance of institutions as sets of rules that enable individuals to predict the behaviour of other resource users and so reduce the costs associated with uncertainty. Institutional economics (North, 1990) uses game theory to analyze how individual rationality may be served by adhering to collective institutions. The purpose of this is to design effective approaches to managing shared resources such as the 'global commons': the seas and the atmosphere.

Alternative Perspectives: Populist, Structuralist and Postmodern

While neoliberal approaches dominate the environmental aspects of development policy, they have been subject to challenge by alternative perspectives that have proved important in mobilizing public opposition, as at the World Trade Organization's meeting in Seattle in November 1999. While the extent to which the neoliberal agenda has been compromised by this opposition is debatable, it is significant that environmental issues have provided one of the most durable platforms for opponents of the neoliberal project. The alternative positions draw on a variety of theoretical perspectives. One of the most important is a populist or communitarian emphasis on the knowledge, social support and cohesion of local communities. Drawing heavily on traditions of rural populism that have sought to defend rural societies from industrial or urban domination, this perspective has variants that emphasize the effectiveness of local institutions in regulating natural resource use, the special role of women as users and managers of resources (ecofeminism, see Shiva, 1994), and the environmental and social advantages of smaller-scale, owner-operated production ('small is beautiful', Schumacher, 1993). These 'people-centred' approaches explicitly place the poor (as both victims and agents of environmental degradation) at the centre of efforts to understand the environmental aspects of development: securing 'sustainable livelihoods' for the poorest is argued to be the key to sustainable development (Chambers, 1988). This argument, which draws heavily on the entitlement theory of food security (Drèze and Sen, 1989), has underpinned campaigns to strengthen local ownership and access rights for otherwise disadvantaged groups as a means to secure the conservation of resources with wider or even global significance. Examples include international support for ownership rights for indigenous people in rainforest areas (Poffenberger, 1990), and community-based conservation of wildlife in Africa (Hulme and Murphree, 2001).

Advocacy of a role for the poor in the search for solutions to environmental problems has been strengthened by the arguments from a number of other theoretical perspectives that have become influential since the early 1990s. Firstly, ecological and anthropological field studies have yielded examples of the part played by local people's indigenous knowledge in sustaining the productivity of the land, water, forests or pastures they use (Warren, 1991; Scoones and Thompson, 1994). In particular, researchers have come to appreciate the extent to which the exploitation and management of biodiverse ecologies such as rainforests hinges on the extensive knowledge of species and their uses that rainforest societies have accumulated (Hecht and Cockburn, 1990). Similarly, a growing appreciation of the extreme fluctuations of rainfall and biomass that are normal in some ecologies, such as the semi-arid rangelands of Africa, has revealed to scientific researchers a logic they had previously ignored in African pastoralists' management strategies (Scoones, 1994).

Secondly, greater awareness of the extent of indigenous environmental management has given rise to a willingness to challenge established, often Eurocentric, notions of pristine wilderness unaltered by human intervention, and to question how these have shaped judgements of environmental change as 'degradation' (Leach and Mearns, 1996). This type of analysis finds support in the postmodern rejection of a normative conceptualization of reality in favour of socially constructed multiple realities, and further strengthens the perception that local or indigenous criteria for resource conservation may be as valid as those originating from scientific study.

Finally, structuralist – or political economy – approaches that emphasize the role of power relations in decisions about how natural resources are to be used or abused (Blaikie, 1985) have been used to argue for improved economic and political rights for disadvantaged resource users relative to international capital or national governments.

Although these alternative environmental perspectives on development are often grouped together under the term 'political ecology', some have observed that political ecology is often apolitical (Peet and Watts, 1996). In particular they argue that the populist heritage of many people-centred alternatives inhibits a rigorous examination of power relations. As a consequence, power relations between local communities and 'external' agencies of the state or market tend to be highlighted, while those within communities may be neglected, leading to idealized and conservative images of 'community' that preclude an understanding of the dynamics of social change and their environmental implications (ibid.).

Despite this, the political ecology alternatives underpin the rights-based advocacy of the control of resources being redistributed in favour of disadvantaged groups, which is the principal counter to the market-based distributive criteria of neoliberal policies. In this sense the environmental debate may be regarded as an ideological proxy for a historical and material struggle for control over natural resources and the wealth they generate. Moreover it is important to note that this struggle defines the meaning of environment in much the same way as the broader 'externality' or 'conflict of interest' interpretation that is the basis of the environmental impact assessment procedures in industrial societies. As such, the environmental agenda of sustainable development may offer an arena in which groups who are relatively disenfranchised politically and economically can pursue their economic and social goals in ways that have legitimacy for those with more power who they seek to oppose.

Sustainable Development: the Environment in Development Practice

It was noted at the beginning of this chapter that the reaching of a consensus on the need for sustainable development represented a triumph for environmentalist groups that had campaigned for environmental concerns to be addressed by mainstream development policy makers. While the promotion of sustainable development can be interpreted as a victory for the opponents of postwar modernization theory, it is also a displacement of much the same struggle to a different terrain, upon which the meaning of sustainable development is disputed between the dominant neoliberalists and the holders of various alternative perspectives. As one commentator at the Rio Conference in 1992 observed: 'this was not a conference about the environment at all, it concerned the world's economy and how the environment affects it. ... [T]his was the first meeting of world leaders since the end of the Cold War. The old East/West agenda is dead, attention is now focussed on North and South' (Sandbrook, 1993, p. 16).

The consensus that emerged from the conference, as set out in 'Agenda 21' (UNCED, 1992), reflects an ideological tension between the neoliberal emphasis on allocation through market mechanisms, and the populist-inspired emphasis on local, participatory and communitarian processes of environmental management. Both are elements of the efforts made under the auspices of the United Nations Commission for Sustainable Development to promote international cooperation on environmental issues. In practice, international cooperation is effected through the negotiation, signature and ratification of international environmental conventions, of which three were established at the 1992 Rio Conference (on biodiversity, climate change and desertification). The progress of these conventions illustrates the opposition of different development perspectives on the environment. The remainder of this section sets out two examples of opposing perspectives that have been translated into practice. The first subsection briefly traces the evolution of the Convention on Climate Change, which addresses the effects of industrialization. The second compares perspectives on the exploitation of tropical forests, an issue considered so contentious at Rio that no convention was proposed, only a declaration of principles.

The Convention on Climate Change and the Kyoto Protocol

The discovery of the hole in the ozone layer over the Antarctica in 1985 was followed by swift international agreement (the Montreal Protocol of 1987) to control the use of the substances that were believed to be responsible – chlorofluorocarbons (CFCs). In 1990 the amended protocol sought the cessation of CFC manufacture by 2000. This international agreement was a prototype for the more wide-ranging international collaboration needed to address a different atmospheric problem: the accumulation in the lower atmosphere of infrared-absorbing gases (principally carbon dioxide, methane and a number of other industrially produced gases) that trap heat that would otherwise radiate out into space, resulting in a rise in the Earth's temperature – the 'greenhouse effect'.

Although the chemist Arrhenius suggested at the end of the nineteenth century that industrialization could cause a greenhouse effect by increasing the concentration of carbon dioxide (CO_2) in the atmosphere, systematic efforts to monitor atmospheric CO_2 started only in 1957. By the 1970s evidence of a rising CO_2 concentration, coupled with the more general environmental concerns noted earlier in this chapter, prompted fear of a human-induced climate change. The 1979 World Climate Conference was followed by a decade of international scientific effort to investigate the evidence and implications of climate change, culminating in the establishment in 1988 of the Intergovernmental Panel on Climatic Change (IPCC) by the World Meteorological Office and the United Nations Environment Programme. Characterized as 'the most extensive and carefully constructed intergovernmental advisory process ever known in international relations' (Grubb *et al.*, 1999, p. 4) the IPCC recommended in 1990 that the total world emission of carbon dioxide must be reduced to 60 per cent of the 1990 level in order to stabilize the concentration of the gas in the atmosphere. At the Rio Summit in 1992 a framework document for a convention on climate change (FCCC), signed by 176 countries to date, recognized the need to protect the climate on the basis of equity, and that states had 'common but differentiated responsibilities and respective capabilities. Accordingly, the developed countries should take the lead' (ibid., p. 38). This involved the developed countries committing themselves to reduce their emissions to the 1990 levels by 2000. The convention also committed all its signatories to develop and publish inventories of greenhouse gas emissions and sinks, and established the Global Environmental Facility (housed at the World Bank) as the institution to monitor these commitments.

In 1995 the IPPC's second assessment report stressed that 'the balance of evidence' pointed to greenhouse gas emissions causing an increase in global temperatures of 1–3.5°C and a 50 cm rise in the sea level by the end of the twenty-first century, a rate of warming that was greater than anything experienced in the past ten thousand years. In the same year in Berlin, the parties to the FCCC agreed that the 1992 commitment to reduce emissions was not being honoured by many OECD members, and agreed to begin a process by which the industrialized countries would commit themselves to a protocol for quantified and legally binding emission-reduction targets within a specified timeframe. The resulting protocol, agreed two years later after 12 days of negotiations in Kyoto and signed by 160 countries, committed industrialized (so-called 'Annex I') countries to reduce their collective emission of six greenhouse gases to an average of 5.2 per cent below the 1990 levels by 2012.

Despite heavy US pressure, recently industrialized countries such as India, China, South Korea and Brazil were not required to commit themselves to emission reductions before 2012. However the US was successful in its attempt to have a number of 'flexibility mechanisms' inserted in the protocol that would allow industrialized countries to meet their emission-reduction commitments through activities undertaken abroad, rather than at home:

- 'Joint implementation' by more than one industrialized country, where one partner (for example the US) could generate 'emission reduction units' (ERUs) by building or modernizing an industrial plant in another industrial country (for example Russia). The ERUs generated could be offset by the investing partner against its own national emission-reduction commitment.
- The 'clean development mechanism', whereby an industrialized country would introduce cleaner technology to a less industrialized country and claim credit (certified emission reductions – CERs) for the emissions reduced.
- 'Emissions trading', where emission reductions achieved (or production foregone) in one country could be 'sold' to another country that was unwilling or unable to reduce the emissions from its own territory.

The Kyoto Protocol resulted from two years of maneouvres and shifting alliances between a number of stakeholders, whose positions are summarized briefly below.

EU governments

The level of environmental concern varies between EU member states, but it is strong in many and growing in others. Strong emission reductions in Germany (following reunification) and the UK (due to the closure of coal mines) in the early 1990s meant that at the time of Kyoto, overall EU emissions were already reckoned to be about 2.5 per cent lower than in 1990. The internal allocation of emission targets within the EU has allowed some of the least industrialized member states to increase their emissions while the EU as a whole is likely to meet its emission reduction commitments under the Protocol of an 8 per cent reduction of the 1990 level.

The US government

The US is responsible for about 25 per cent of the world's greenhouse gas emissions, and is regarded as the key to securing the credibility and leadership of the industrialized countries in respect of emission reductions. The willingness of the former Democrat administration in the US to achieve emission reductions was constrained by the Republican-controlled legislature, which reflected the hostility to emission control among US consumers, corporations and labour unions. The US position at Kyoto was subject to intense lobbying by US industrial interests that were keen to ensure that any international agreement would not subject them to emission-reduction costs from which their foreign competitors would be exempt. Hence US acceptance of legally binding quantitative targets for emission reductions was conditional on the inclusion of flexibility mechanisms to ensure that the US commitment would not necessarily mean changes in domestic energy use in the US. The key opportunity for this to be achieved was presented by the collapse of industrial output in Eastern Europe following the break-up of the Soviet Union. This meant that at the time of the Kyoto meeting, emissions in these so-called 'economies in transition' (EITs) were already 20–50 per cent below their 1990 levels, representing 'surplus' reductions that the US could offset against its own commitments through transfers under the protocol's joint implementation mechanism.

Other OECD governments

Outside the US and EU, OECD members included those with strong environmental traditions and relatively low per capita emissions (Japan, New Zealand, Canada, Norway and Switzerland), and some, notably Australia, with high energy production and consumption patterns. The attentions of the former were focused on the relatively high marginal cost of achieving emission reductions in their (already efficient) energy sectors; while the latter were concerned about the high political cost of emission reduction. For different reasons, therefore, both groups allied themselves with the US in advocating flexibility mechanisms to achieve emission reductions.

Economies in Transition (EITs)

As noted above, the economic collapse of these countries in the early 1990s resulted in a rapid decline in emissions (by as much as 50 per cent in Ukraine) by some of the highest polluting industries in the world. The question of emission reduction was irrelevant to many of these governments until they realized that emission quotas from this lost industry might be exchanged for new investment from the US or Japan, whereupon they joined the US-led alliance in advocating flexibility.

Developing countries (the G77 and China)

Comprising 120 countries in all, three important subgroups can be identified. The Association of Small Island States (AOSIS) had 42 members, many of which were extremely vulnerable to a rise in the sea level, and consequently advocated the strongest measures for emission reduction. The Organization of Petroleum Exporting Countries (OPEC) campaigned against measures that would reduce oil consumption, and for a time allied with US corporate interests in the 'Global Climate Coalition'. The majority of countries in Africa and Latin America, together with India and China, emphasized economic development as their priority, and national sovereignty over natural resource use. They proved united in their opposition to any action outside the domestic reduction of emissions by industrialized countries. They successfully opposed the inclusion of emission-reduction commitments by recently industrialized countries, but failed to block the flexibility mechanisms and emission-trading elements of the protocol.

By the time the Kyoto proposals were discussed again 10 months later in Buenos Aires, the resistance of many US industrialists had diminished as it had become clear that emission reduction would be achievable through tradeable mechanisms, and a number of industrial corporations were beginning to look for opportunities to act as 'carbon traders' by building wind, solar and other 'clean energy' facilities in non-industrialized countries and selling the carbon credits so acquired to industrialized countries. The details of the implementation of the Kyoto Protocol, upon which ratification would depend, were to be worked out at a meeting in 2000 in The Hague, but developments in the two years after the Kyoto meeting led observers to conclude that 'it is hard to avoid the conclusion that a general market would emerge in emission credits' (Grubb *et al.*, 1999, p. 200). If the protocol was thus to be interpreted as a triumph for neoliberalism, the same observers pointed to the potential limits of this victory.[1]

Firstly, implementation of the protocol would have only a modest effect on global warming (a 4–14 per cent reduction in the *rate* of temperature or sea-level rise), its main impact being to change the culture of energy consumption and promote a search for technological alternatives to fossil fuels, providing the basis for faster, global emission reductions after the end of the existing commitments in 2012. Secondly, from a purely economic standpoint, evolving market-based mechanisms for implementing the protocol through a proliferation of projects to generate emission reductions via flexibility mechanisms – action abroad, rather than domestic reform of energy use – risked an inflationary effect on the value of the (fixed) amount of emissions to which the industrialized countries had committed themselves under the protocol, undermining any incentive for technological innovation. Thirdly, from a political standpoint, failure to demonstrate domestic reform would undermine the 'moral leadership' of the industrialized countries on emission reduction, and with it any hope of extending future reductions to developing countries. As the countries outside the protocol's Annex I (for example China, India, Brazil and South Korea) were projected to produce about 50 per cent of global greenhouse gas emissions by 2012, this was the most critical issue of all: 'in climate change, unlike most global negotiations, the developed world countries are increasingly asking the developing countries for action, rather than the other way around' (Grubb *et al.*, 1999, p. 252).

Managing the Amazonian Rainforest

The management of tropical forests illustrates particularly sharp contradictions between theoretical and practical approaches to the environmental aspects of development. International environmental interest in tropical rainforests has increased with growing recognition of their importance as repositories of biodiversity, and as sites of absorption (or 'sequestration') of atmospheric carbon dioxide (however the significance of this function for strategies under the FCCC is contested (FAO, 1999, pp. 30–3) and investment in carbon sequestration through afforestation projects had been excluded, at the time of writing, from the CDM under the Kyoto Protocol). As the largest area of rainforest, the Brazilian Amazon has attracted particular attention and there has been pressure for the 'internationalization' of its management. In order to understand the impact of such a development, we shall draw on Hecht and Cockburn (1990) to summarize some key sets of socioeconomic interests that are shaping the current environmental debates on the management of the Amazon rainforest.

International capital initiated, and continues to supply, the main dynamic of changing resource use in the Amazon. The first investors were Portuguese in pursuit of gold, while the nineteenth- and early twentieth-century rubber boom was financed by French and later US investors. Multinational companies have been heavily involved in the large-scale development of iron ore and tin mining since the 1980s, and from the late 1990s in the felling of hardwood for plywood manufacture and investigating rainforest plants and animals for their potential pharmaceutical value. For international capital the Amazon remains, quite simply, a natural resource cornucopia.

The Brazilian political leadership has retained, since its colonial origins, an essentially military character, preoccupied with territorial occupation and the security of national frontiers. The relatively inaccessible and sparsely populated frontiers in the Amazon basin, openly contested by neighbouring Bolivia at the height of the rubber boom, have always been a source of concern. The military governments that ruled Brazil for much of the twentieth century sought above all to improve their access to the Amazon region, and fears of insurgency following the Cuban revolution resulted in a sustained programme of road construction and the provision of incentives for entrepreneurial activities in the rainforest. While international capital enabled much of this 'march to the west', the military governments' main implementing partner was Brazilian landed and industrial capital.

Large landowners, in the tradition of the irregular bands of adventurers (*bandeirantes*) who pioneered the exploration and exploitation of Brazil under the Portuguese, have been the main beneficiaries of the government's fiscal incentives since the 1960s to acquire and clear forest in the Amazon region. The low costs and speculative nature of this land acquisition (primarily serving as a hedge against high rates of inflation) by individual and corporate Brazilian interests, coupled with a chaotic land titling regime, served to promote forest clearance for ranching as the means to establish unequivocal, if unproductive, ownership rights.

The indigenous rainforest people – whose number before European colonization was estimated at six to twelve million but has now fallen to just 200 000 (Hecht and Cockburn, 1990, p. 3) – have been decimated by disease and much of the rainforest they inhabited has been expropriated.

Rubber tappers, brazil nut gatherers and small-scale farmers have made a living in the Amazon rainforest for many generations and number some two million, to which a further two to three million small-scale settlers from north-eastern and southern Brazil have been added since the construction of roads through the region in the 1960s. Since the 1980s small-scale agriculture and the extraction of rainforest resources has been supplemented by small-scale gold mining by around half a million *garimpeiros*, many of whom may have been or still are farmers.

In common with many other frontiers of European expansion, the struggle between these competing interests has for the most part been characterized by lawlessness and violence. The growth of international environmental interest in the Amazon has opened international channels for lobbying for the rights of indigenous people and other groups that are identified with sustainable extractive use of the rainforest, and has assisted local campaigns to formalize property rights for such groups in the form of reserves, covering some 28 per cent of the rainforest. A second consequence of the internationalization of the Amazon has been the withdrawal of the incentives for logging and the imposition on large landowners of a requirement to maintain a minimum of 50 per cent of their Amazonian holdings as rainforest. However the policy debate in Brazil on the future of the Amazon exemplifies the use of environmental discourse as a proxy for the political economy of natural resource use. In May 2000 a proposal to raise the proportion of rainforest required in large landowners' Amazonian holdings from 50 per cent to 80 per cent was dropped as part of a package in which GEF funding would be used to secure supervision of the conservation of 10 per cent of the Amazon. Press reports (Associated Press, 14 May 2000) suggested that the conservation area would include reserves inhabited by some 20 000 people, 'on the basis that they would be allowed to stay and play a major role in protecting the natural resources'. In the face of environmentalists' accusation that it was pandering to wealthy landowners, the government withdrew its support for the proposal.

The following month the government perceived a challenge to its sovereignty over Amazonian natural resources when the Brazilian parastatal Bioamazonia drew up an agreement that would give the Swiss-based multinational Novartis Pharma the right to collect samples in the rainforest for testing for medicinal or other marketable substances. The government's hastily promulgated 'temporary measure' suspending the agreement was heavily criticized by environmental and political opposition groups, who perceived it as a move by the government to assert its authority over the granting of international access to genetic resources and indigenous knowledge, thereby overriding the property rights of rainforest peoples that had been a cornerstone of legislation pending since 1995 (projeto de lei do Senado no. 306 de 1995).

These legislative debates in Brazil suggest that the environmental agenda has opened up a terrain on which international support can be marshalled by movements representing indigenous people, rubber tappers, small-scale settlers and other poorer groups with livelihoods in the Amazon, constituting an unprecedented counterweight to the historical dominance of Amazonian interests by the Brazilian military and domestic and international capital. However, as well as the obvious difficulty of implementing legislation to protect the rights of the poor in a region accustomed to centuries of gun law, the engagement of international environmental organizations with social movements in the Amazon also exposes two weaknesses in the alternative approaches to sustainable development. The first of these is the divergence between Northern perceptions of the Amazon as primarily a pristine and therefore an essentially non-human resource to be preserved, and the agenda for development and social change (for example access to education and health services) pursued by those living in the rainforest.

A second, related, weakness is the failure of many alternative approaches to resource use to address the realities of market relationships, from which indigenous forest users are not protected simply by virtue of establishing property rights in the form of extractive reserves. According to one evaluation of the Amazonian extractive reserves that the governments of Brazil and Bolivia leased to groups such as rubber tappers and brazil nut gatherers: 'there are considerable doubts about economic viability. There is high dependence on outside support, and low product prices and marketing diseconomies of scale have forced extractivists into less benign forms of land use, such as cattle ranching' (Richards, 1995). One might add that the same economic logic would make it attractive for forest users to diversify into gold-mining. Yet this would pose an enormous environmental threat in that the mercury used in gold extraction could result in wholesale contamination of the aquatic ecology, and with it much of the Amazonian food chain.

Conclusion

This chapter has identified that environmental agendas are a fundamental characteristic of industrial society, involving a reappraisal of
the relationship between humanity and nature; and has traced how
the growth of environmental concerns in the postwar period has
undermined the model of industrialized consumer society upon which
modernization theory is based. Environmental agendas also serve to
protect the interests of those social groups who directly or indirectly
are disadvantaged by having to bear a disproportionate share of the
costs of development. Hence environmental legislation, such as the
requirement for environmental impact assessments, can provide the
formal basis for legitimating protests against and opposition to
development that will produce inequitable outcomes. More broadly,
acceptance of the principle of impact assessment underpins the
growing call for wider consultation on policies with environmental
impacts, which – as public opposition to genetically modified food
demonstrated in 1999 – will demand a rethinking of the governance of
science and technological change by society (ESRC, 1999).

Despite these trends in industrial societies and the international
consensus on sustainable development, international initiatives to
manage global environmental problems have been dominated by
neoliberal market models that permit wealthy, high-energy-consum-
ing societies to use their purchasing power to avoid a reduction in
their consumption levels. It is quite clear from the negotiations
leading up to the Kyoto Protocol that many developing countries
consider such an outcome inequitable, as it will perpetuate the
international disparities in consumption and living standards. Yet
the shared nature of such environmental problems implies that only
concerted action will be effective: an equitable outcome is more likely
to be associated with effective action. The lesson and challenge for
future environmental and development policy is therefore to define
the principles and processes by which markets can be regulated to
produce a more equitable outcome.

Note

1. The swift repudiation of the Kyoto Protocol by US President G. W. Bush,
    following his election in 2001 placed in jeopardy even these modest aims.

9

Neoliberalism, the World Bank, and the New Politics of Development

PAUL CAMMACK

The time is evidently past for public officials to be expected to sit on the developmental sidelines, limiting their role to fixing general rules and providing certain basic services and incentives for those private entrepreneurs who are the major players in the complicated and exciting game of fashioning profound changes to economic and social systems (LaPalombara, 1963, p. 4).

Despite the uncertain outlook for the twenty-first century, a certain measure of optimism is justified now that more and more countries are opting for a market-friendly approach. With strong international cooperation, the opportunities for development will be brighter. There is more agreement today than at any other time in recent history about what needs to be done and how to do it. What remains to be done is to put these ideas into practice everywhere (World Bank, 1991, p. 157).

Knowledge management is expected to change the way in which the World Bank operates internally, and to transform its relationships with all those it deals with on the outside (World Bank, 1999a, p. 140).

Thinking about development has been transformed in recent years, with far-reaching consequences for development studies. The World Bank and its allies around the world have had outstanding success in overturning the assumptions on which debates about development had rested since the Second World War, establishing a new neoliberal orthodoxy that is faithful to the disciplines required for capitalist accumulation on a global scale, and generating a legitimizing ideology that obscures the presence of those disciplines at its core. If alternative approaches to development are to reclaim the space occupied by the new orthodoxy, its subterfuges and contradictions must first be exposed. With this in mind, this chapter lays bare the mystification involved in presenting an approach that is systematically tailored to meeting the needs of capitalism on a global scale but gives the impression of being principally intended to reduce poverty and other inequalities.

The establishment of neoliberalism as the new development orthodoxy is part of a profound shift in power in the global political economy. In the mid-twentieth century, successive events severely shook the confidence and credibility of the leaders of the capitalist world. The First World War, the Russian Revolution, the stock market crash and subsequent depression, the rise of fascism, the Second World War and the proliferation of anti-imperialism in the colonized world all called the prospects of global capitalism into question. The economic liberalism that had become the dominant global discourse of development after the industrial revolution was regarded with great scepticism, and the advocates of capitalism were divided and demoralized. The Soviet economic miracle and the revolution in China promised egalitarian alternatives, while the compromises adopted in postwar Europe in an effort to stem proliferating class conflict and restore growth threatened the authority of capital over labour. The loss of faith in economic liberalism was also a crisis of capitalist hegemony, in which the fundamentals upon which capitalism depended were challenged or denied. As LaPalombara's (1963) lament suggests, societies across the world neither respected nor consented to the norms upon which capitalism depended.

In the last quarter of the twentieth century the compromises of the postwar period were thrown out one by one, and liberal principles – long in partial eclipse – were reasserted. This reimposition of liberal principles – or 'neoliberal revolution' – was accompanied by a restructuring of the relationship between capital and the state, and between the state and society, with the aim of restoring the unfettered operation of market forces. These reforms were implemented in the advanced capitalist economies – notably the UK and the US – as much as in the developing world. Meanwhile the restructuring of international institutions, culminating in the creation of the World Trade Organization in 1995, hastened, reinforced and complemented processes that were under way at the national level, as individual countries were explicitly invited to lock themselves into irreversible reform. At the same time, the Soviet experiment with a state-controlled economy was brought to an end, along with those of Eastern Europe.

As noted above, it was possible by 1990 for the World Bank to claim – somewhat ahead of time – a consensus in favour of 'market-friendly' policies. This situation, barely imaginable a generation earlier, reflected the success of a protracted campaign by the advanced capitalist states under the leadership of the US, supported by global business and coordinated through transnational alliances and international institutions. An increasingly explicit and coherent agenda was advanced in opportunistic response to a series of crises – of global trade and finance, social democracy and the welfare state in the West, of Third World debt, and of state socialism in China and the Soviet Union.

As the twenty-first century dawned, a bid was under way to establish the global hegemony of capitalism. The essential elements of a global capitalist system – the authority of capital over labour, the unimpeded operation of capitalist markets for labour, goods and investment, the receptiveness of governments to the needs of capital, the presence of domestic and global regulatory orders capable of reinforcing the disciplines essential to capitalist reproduction, and the dissemination of ideologies justifying capitalism and dismissing alternatives – were in place, together, for the first time. 'Development' had been reinvented, not as a form of resistance to the logic of capitalism, but as a programme for surrendering to it.

Advocates of alternative strategies of development are now faced with a new and powerful doctrine for capitalist development, supported and allegedly vindicated by world-historical changes in recent decades and the global shifts in power and authority they reflect. This new doctrine overturns the assumption from which development studies emerged – that domestic and international policies that worked against market forces were essential to bring about development. It virtually abolishes the idea of development as a specific concern, in favour of a universal set of prescriptions applied to developing and developed economies alike.

The presentation of this new orthodoxy in seemingly authoritative texts is part of a concerted process of reestablishing the authority of the attitudes, ideas, behavioural norms and practices that capitalism requires, and embedding them so profoundly that they no longer appear as requisites for capitalism, but as natural aspects of everyday life. It is essential to be alert to this process, and to the rhetoric mobilized to accomplish it. Contemporary proponents of capitalist development have managed to secure the commitment of states around the world and international organizations to principles that are favourable to capitalism. And they have sought to win support for their goals (and neutralize opposition) by cloaking their commitment to capitalist discipline in arguments and language that disguise its logic, and promote it as a solution for the very conditions – poverty and inequality on a global scale – that it itself produces. The World Bank and other institutions, far from disseminating recipes for development that will benefit all sectors of society, are constructing a legitimizing ideology that conceals the contradictions of capitalism as a global system, translates its structural requisites into a universal programme, and re-presents it as a remedy for the very human ills it generates. This chapter examines the emergence and legitimization of the new orthodoxy, as reflected in the series of *World Development Reports* produced by the World Bank in the 1990s, contrasting it briefly with the failure of advocates of free enterprise and capitalist development to win acceptance for such an orthodoxy in the 1960s and 1970s.

Capitalist Hegemony Under Threat: the Failure of the 'Doctrine for Political Development'

In his last public statement Joseph Schumpeter in a talk entitled 'The March into Socialism', delivered to the American Economic Association in New York on 30 December 1949, a week before he died – identified a visible trend towards socialism, understood as 'that organization of society in which the means of production are controlled, and the decisions on how and what to produce and on who is to get what, are made by public authority instead of by privately-owned and privately-managed firms' (Schumpeter, 1970, p. 415). He listed six policies that were accepted by the great majority of economists: state-managed stabilization policies to prevent recession or depression; redistributive taxation to bring about greater income equality; measures to regulate prices; public control over the labour and money markets; indefinite extension of 'the sphere of wants to be satisfied that are, now or eventually, to be satisfied by public enterprise'; and all types of (social) security legislation (ibid., p. 418). He then commented: 'I believe that there is a mountain in Switzerland on which congresses of economists have been held which express disapproval of all or most of these things. But these anathcmata have not even provoked attack' (ibid.). The dismissive reference to the Mont Pelerin Society, founded by Hayek in 1947 to combat the rising tide of collectivism and reaffirm the virtues of classical liberalism (Desai, 1994, pp. 43–4), shows how faith in the market had dwindled over decades of war and capitalist crisis.

Development studies, which emerged as a new field of enquiry in the years after the Second World War, was profoundly marked by the neo-Keynesian consensus that dominated economic thinking and practice in the period. The near-universal assumption that states could and should intervene directly in production and distribution made possible the idea of development as an active process, and until the 1970s debates on development took place 'in the shadow of Keynes' (Toye, 1987, pp. 22–45; Preston, 1996, pp. 154–6). In addition, developmentalist policies were partially facilitated by the Bretton Woods institutions, despite successful US opposition to Keynes' plan for the IMF and World Bank to operate as active agents of development and redistribution across the global economy. As Leys (1996) summarizes it, the developmental framework they created facilitated national economic management, as its different elements were designed to permit national governments to manage their economies so as to maximize growth and employment. Capital was not allowed to cross frontiers without government approval, which enabled governments to determine domestic interest rates, fix the exchange rate of the national currency, and tax and spend as they saw fit to secure national economic objectives. National economic planning was seen as a natural extension of this thinking, as were domestic and international arrangements to stabilize commodity prices. It is not a great oversimplification to say that development theory was originally just a theory about the best way for colonial, and then ex-colonial, states to accelerate national economic growth in this international environment. The goal of development was growth; the agent of development was the state and the means of development were these macroeconomic policy instruments. These were taken-for-granted presuppositions of development theory as it evolved from the 1950s onwards (ibid., pp. 6–7).

Thinking about development in the postwar period, in sharp contrast to the current situation, was shaped by the weakness of orthodox economic liberalism. This was in turn reflected in contestation rather than in the dominance of a single orthodoxy in development studies in the 1950s and 1960s, as 'modernization theory' – a liberal doctrine with conservative goals – failed to repel the challenge by the dependency and world-system approaches (Cammack, 1988).

Modernization Theory and Development Studies

Modernization theory figured in development studies as a defensive response to the hegemony of nationalist developmentalism in the postwar period. Governments in Western Europe turned to a combination of welfare, neo-Keynesian economic management and the repression of the radical left in an effort to rebuild capitalist accumulation and social harmony, and in the emerging Third World, created by decolonization, new states adopted parallel ideologies of 'nationalist developmentalism', to which the active state was central (Preston, 1996, pp. 158–9). While development studies advocated state activism and intervention in the market, social scientists in the US, doubtful about the capacity of even European elites to hold the line on behalf of capitalism, sought vainly to promote conservative social and political strategies on behalf of their even weaker non-Western counterparts. In this context, modernization theory was deployed in a defensive and highly ideological manner. Leading US scholars – Almond, Coleman, Huntington, LaPalombara and Pye – saw modernization as a source of instability, and looked for means of defending the interests of the West (by which they meant the global capitalist complex led by the US) against the threat of radicalism and revolution around the world. They emphasized the need for elite social, political and institutional control in order to overcome the mismatch between modernization pressing in from outside, and what they saw as 'premodern' internal social and psychological attributes (Cammack, 1997).

The Doctrine for Political Development

LaPalombara, Pye and others devoted their energy to propagating a 'doctrine for political development' (Pye, 1965, p. 12) that would tilt the balance back in favour of free enterprise and respect for the authority of pro-Western elites (Cammack, 1994, 1996). The fruits of their labour were nine weighty volumes of *Studies in Political Development*. The series sought but failed to build a new orthodoxy favourable to free market capitalism on a global scale. The problems involved were identified by LaPalombara (1963), who well knew just how little the assumptions of the age were hospitable to this project. He pinpointed a central dilemma for Western promotors of development – the contradiction between the assumption that economic development required state intervention on a massive scale, and the end goal of economies based on private enterprise. Concluding that economic development and political democracy were unlikely to emerge unless 'the bureaucracies of the new states make quite deliberate efforts to encourage the flourishing of the private sector' (ibid., p. 25), he recommended 'the use of democratic ideological indoctrination as a means of controlling bureaucracies', and concluded with the hope that the hegemony of economic liberalism and the private entrepreneur might one day be restored.

LaPalombara's comments remind us of something that loose talk of globalization obscures: what changed in the last quarter of the twentieth century was not the nature and extent of connectedness among societies and economies around the globe, but the extent to which those societies and economies were organized in order to enforce the disciplines that specifically *capitalist* development requires.

Capitalist Hegemony Restored: the Triumph of the New Politics of Development

Point by point, the neoliberal revolution has thrown the six components of postwar political economy identified by Schumpeter into reverse. State-managed stabilization policies to prevent recession or depression have given way to internationally managed policies of restructuring, often deliberately inducing domestic recession; redistributive taxation to bring about greater equality of incomes has been abandoned in favour of fiscal reform that rewards entrepreneurship and accentuates inequality; measures to regulate prices have been dropped; public control over the labour and money markets has been systematically stripped away; the indefinite extension of 'the sphere of wants ... to be satisfied by public enterprise' has been thrown into reverse; and social security legislation has been restructured to promote rather than work against market forces.

When Schumpeter declared (in the preface to the third English edition of *Capitalism, Socialism and Democracy*, published in 1949) that 'a modern conservative government, should the next elections produce one, will ... have to manage readjustment in the given situation and in a society in which the labor interest dominates and the free-enterprise "beacon light is quenched in smoke" ' (Schumpeter, 1970, p. 409), he was stating the common sense of the age. Fifty years later the opposite assumption prevailed. It was generally assumed, and accepted by the Labour government in the UK and by the vast majority of governments around the world, that business interests dominated. The beacon of free enterprise was again burning brightly, and planning and state intervention were now 'quenched in smoke'.

Against this background, the World Bank's *Entering the 21st Century* (1999b) marked the consolidation of a process that had been under way for a decade – the definition of a comprehensive development framework (CDF) identifying both the policies needed at the national and global levels to bring capitalist development about, and the means by which they were to be implemented. Along with the promised report on poverty alleviation (World Bank, 2000b), it was intended to mark the culmination of a sequence of publications through which the elements of the CDF were fashioned, refashioned and finally fused into a coherent whole. The 1990 report, *Poverty*, began the process by examining the incidence of poverty across the global economy, and proposing how it should be addressed. The 1991 report, *The Challenge to Development*, then set out the first version of the new framework. Among the most significant of the reports that followed were *Workers in an Integrating World* (1995b), *From Plan to Market* (1996) and *The State in a Changing World* (1997). This trio was flanked by reports on *Development and the Environment* (1992b), *Investing in Health* (1993b), *Infrastructure for Development* (1994c) and *Knowledge for Development* (1999a). The key elements of the framework were in place by the mid 1990s, but it was only at the end of the decade that a way was found – by recourse to the mystificatory language of globalization and localization – to conceal the logic of capitalist discipline.

Defining the New Orthodoxy

The Foreword to the World Bank's *World Development Report 1990* proposed that global poverty should be addressed by making the poor work. They were to be first equipped, then obliged, to sell their labour in competitive national and global markets:

> A review of development experience shows that the most effective way of achieving rapid and politically sustainable improvements in the quality of life for the poor has been through a two-part strategy. The first element of the strategy is the pursuit of a pattern of growth that ensures the productive use of the poor's most abundant asset – labor. The second element is widespread provision

to the poor of basic social services, especially primary education, primary health care, and family planning. The first component provides opportunities; the second increases the capacity of the poor to take advantage of these opportunities (World Bank, 1990, p. iii).

Under cover of the ambitious goal of 'the eradication of poverty from the world' (ibid., p. 7), the World Bank proposed the capitalist exploitation of labour on a global scale, and assumed the mission of driving this logic through every aspect of social organization. To this end the report called for policies that would harness market incentives, social and political institutions, infrastructure and technology to that end (ibid., p. 3).

This was to be achieved by excluding the 'nonpoor' from social welfare, 'targeting' benefits to prevent potential workers from surviving outside the labour market, and creating 'safety nets' to support domestic reproduction and propel workers back into the labour market when they temporarily fell out. The logic of the provision of basic social services – primary health care, family planning, nutrition, and primary education – was that governments should organize themselves to provide businesses (capital) across the world with an adequate number of healthy and educated workers, and impose disciplines that would keep them available for exploitation. At the local level, public employment schemes were to cater exclusively for 'those in need': 'Since poor people are willing to work for low wages, public employment programs can offer wages that screen out the nonpoor so that resources can be used more effectively' (ibid., p. 97). At the global level, other institutions should follow the lead of the World Bank, denying aid to countries that were not 'serious about reducing poverty' (ibid., p. 137) – or in other words, were unwilling to restructure their economies and societies comprehensively along the lines required by the Bank:

> These principles ... should be regarded as applicable to the aid community as a whole. If the aid strategy outlined here were adopted and followed consistently by bilateral donors, nongovernmental organizations, and multinational agencies, its effectiveness would be greatly increased (ibid., p. 4).

The sequence of *World Development Reports* from 1990 to 2000/2001 began, then, with a clear statement of intent, and a bid for leadership of the world community in making a global reality of the efficient capitalist exploitation of labour – precisely as analyzed from a critical perspective in Marx's *Capital*. The next eight volumes lay out the programme systematically, showing just how the basic principles involved could be extended to 'market incentives, social and political institutions, infrastructure and technology'. In so doing they signalled that the postwar development world had been replaced by a new global system of direct enforcement of the fundamental disciplines of capitalism. This enterprise was rounded off, as we shall see, by an attempt to conceal the logic of capitalist exploitation – visible beneath the 'preference for the poor' with which it was thinly veiled in 1990 – by controlling hearts and minds across the globe, and re-presenting the whole package as a benevolent response to forces of 'globalization' beyond the reach of human agency.

The process of rolling out the new orthodoxy gathered momentum in the 1991 report. 'Experience shows', intoned World Bank president Barber Conable in the foreword, 'that success in promoting economic growth and poverty reduction is most likely when governments complement markets; dramatic failures result when they conflict. The Report describes a market-friendly approach in which governments allow markets to function well, and in which governments concentrate their interventions on areas in which markets prove inadequate' (World Bank, 1991, p. iii). The successive paragraphs set out an approach in which governments would (1) provide a stable macroeconomic foundation in order to inspire the confidence of the private sector, (2) create a competitive environment within which enterprise could flourish, (3) integrate their economies into the global economy and (4) 'invest in people' to supplement the market where needs were unmet in the areas of health, education, nutrition and family planning.

Within this framework, the state was called upon to define and protect property rights, to provide effective legal, judicial and regulatory systems and an efficient civil service, and to protect the environment. In other words the state was not to be downgraded, but reoriented in order to underpin and support market-friendly policies. The contrast was not between state intervention (bad) and *laissez-faire* (good), as 'in several respects, government intervention is essential for development' (ibid., p. 5). Rather intervention should be market friendly. In sum, governments should combine a 'sound policy climate with market-friendly interventions', intervening reluctantly where markets were not working, making intervention open (simple, transparent and subject to rules) when it did occur, and subjecting intervention to the checks and balances of domestic and international markets.

As set out in 1991, then, the development framework was built on four principal pillars – human development (investing in people), the domestic economy (the climate for enterprise), the international economy (integration into the global economy) and macroeconomic policy (the macroeconomic foundation). Each was explicitly oriented towards capitalist development. A stable macroeconomic foundation would restore the confidence of the private sector by keeping in place a microeconomic incentive structure that would impose market discipline:

> In reappraising their spending priorities, implementing tax reform, reforming the financial sector, privatizing state-owned enterprises, and using charges to recover the cost of some state-provided services, governments can meet the goals of microeconomic efficiency and macroeconomic stability at the same time (ibid., p. 9).

Integration into the global economy would be 'critical in encouraging domestic producers to cut costs by introducing new technologies and to develop new and better products' (ibid., p. 8), while the creation of a climate for enterprise would 'confront entrepreneurs with the information that is embodied in prices, and ... equip them (by means of investments in infrastructure and institutions) to respond' (ibid., p. 7). Rounding this off, investment in people, through appropriately targeted public programmes, would meet needs of interest to private enterprise, but not usually provided by the private sector itself. The whole programme implied 'rethinking the state', with governments urged to do less in areas where markets could be made to work, and more where they could not be relied upon. It would also produce a global programme for reform, covering the industrial countries, the multilateral agencies and the developing countries. While developing countries were to invest in people, improve the climate for enterprise, open economies to international trade and investment, and get macroeconomic policy right, the industrial countries would roll back restrictions on trade and reform macroeconomic policy; and they were urged, in conjunction with multilateral agencies, to provide increased financial support for development, support policy reform and encourage sustainable growth (ibid., p. 11).

Against the background of this comprehensive approach to development, successive *World Development Reports* in the 1990s set out to define market-friendly approaches to key development issues, or in other words to frame policy within the logic of a procapitalist, neoliberal framework. Each report identified the appropriate roles for governments and international institutions oriented towards supporting and supplementing markets, and asserted the capacity of procapitalist policies to achieve developmental and welfare goals. Throughout, the underlying claim was that there was no alternative to promarket policies. At the same time, promarket policies were consistently passed off as *pro-poor* policies, and women and ethnic minorities were routinely identified as principal beneficiaries. Taken together, these reports represented a major effort to impose the logic of uncompromising neoliberalism on every aspect of development, combining the maximum scope for market forces with a thoroughly supportive and complementary role for states and international agencies, and to assert the ability of the recommended policies to address universal welfare goals. Thus the first three post-1991 reports spelt out the essential parts to be played by the state (in partnership with private enterprise and in accordance with its logic) in the protection of the environment, the promotion of health and the provision of infrastructure. In each case, policies to extend, support and supplement the market were advocated, the logic being to provide the physical and human environment without which capitalism could not flourish.

Throughout, adherence to the agenda set out in 1991 was explicit. The 1992 report (World Bank, 1992, p. 65) proposed policies on the environment that were set in the context of the four elements of the market-friendly approach described in the 1991 report. In conformity with this philosophy, the report advocated economic incentives (price and tax regimes) where possible, supplemented by direct regulation in a minority of special cases. On health, a year later governments were called upon to 'foster an economic environment that enables households to improve their own health', and to redirect their spending 'to more cost-effective programs that do more to help the poor'. These ends were to be achieved by market-oriented policies, in which 'government financing of public health and essential clinical services would leave the coverage of remaining clinical services to private finance, usually mediated through insurance, or to social insurance' (World Bank, 1993b, p. iii).

The subsequent report, on infrastructure, stressed that 'the challenge is to determine those areas in which competitive market conditions can work and those that require public action' (World

Bank, 1994, p. 35), and governments were urged to run public utilities on commercial principles, establishing public entities as quasi-independent corporations, insulating infrastructure enterprises from non-commercial pressures and constraints, drawing up explicit contracts between governments and public or private managers or private entities involved in infrastructure services, and pursuing pricing strategies designed to ensure cost recovery (ibid., p. 37). At the same time they were to pursue legitimacy by developing strategies to persuade 'users and stakeholders' that they would share 'ownership' of the policies adopted:

> To promote more efficient and responsive service delivery, incentives need to be changed through commercial management, competition, and user involvement. *Commercial management* – including financial autonomy, accountability, and well-defined objectives – focuses providers of infrastructure services on increasing efficiency and meeting customer demand. *Competition* provides users with choices that can better meet their needs and compels providers to become more efficient and accountable. *Involvement of users and other stakeholders* in the design, operation, and maintenance of infrastructure is also key to better performance, particularly in areas where competition is constrained (ibid., p. iii).

In sum, the *World Development Reports* from 1992 to 1994 – the principal vehicle with which the World Bank sought to orchestrate the approaches of governments and international organizations around the world – presented the policies and policy approaches required to deliver and reproduce the *environment*, the *people* and the *services* that global capitalism required, in ways that would contribute most effectively to the smooth functioning and expansion of markets.

Workers, Capitalists and the State in the New Politics of Development

Against this background, the reports published in 1995, 1996 and 1997 turned their attention explicitly to the principal actors in the capitalist system – workers, capitalists and the state – and proposed a set of policies through which the transition to and operation of a fully capitalist economy could proceed. The first, *Workers in an Integrating World*, took as its starting point the assertion that 'about 99 per cent of the 1 billion or so workers projected to join the world's labor force over the next thirty years will live in what are today's low and middle income countries' (World Bank, 1995, p. 7). It therefore proposed a programme for completion of the process of proletarianisation ('primitive' or 'original' accumulation) first identified and analyzed by Marx in Chapter 26 of *Capital* (volume one), and the creation of institutions to regulate labour to the benefit of capital. First, 'fears that increased international trade and investment and less state intervention will hurt employment' (ibid., p. 2) were dismissed. Governments were to pursue a four-point programme, pursuing 'market-based growth paths', taking advantage of 'new opportunities at the international level by opening up to trade and attracting capital', constructing a framework for labour policy that would complement informal and rural labour markets, support collective bargaining in the formal sector, provide safeguards for the vulnerable, and avoid biases that would favour relatively well-off workers, and designing transitions to be as rapid as possible without excessive or permanent costs for labour (ibid., pp. 2–3). The Foreword to the report, under the name of new president of the World Bank, James D. Wolfensohn, was uncompromising about the context in which these policies were to be applied:

> What makes the Report even more timely is the growing impact of two distinct global trends: reduced government intervention in markets, and the increased integration of trade, capital flows, and the exchange of information and technology. In such a climate of profound change, basic decisions about wages and working conditions are driven by global competitive pressures. The harsh reality of a global market is that policy failures are punished hard – through currency movements, shifts in market share, and, ultimately, through fluctuations in employment and wage levels (ibid., p. iii).

Against this background, the report advocated forms of regulation that would promote the development of capitalist-friendly labour markets. Minimum wage legislation was ruled out in middle- and low-income economies with large agricultural and informal sectors (ibid., pp. 74–6); health and safety legislation would be governed by market principles, set at a level 'at which the costs are commensurate with the value that informed workers place on improved working conditions and reduced risk' (ibid., p. 77); and trade sanctions would not be used to enforce even basic rights for workers (ibid., p. 79). Unions would have a strictly limited role. They would involve workers in activities that would improve efficiency and productivity, and promote health and safety legislation, but they would not be enabled to act as monopolists, distort labour markets or oppose programmes of reform and structural adjustment. Competitive product markets would limit unions' ability to obtain higher wages for their members unless they delivered higher productivity in return (ibid., p. 82). Collective bargaining was to take place at the enterprise rather than the sectoral or national level, the ideal model being provided by Hong Kong, where the bargaining position of unions was weak, and 'most unions are in the business of providing insurance and social assistance to their members rather than fighting for higher wages' (ibid., p. 83). Effective unions, from the World Bank's point of view, were those that eliminated the need for large-scale state regulation and intervention, and pressed firms to adopt more advanced methods of production, but did not protect jobs or distort markets. Unions were to be allowed to exist and represent their members, but not to pursue job security or push wages above the market rate – in other words, they were to become part of an institutional framework to promote and enforce the discipline of capitalist competition.

Although its apparent focus was on the transitional economies, the key to the broader purpose of the 1996 report, *From Plan to Market*, can be found in the closing sentences of the Introduction:

> Many other countries have market or mixed economies resting on weak foundations and have at one time or another adopted parts of the planning model. The process of transition is therefore of interest to a wide-ranging set of countries and peoples (World Bank, 1996, p. 6).

In accordance with this orientation, the report went beyond a consideration of appropriate strategies of transition to set out in a comprehensive manner the essential institutions of a market or capitalist economy. Conceptualizing transition as 'a passage from one mode of economic organization to a thoroughly different one' (ibid., p. 3), it moved from reinforcing the lessons of previous reports – 'the utter necessity of both liberalizing economies through opening trade and market opportunities and stabilizing them through reducing inflation and practicing financial discipline' – to 'discussing the institutions that make market-based economies work' (ibid., p. iii). Its stated purpose, then, was to define for all economies in the global capitalist system – not just those in transition – a comprehensive set of institutions that would eradicate any vestige of planning, and implement the logic of capitalist exploitation, competition and accumulation throughout all economic, social, political and cultural systems.

In this context the bridge between liberalization and stabilization on the one hand (ibid., pp. 22–43) and the institutions of market-based economies on the other (ibid., Part II) was provided by a lengthy discussion of the need for clear and comprehensive property rights (ibid., pp. 44–65). Whereas the previous report had addressed the need to subject workers to competitive labour markets, the focus in the 1996 report was on creating a legal framework that would both define and enforce property rights, and force capitalists to compete: 'Transition requires changes that introduce financial discipline and increase entry of new firms, exit of unviable firms, and competition' (ibid., p. 44). The disciplines of capitalism were to be applied to workers and capitalists alike, and the strategic objective of privatization was to reorganize ownership in order to respond to the needs of the market economy. In this key strategic context, the example of New Zealand was invoked to spell out the lesson that even where state entities could be successfully reoriented along commercial lines, 'privatization was required, not necessarily to improve performance in the short run but to *lock in the gains of earlier reforms*' (ibid., Box 3.3, p. 50, emphasis added).

Against this background, the second part of the report defined a comprehensive institutional framework informed by the logic of economic liberalism. It called for market-oriented laws enforced by market-oriented institutions, complemented at the micro level by market-oriented incentives (ibid., p. 88). The logic was explicit, and systemic in scope:

> Economic laws in market economies have at least four functions: defining and protecting property rights; setting rules for exchanging those rights; establishing rules for entry into and exit out of productive activities; and promoting competition by overseeing market structure and behavior and correcting market failures (ibid.).

This was followed by a detailed description of institutions that were deemed appropriate to a capitalist economy: property rights, contracts, company and foreign investment law, bankruptcy law and competition law, independent judicial institutions (and constraints on state power), and new financial institutions, including 'fully independent and market-oriented' supervisory agencies (ibid., p. 102), private banks, non-bank financial intermediaries and capital markets (ibid., pp. 88–109).

Against this background the report advocated 'better and slimmer government', and identified four areas for government intervention:

the provision of pure public goods and goods with positive externalities; the provision or regulation of natural monopolies; and provision
or regulation in areas where imperfect information might lead to
market failure (ibid., p. 111). In sum, robust empirical evidence
supported the view that government spending tended to be productive
and promoted economic growth in cases where it corrected proven
market failures and truly complemented private activity – as did some
types of infrastructural investment, preventive health care and basic
education – but rarely otherwise (ibid., p. 115).

The 1996 report, a comprehensive treatment of institutions that
were appropriate to a capitalist economy, concluded by stressing the
significance of 'institutional reform and managing the realignment of
the state' (ibid., p. 146). Its successor, *The State in a Changing World*
(World Bank, 1997), described in detail the 'effective state', which
would enforce and support the disciplines essential to a capitalist
economy – or in World Bank rhetoric, would act as a 'partner,
catalyst, and facilitator' rather than a direct provider (ibid., p. 1).
With the key features of this 'effective state' already defined, the
report was principally concerned with securing its adoption and
legitimization. A bid to consolidate the hegemony of the neoliberal
state, it revealed with indelicate transparency the strategy of presenting the disciplines of capitalism as if they were avenues of freedom
and empowerment. In so doing, it exposed the disciplinary content of
'participation and decentralization' as essential aspects of contemporary development policy. At the outset, a clear statement of the
need to redefine the state and reeducate the people – *'[g]etting
societies to accept a redefinition of the state's responsibilities* will be
one part of the solution. This will include strategic selection of the
collective actions that states will try to promote, coupled with greater
efforts to take the burden off the state, by involving citizens and
communities in the delivery of collective goods' (ibid., p. 3; emphasis
added) – was immediately translated into the mystificatory language
of empowerment: 'making the state more responsive to people's
needs, bringing government closer to the people through broader
participation and decentralization' (ibid.). In other words the report
simultaneously provided a recipe for the disciplinary state and the
rhetoric for selling it to the people.

The report insisted first upon the need for an authoritative state
capable of imposing the disciplines required for capitalism to succeed.
The true neoliberal state was not the 'minimal' state that left everything to the market, but a capable or 'effective' state that could create
and sustain the environment in which market discipline could work:

'A clearer understanding of the institutions and norms embedded in markets shows the folly of thinking that development strategy is a matter of choosing between the state and the market. ... Countries need markets to grow, but they need capable state institutions to grow markets' (ibid., p. 38).

This perspective was reinforced by the World Bank's version of the folly of postwar developmentism (ibid., p. 29), and the results of a survey of entrepreneurs from 3600 firms in 69 industrial and developing countries, focusing on the weakness of the institutional framework provided by the majority of states around the world. The point could not be made more clearly: the 'effective' state was the state that was effective from the point of view of capitalist competition and accumulation.

The report then outlined the appropriate institutional framework – a policy hierarchy in which macroeconomic discipline would be guaranteed by strong central control over policy and spending (locked in place by an independent central bank) and commitment to disciplinary multilateral organizations such as the World Bank itself, the IMF and the WTO (ibid., pp. 50–1, 101). Discipline was to be diffused through the system by incorporating contracts and internal competition into direct public provision, and contracting out to private and non-governmental providers where possible (ibid., pp. 61–98). Within this framework, decentralization and participation would play the triple role of exerting pressure on the state to deliver essential services efficiently, sharing the cost of delivery with the 'beneficiaries' themselves, and inducing people to experience as empowerment, tightly controlled and carefully delimited forms of market-supporting activity: 'The message, here as elsewhere, is that bringing government closer to the people will only be effective if it is part of a larger strategy for improving the institutional capability of the state' (ibid., p. 111). Participation could either improve or undermine the capability of the state (ibid., p. 120); it was good if it served to reinforce the efficiency and authority of the neoliberal state, bad if it did not (ibid., pp. 129–30). If citizens were to vote in a plebiscite to index pensions to wages, or to reverse privatization legislation, as they had in Uruguay in 1989 and 1992 respectively, constitutional reform to rule out further surprises would in order (ibid., p. 148). The goal, in sum, was to bring government closer to the entrepreneur, and to lock the rest of the population into the discipline of the market.

The emphasis of the 1997 report was strategic, focusing on engineering and legitimizing neoliberal reforms. Its significance in this regard has been noted (Gill, 1998; Panitch, 1998), though without setting it adequately in the context of its predecessors. Governments were urged to take advantage of crises to push through reform (World Bank, 1997, pp. 144, 150–1), and to sequence reforms in a manner that could weaken opposition to them:

> This, in turn, may call for a two-stage strategy to circumvent resistance. During the first phase, an opting-out mechanism might be put in place, to allow people to switch to private providers if they want to. Wider recognition of the benefits of better services can then make it easier to carry out the second phase: getting rid of the public providers (ibid., p. 153).

From this report onwards, then, the emphasis shifted from defining the constituent institutions of a global capitalist economy to creating a legitimizing mythology for them. The disciplinary context would now be presented as natural and inevitable, effectively beyond human control, and the practices necessary to sustain it would be turned on their heads and presented as instances of opportunity, choice and self-realization. But as the quotation above suggests, the iron hand could sometimes slip from the velvet glove. To counter this eventuality, the subsequent reports set out a strategy for the repackaging, dissemination and global management of neoliberal doctrines as objective knowledge, and adopted the mystificatory language of globalization and localization in order to divert attention from the concerted and purposive action by governments and multilateral agencies to bring about the global sway of capitalism.

Legitimizing the New Politics of Development

In the consecutive reports from 1990 to 1997 the strategy of the World Bank was to promote procapitalist policies, extend them to every aspect of social and economic organization, and claim that they would reduce poverty to the benefit of all. There was a potential danger in making so clear the extent to which claims about addressing of social needs was closely tied to the logic of capitalist accumulation and the global implementation of capitalist markets, especially as the World Bank's own figures showed a relative decline in GDP per capita in the poorest two-thirds of countries since 1980 against a steady increase in the richest third, and a steady increase in the absolute number of poor (World Bank, 1999b, pp. 14, 25). In this respect, *Knowledge for Development* (World Bank, 1999) and *Entering the 21st Century* (World Bank, 2000b) were vital efforts to establish the global hegemony of neoliberal ideology.

The global hegemony of the neoliberal orthodoxy preached by the World Bank was not expected to come about by chance. Alongside predictable advocacy of the global privatization of commercially exploitable knowledge (intellectual property rights), and developing-country access to knowledge through liberalization and the encouragement of private inward investment, the 1998/99 report (World Bank, 1999a) set out complementary national and global 'knowledge strategies'. National governments were advised to 'seek ways to improve information flows that make a market economy function better' (World Bank, ibid., p. 149), but at the same time the report barely attempted to conceal the fact that in all relevant areas – access to new communication technologies, the ability to capture the commercial benefits of new knowledge, and the capacity to address information problems that could provoke market failure – the developing countries were at a massive disadvantage. The obvious implication was that an approach to knowledge that began by asserting the priority of extending property rights aggressively into the realm of ideas would inevitably exacerbate the disparities in wealth and power that already shaped the global economy. The response of the World Bank was to propose itself as the lead institution for a global policy of knowledge management that was intended to cement developing countries' institutionalized commitment to neoliberal ideas and policies. First, the report rebranded the neoliberal doctrines elaborated over the previous decade as 'know-how' or 'expertise' – value-free objective knowledge. Second, it announced a 'knowledge management system' (launched in 1996 and modelled on similar systems pioneered by international consultancies such as Arthur Andersen, Ernst and Young, and Price Waterhouse), which was intended to act as a rapid-response taskforce capable of producing market solutions on demand. Third – confirming the Bank's sophisticated understanding of strategies for hegemony – it proposed 'to incorporate local knowledge from countries and sectors in which the Bank is active':

Gathered through field interviews, participatory community assessments, and focus-group meetings with NGOs, this knowledge is being catalogued by country, region, sector and theme, to be made widely available to practitioners everywhere. By taking into account and complementing traditional practices in the least-developed countries, this approach should make knowledge available to far greater numbers of the poor. It may also ensure greater acceptance of development solutions (ibid., p. 140).

Hence the World Bank is now mobilizing massive resources for an explicit strategy of establishing the new neoliberal orthodoxy as the common sense of the age. In a complementary strategy, the 1999/2000 report (World Bank, 2000b) latched onto 'globalization' to preach the inevitability of the new orientations it proposed. At the same time it brought the desired patterns of behaviour and organization required to ensure the embedding of pure capitalist disciplines (including its own covert strategy identified above) under the term 'localization', presented as an empowering force that would ensure human agency in the process. With globalization and localization, policy makers around the world would be confronted by 'forces that bring new opportunities but also raise new or greater challenges in terms of economic and political instability'. Their task would be to contain this instability, and to provide 'an environment in which a development agenda can be implemented to seize the opportunities' (World Bank, 2000b, pp. iii–iv). This was to be achieved by a 'broad pragmatism', 'realizing that development must move beyond economic growth to encompass important social goals – reduced poverty, improved quality of life, enhanced opportunities for better education and health, and more' (ibid., p. iii). The reference to a 'market-friendly' approach, which had defined the 1991 report, had disappeared, as had the focus of the four key lessons on creating a competitive domestic and international environment. Instead a new and mystificatory set of 'four critical lessons' was identified, in which all reference to the promotion of competition and the privileging of global trade was airbrushed out:

First, macroeconomic stability is an essential prerequisite for achieving the growth needed for development. Second, growth does not trickle down; development must address human needs directly. Third, no one policy will trigger development; a comprehensive approach is needed. Fourth, institutions matter; sustained development should be rooted in processes that are socially inclusive and responsive to changing circumstances (ibid., p. 1).

The new orthodoxy is now presented as if its internal logic derived directly from the goal of moving towards the abolition of poverty and inequity. The specificity of the policies proposed is obscured, and the role of institutions in embedding the domestic and global disciplines of capitalist reproduction is concealed. Macroeconomic stability is presented as the key to growth, which is in turn the key to universally beneficial development, reversing a line of causation in which priority is actually given to capitalist accumulation, institutions are shaped accordingly and the disciplines they embody set limits to the extent and distribution of development.

The effect is to present a set of policies infused with the disciplines and class logic of capitalism as if they were of universal benefit. The intention, as always with such legitimizing strategies, is to disguise the purposive action of specific human agents bent on establishing the hegemony of a particular social form of organization of production, presenting the process as if it were the natural outcome of abstract forces too powerful for humanity to resist. The purpose of this chapter has been to expose this sleight of hand, so that space can be reclaimed within which alternatives to systematically procapitalist development can be explored.

Conclusion: the New Orthodoxy in Development Studies

The *World Development Report 1998/1999* declared that 'knowledge *is* development' (World Bank, 1999a, p. 130). The truth is that for the World Bank, development is *capitalism*, pure and simple. Over little more than a decade the vocabulary of development has been hijacked to project capitalism as the answer to the human aspiration for a better life, then to mask the logic underlying uncompromising neo-liberalism. As a lead institution for the forces seeking to achieve the hegemony of capitalism on a genuinely global scale, the World Bank has succeeded brilliantly over the last decade in articulating and propagating a new orthodoxy in the field of development studies – a 'new politics of development' that is simply a recipe for establishing capitalism on a global scale. It should be seen, precisely, as an orthodoxy – *a doctrine certified as correct by an authoritative institution*. A starting point for a critical approach to development studies today is to recognize both the ascendancy of the new neoliberal orthodoxy and its character as ideology.

10

Conclusion: Orthodoxy and its Alternatives in Contemporary Development

MARTIN MINOGUE AND UMA KOTHARI

The purpose of this book, as explained in Chapter 1, has not been to present an encyclopaedic account of the whole field of development thought and practice, an account that could not be contained in one volume. Rather the intention has been to consider key issues in the contemporary development agenda, which may indeed have their origins in alternative discourses, and to demonstrate that in each of these key areas, development practice is dominated by a set of ideas that can be described as constituting a prevailing orthodoxy. In each area it is also possible to find multiple, sometimes divergent and conflicting strands in both literature and practice that represent, to varying degrees, alternative ways of conceptualizing development. In short we seek to challenge both the adequacy and appropriateness of these stereotypical orthodoxies and to propose different conceptual and practical strategies for development.

The notion of challenging the orthodoxy rests on the existence of a clear orthodoxy that can be defined and is ideologically dominant, and that this intellectual dominance is translated into practice. As the preceding chapters demonstrate, there are various positions on what constitutes the orthodoxy and the ways in which it can be challenged. The most critical position taken is that dominant patterns of thought and practice mask unstated, even concealed intentions that contradict stated aims (see Chapters 3, 8 and 9). A modified position is that existing thought and practice are characterized by flawed assumptions and inadequate or inconsistent application (Chapters 5 and 7). A more optimistic view is that, over time, repeated challenges to the

179

orthodoxy produce some absorption of alternative approaches into mainstream practice, so holding out the promise of a transformative response to criticism (Chapters 4 and 6). Let us now examine these approaches in more detail, reflecting on the key issues that have emerged in this book.

Neoliberalism and Globalization

As discussed in Chapter 1, neoliberal thought is now dominant in development discourse and action. It is, according to Paul Cammack (Chapter 9), 'the new development orthodoxy' and 'virtually abolishes the idea of development as a specific concern in favour of a universal set of prescriptions for developing and developed economies alike'. These prescriptions are nothing less than the prerequisites for a capitalist economy. While, as Cammack argues, this represents an overturning of the statist development orthodoxies of the 1960s (and indeed of the institutionalized socialist version of state-led development), it might also be regarded as the reemergence of a type of capitalism temporarily arrested by the statist modernization (development) project.

Cammack uses the successive annual reports of the World Bank to illustrate the extent to which this revitalized mode of thought has embedded itself in leading development agencies. This, it is contended, amounts to the construction of 'a legitimizing ideology' that supports capital expansion while concealing the problems created by capitalist development. Cammack traces the process by which the Keynesian consensus, in the development field as elsewhere, was overturned and replaced by a less constrained, more triumphal capitalism. He argues that this newly dominant capitalism obliges labour to operate in ever more competitive national and global markets, a process clearly identified in the 1990 World Development Report's proposal, as Cammack expresses it, 'that global poverty should be addressed by making the poor work'.

Cammack goes on to suggest that the linkage of market-friendly (or procapitalist) policies to socially beneficial outcomes was a consistent feature of World Bank reports in the 1990s. A major consequence has been a reorientation of the state, which is advised to reduce its direct involvement in social and economic problems while assisting the market to fill the consequent vacuum in social and economic provision. For Cammack, much of development discourse is a subterfuge, and it is necessary (though not of course sufficient) to demonstrate the intellectual dishonesty and concealed relations of economic and political power involved. These powerful interests act to promote market-friendly development strategies and policies, and by implication to resist, rule out or emasculate alternative, non-market approaches. One reason for revealing the 'capitalist project' is to strengthen the possibility of establishing and implementing such alternatives.

Social Development

The claim of virtually all major aid donors is that the principal object of their development interventions is to reduce poverty and improve the quality of life for all. In this formulation the intended outcome of economic growth objectives is social development. In Chapter 4 Maia Green examines the various meanings of 'social development', pointing out that it 'stands ambiguously between classification as a discipline and classification as professional practice'. At the same time 'there are no accepted theories or bodies of research that provide the foundation for social development practice.' Green suggests that the failure of economistic models has allowed social development to gain ground, but she is concerned to identify the weaknesses in the social development paradigm that limit the effectiveness of social development interventions.

One weakness is the marginalization of social development within development agencies and discourse. Another is the tendency to focus on specific target groups and the transformation of social relations between them, without an adequate understanding of either the actual social relationships between social groups and categories, or of the wider socioeconomic context that may condition possible outcomes. This can lead to the stereotyping of particular groups and communities, but if these communities challenge the assumptions made about them they are 'viewed as ... having the wrong kind of social relations and institutions'. Such misrepresentations of social categories and realities abound; for example 'much gender programming still homogenizes women as a category associated with the domestic, irrespective of life cycle and aspirations'. All this may mean that 'planners and policymakers ... have little understanding of the broader processes of social change in which development interventions come to be embedded'.

Green suggests that this failure to embrace either the context or the history of social relationships is a fatal flaw in current approaches to social development. Stakeholder analysis is too static, representing stakeholder relationships 'in relation to the project rather than to each other'. Participation, while 'now part of the standard toolkit ... may in practice replicate existing social divisions, be appropriated by the elite and the articulate, and exclude poorer and marginalized groups, including women'. Well intentioned attempts to strengthen civil society and social capital are weakened by 'the fact that social capital as an asset is visible only to outside experts who are keen to place an economic value on social institutions'.

In alluding to the failure of economistic models, Green is more concerned with correcting their shortcomings as instruments of social development than with castigating them. She accepts that much social thinking is ideological, but this leads her not down the path of ideological contestation, but rather in the eminently practical direction of how to make social development interventions more effective. Since current approaches are seen as 'little more than statements of desired outcomes', she calls for social development policies that are more clearly rooted in existing social realities and relationships, an implied criticism of the 'blueprint' mentality of aid donors. Green takes the view that if the social needs of poor and marginalized members of society are to be met, then social development must be less marginalized within development agencies.

Social Capital

The origins, meanings and applications of the concept of social capital are elaborated by Paul Francis in Chapter 5. He locates the term and its usage in notions of 'civil society' and 'social exclusion'; concepts that are 'associated with new and sometimes far-reaching thinking on a wide range of questions, including the non-economic dimensions of poverty, the role of civil associations in governance, and the importance of social networks and values in economic life'.

'Civil society' is taken to refer to 'the institutions that exist between the individual on the one hand, and the state and the economy on the other'. Francis draws attention to the breadth and relative incoherence of the concept, and suggests that its cultural specificity (to developed societies) 'risks at best, inappropriateness, and at worst imposing a form of cultural imperialism'. Even if there is a case for seeing an active civil society as an essential component of development, this 'tells us little about how the appropriate range of institutions that make up the sector can be nurtured'.

Social exclusion is seen as potentially valuable in its 'encapsulation of the multifaceted character of poverty' and in capturing the interlocking nature of the different types of deprivation associated with poverty. But as Francis points out, the meaning of exclusion depends on what is regarded as inclusive in a society, so that 'differing conceptions of what society is and what exclusion from it constitutes' will lead to different proposals for promoting social inclusion.

Given the uncertainty surrounding these ideas, it comes as no surprise to find that the concept of social capital is beset with problems of definition, though Francis gives us a common-sense description of it as 'the metaphorical glue that holds groups and societies together and enables them to get things done', along with the 'recognition that economic activity cannot take place without social values, norms and structures'. He outlines the various models of civil society that have been presented, and shows that insofar as these models see development 'as a transition from one kind of social capital to another', they reflect the modernization narrative of an earlier period. In this structural–functional scenario the construction of social capital has an obvious appeal to those responsible for the realization of development policies and strategies (though Francis reminds us that social capital has many negative consequences and implications) and is 'increasingly used to describe a wide range of development interventions'. While it is seen as 'a new key to poverty alleviation', Francis warns us that social capital is more typically the province of the better-off and the better-organized than of the poor. Meanwhile its conceptual incoherence and breadth mean that it is in danger of explaining 'everything and nothing'.

In pointing to the methodological and analytical weaknesses of the concept of social capital, Francis offers diverse interpretations of its value. On the one hand social capital offers the basis for a new set of tools of social analysis, and a genuinely transformative challenge to the dominant economic model of development. On the other hand it is embedded in a contradiction, in that it is being promoted as a 'communitarian' construct at a juncture when the economic development process itself is eroding the communitarian ties and relationships that are central to its realization. The damaging judgement must be that at present social capital is a weakly designed and incoherent framework and cannot possibly be a sound policy vehicle.

Gender, Eurocentrism and Development

In Chapter 4, Maia Green analyses gender 'as a key target for development outcomes and interventions' because of its significance in constructing effective poverty-reduction strategies. She considers that narrow approaches that focus mainly on women are too static, and calls for more attention to the processes of inequality and transformation. Uma Kothari (Chapter 3) is concerned with both cultural and gender blindness in development thought and practice, and with the continuities between the colonial and postcolonial periods. She is principally concerned with the ways in which knowledge is constructed and ordered, so that subjects such as development studies help to reproduce and sustain unequal relations of power. She identifies the male and Western bias within development theory and practice before presenting the feminist and postcolonial challenges to these.

According to Kothari, one way in which power inequalities are sustained is through the 'masculinist discourse' within development, which for some time meant that 'women were virtually invisible to development planners and policy makers'. This was in part the product of the absence of research into or information about women's roles and needs, partly because economic activity (up to the 1970s the principal concern of development planners) was seen as a male province. This male bias seriously distorted development policy and its outcomes. New approaches, now labelled 'gender and development', have tried to redress these distortions by focusing on the socially constructed relations between men and women, with particular reference to the sexual division of labour and understandings of the household. Kothari suggests that while it is now widely accepted by development agencies that men and women should benefit equally from the processes of change, and that gender inequalities should be reduced, the masculinist discourse persists in various forms within the aid system.

Another related way in which power inequalities persist is through the Eurocentric bias in the theory and practice of development. Kothari points to the colonial legacy of development studies and suggests that its imperialist past is evident in the continuing preoccupation with ideas about modernity and progress, and in the ways in which Third World people are represented. She goes on to demonstrate how postcolonial theory has attempted to decentre Western knowledge and representations before stressing the need to bring together feminist and postcolonialist critiques. 'Postcolonial feminism' calls for a rethinking about the ways in which other people and places are represented. This means deconstructing the dominant (and politically motivated) representations and recovering the voices and identities of those marginalized by these representations. The main thrust is that 'particular forms of power relations and forms of knowledge prevalent in colonial times are apparent in strands of contemporary development discourse, including gendered and racial distinctions'. Kothari calls for 'a strategic engagement between feminist and postcolonialist thought that will transcend both perspectives rather than simply seek an alliance between them'.

Like Cammack, Kothari emphasizes the degree to which development policy and practice are produced and owned by Western interests, and argues for a process of 'decentring' to return responsibility for the development agenda, and its realization, to non-Western peoples; a similar process of 'decentring' of male bias and self-interest is essential if development policy and practice are to address unequal power relations at all levels.

Participation

When discussing the debates and practices associated with participation, McGee (Chapter 6) asserts that 'paradigm shifts in development usually take the form of modifications to Northern donor and policy-maker perspectives, rather than considering anything that happens in the South'. While Green (Chapter 4) emphasizes the limitations of participatory practice, McGee is concerned to give a more nuanced account of the changing nature of participation. She identifies two schools, an earlier one labelled 'participation in projects', and a later one labelled 'participatory development'. The first was characterized by a largely technical concern to improve the efficiency of donor-designed and donor-driven projects, treating those involved as objects or targets; the second was based on 'the notion of people as conscious agents in social and political life', and sought to locate development activity inside people's everyday world.

Alluding to the importance of differing methodologies between the mid 1980s and the mid 1990s, McGee contrasts the 'toolkit' tendency of the project school with the preference of the participatory process school for methodologies such as participatory rural appraisal, which promised to provide 'frameworks for analysis and awareness-raising that would be capable, over time, of convincing a critical mass of people of the need for transformation', and also capable 'of mobilizing a critical mass of development actors ... radically in order to transform the development paradigm, making it more democratic, equitable, inclusive and pluralist'. Methodology, in this case, was not merely a toolkit for specific purposes, but 'the key to how development was conceived and by whom, and what sort of development was promoted and how.'

The threat this approach offered to the political *status quo*, both globally and locally, perhaps explains the 'mainstreaming' of participatory development discourse by major donors, and the linking of it to governance and democratization agendas. McGee usefully reminds us, however, that the 'participation in projects' orthodoxy remains precisely that, because it is still 'the dominant form in which participation policies are put into practice in development work around the world'. Nonetheless, McGee concludes that donors appear to have accepted many of the principles of the participatory development approach, so this 'subsuming of the radical alternative by the orthodoxy' is genuinely transforming the mainstream development agenda.

Good Governance and Development Management

Many proponents of development suggest that the key to progress lies not in debating contested ideas and values, but in the practical task of 'getting things done'. It is also clear from several chapters in this book that elements of a 'good governance' agenda are in operation across the whole field of development practice. In Chapter 7 Martin Minogue outlines the origins of this relatively new orthodoxy, which is 'much more than the more efficient management of economic and social resources or the improved delivery of public services' – it also entails 'strategies to strengthen the institutions of civil society, to make governments more open and accountable, and even to transform the political context (through democratization) of the developing and transitional economies'. He argues that while many of the component parts of good governance are not new, what is new is political conditionality. This agenda is evidently rooted in the collapse of socialism, which brought 'renewed confidence in the demonstratable power of the capitalist democracies', but it is also an attempt to make good the failures of economic conditionality, while simultaneously allowing donors to respond to domestic political pressure for more effective use of development aid budgets. Unsurprisingly, in practice much 'good governance' spending by donors is allocated to efforts to improve the administrative capacity and performance of developing country governments through the introduction of Western-derived management reforms.

Minogue challenges the major assumptions that underpin the 'good governance' orthodoxy. Donors, it is suggested, operate with a highly oversimplified model of the causal relations between economic and political change, and between democratization and development, a model for which there is little hard evidence. Indeed the presumed link is rejected by radical critics as 'no more than a Western project to maintain the West's dominance in the post Cold War world', and one that is ahistorical in its disregard for the legacies of the colonial system.

A further set of ethnocentric assumptions is considered by Minogue in relation to the positioning of human rights at the centre of the good governance agenda. 'Universality' proposes that there is 'a universally applicable morality', from which can be deduced 'a universally valid set of criteria for human rights claims'. But universality, it has been argued, 'is complemented by "universalization", a process by which those who are powerful identify their own values as universal values, then seek to extend them . . . choosing the form of humanity for others is an exercise in power, not in morality'. 'Relativism' proposes that there can be 'plural moralities, reflecting the different sets of values held by different societies' and 'defends culture itself as "the supreme ethical value" and cultural relativism as a universal moral principle'. In more practical terms it is suggested that 'alternative social values exist in non-Western societies that offer an equally valid basis for development priorities and choices'.

This debate is directly relevant to the critique of the political conditionality policies that underpin good governance strategies, for it suggests that the political certainties promoted by major aid donors have neither an ethical nor an empirical foundation. It is also a policy that is inconsistently applied by donors. Minogue concludes that on current evidence, 'governance will . . . fail as a universalizing project, representing as it does the attempted imposition of a Western model' at a time when the economic and cultural values of the West are increasingly under challenge. The element of triumphalism evident in Western proclamations of the virtuousness of Western political values and institutions is undermined by the equally evident weaknesses of and inconsistency in the attempts to implement good governance policies. Perhaps such ineptness of practice is desirable if the underlying concepts are so flawed. But this strategy at least represents a belated recognition of the importance of the political factor in development, hitherto a much neglected constituent; and the alternative we might envisage in this field, therefore, is not to abandon the ambition to construct an appropriate political model of development, but to ensure that such an approach is informed by greater respect for the diversity of political cultures, and by a better understanding of the dynamics of political systems.

Environmentalism

Like governance, environmental issues cut across virtually all areas of development policy, particularly in relation to economic growth, industrialization, trade, agricultural development, food production, natural resource utilization and poverty. This intermeshing of environmental and development issues gave rise to the concept of 'sustainable development', a term as notable for its ambiguities as any other in the development lexicon. In Chapter 8 Philip Woodhouse traces the mixed origins of environmental thought. The earlier forms are found in debates on the relation of humanity to nature, interpreted first through the Enlightenment rationalist perspective, and later in attempts to come to terms with the deleterious consequences of the Industrial Revolution.

The need to regulate industrialization was born out of the perception that its environmental costs and benefits were unevenly distributed, with developers capturing the benefits, and society more generally incurring, or suffering from, the costs. Regulatory approaches based on the principle that 'the polluter pays' eventually gained ground and are now standard environmental practice. This now includes provisions for prior environmental impact assessment of development projects. Woodhouse points out the distinction between the conservationist agenda, which is associated with 'environment as nature', and the essentially utilitarian perspective, which permits the exploitation of nature (within limits) and is primarily concerned with questions of ownership, use and management. It is the latter, utilitarian perspective that was incorporated into the normative, 'modernization' model of development. Initial fears about natural limits to growth proved unfounded, but the environment was forced onto the international political agenda by the problem of stratospheric ozone depletion, renewing anxiety about the long-term effects of industrialization and strengthening the hand of environmentalists.

This merely set the stage for a new struggle with the advocates of institutional economic strategies (which, of course, includes the major development agencies). Their approach is to treat environmental resources as 'natural capital', and to apply to this the full rigour of neoclassical economic methodology. While this helps to integrate environmental analysis into mainstream development debates, it leaves profoundly important issues of ownership, distribution and rights in dispute. Unsurprisingly this orthodoxy has been subjected to 'alternative' challenges, not least the populist or 'people-centred' approach, which 'places the poor (as both victims and agents of environmental degradation) at the centre of efforts to understand the environmental aspects of development', and provides a focus for political opposition to the neoliberal project. A different strand gives special weight to indigenous and local knowledge of natural resource use, and challenges Eurocentric notions of what constitutes environmental (and related social) realities. A third approach emphasizes 'the role of power relations in decisions about how natural resources are to be used or abused'. Overall this 'political ecology' movement underpins 'a rights-based advocacy of the control of resources being redistributed in favour of disadvantaged groups, which is the principal counter to the market-based redistributive criteria of neoliberal policies'.

Woodhouse illustrates the ways in which the tensions between these contending paradigms are played out in the international arena by reference to debates on and negotiations over climate change, and on the development of tropical rainforests. While the negotiations on managing climate change appear for the time being to represent a victory for the neoliberals, the 'internationalization of the Amazon' seems to demonstrate the possibility of effective coalitions being established between local and international groups concerned to limit the social and environmental damage caused by exploitation by powerful economic and political interests.

Woodhouse is concerned to present environmentalism as something that may provide a means for progress, through its challenge to the 'model of industrialized consumer society upon which modernization theory is based', and through its assertion of the interests of those disadvantaged groups that bear a disproportionate share of the costs of development. He sees some hope in the international consensus on the need for sustainable development, but it is clearly essential to erode the dominance of neoliberal market models that mainly support vested interests in high-consumption societies. Ultimately the 'shared nature' of environmental problems should lead to concerted collective action, a process that is likely to produce both equitable and sustainable outcomes.

Conclusion

As the preceding chapters have demonstrated, development discourse is a kind of subterfuge, and it is necessary (though not, of course, sufficient) to demonstrate the intellectual dishonesty of and concealed relations between the economic and political powers involved. These powerful interests act to promote market-friendly development strategies and policies, and by implication to resist, rule out or emasculate alternative non-market approaches. One reason for revealing the 'capitalist project' is to strengthen the possibility of establishing and implementing such alternatives. In the language of policy analysis, there seems to be ample 'room for manoeuvre', for the 'development policy space' is occupied by a multiplicity of actors and activities, while the big players (the main aid donors and the more influential nation-states in both the North and the South) are not so confident about their capacity for effective intervention that they can ignore the lessons born of practice that the real world of development is apt to provide.

In Chapter 6 McGee highlights the dilemmas associated with attempting to present a well-founded critique of dominant ideas and practices while at the same time suggesting practical alternatives. Her analysis shows that both the orthodox approach to participation and the suggested alternatives to make good the deficiencies of that orthodoxy have been brought within the mainstream policies and practices of chief practitioners. This may be regarded positively, as a process whereby criticisms of traditional practice have compelled the major aid donors to incorporate more innovative and radical ideas into their strategies and practices. In other words the convergence of different perspectives might produce a new, more effective consensus on the way forward. On the other hand, some of the contributors to this book would undoubtedly see this process as an attempt by powerful institutions to neutralize radical ideas by taking them over, controlling their operation and emptying them of radical content. Clearly development is a terrain upon which these battles of ideas and disputes about action will continue to be fought out. We must hope that the result is not, as was said of the *Pax Romana*, to bring about desolation and call it peace.

Bibliography

ACORD (1991) 'ACORD's Experience with Participatory Techniques and Annotated Bibliography', *Research and Policy Programme Document*, 3 (1, 2) (April).

Ahmad, A. (1995) 'The Politics of Postcoloniality', *Race and Class*, 36 (3): 1–20.

Allen, J. and C. Hamnett (eds) (1999) *A Shrinking World: Global Unevenness and Inequality* (Oxford: Oxford University Press).

Allen, T. and A. Thomas (2000) *Poverty and Development in the 21st Century* (Oxford: Oxford University Press).

Amin, S. (1989) 'Eurocentrism', *Monthly Review Press* (New York).

Amin, S. (1990) *Delinking* (London: Zed Books).

Amos, V. and P. Parmar (1984) 'Many Voices, One Chant', *Feminist Review*, 17: 3–19.

Appadurai, A. (1990) 'Disjuncture and Difference in the Global Political Economy', in M. Featherstone (ed.), *Global Culture* (London: Sage).

Arrow, Kenneth J. (1999) 'Introduction', in P. Dasgupta and I. Serageldin (eds), *Social Capital: A Multifaceted Perspective* (Washington, DC: World Bank).

Atkinson, A. B. (1998) 'Social Exclusion, Poverty and Unemployment', in A. B. Atkinson and J. Hills, *Exclusion, Employment and Opportunity*, CASE Paper 4 (London: Centre for Analysis of Social Exclusion, London School of Economics).

Atkinson, A. B. and John Hills (1998) *Exclusion, Employment and Opportunity*, CASE Paper 4 (London: Centre for Analysis of Social Exclusion, London School of Economics).

Aubrey, L. (1998) *The Politics of Development Co-operation. NGOs, Gender and Partnership in Kenya* (London: Routledge).

Aycrigg, M. (1998) 'Participation and the World Bank: Successes, Constraints and Responses – Draft for discussion prepared for International Conference on Upscaling and Mainstreaming participation of Primary Stakeholders: Lessons Learnt and Ways Forward', Social Development Paper no. 29 (Washington, DC: World Bank, November).

Barker, F., P. Hulme and M. Iversen (eds) (1994) *Colonial Discourse and Postcolonial Theory* (Manchester: Manchester University Press).

Barrington M. Jnr (1969) *Social Origins of Dictatorship and Democracy: Lord and Peasant in the Making of the Modern World* (Harmondsworth: Penguin).

Barya, J.-P. (1993) 'The New Political Conditionalities of Aid: An Independent View from Africa', *IDS Bulletin*, 24 (1): 16–23.

Bauhn, P. (1998) 'Universal Rights and the Historical Context', *European Journal of Development Research*, 10 (2): 19–32.

Bauman, Z. (1998) 'On Universal Morality and the Morality of Universalism', *European Journal of Development Research*, 10 (2): 7–18.

Baylies, C. (1995) 'Political Conditionality and Democratisation', *African Political Economy*, 22 (65): 321–37.

Baylis, J. and S. Smith (eds) (1999) *The Globalization of World Politics* (Oxford: Oxford University Press).

Beale, J. (1997) 'Social Capital in Waste – A Solid Investment?', *Journal of International Development* 9 (7): 951–61.

Berkowitz, P. (2001) 'Sensitivity Isn't Enough', *London Review of Books*, 22 (17): 17–18.

Bhabha, H. (1984) 'Of Mimicry and Men: The Ambivalence of Colonial Discourse', *October*, 28 (Spring): 125–33.

Bhatnagar, B. and A. C. Williams (eds) (1992) 'Participatory Development and the World Bank: Potential Directions for Change', World Bank Discussion Paper 183 (Washington, DC: World Bank).

Bhavnani, K.-K. and M. Coulson (1986) 'Transforming Socialist-Feminism: The Challenge of Racism, *Feminist Review*, 23: 81–92.

Biggs, S. and G. Smith (1998) 'Beyond Methodologies: Coalition-Building for Participatory Technology Development', *World Development*, 26 (2): 239–48.

Blackburn, J. and J. Holland (eds) (1998) *Who Changes? Institutionalizing Participation in Development* (London: Intermediate Technology Publications).

Blaikie, P. (1985) *The Political Economy of Soil Erosion in Developing Countries* (Harlow: Longman).

Blunt, P. (1995) 'Cultural Realism, "Good" Governance and Sustainable Human Development', *Public Administration and Development*, 15: 1–9.

Booth, D. (1994) *Rethinking Social Development* (London: Longman).

Booth, D., J. Holland, J. Hentschel, P. Lanjouw and A. Herbert (1998) 'Participation and Combined Methods in African Poverty Assessment: Renewing the Agenda', report commissioned by the UK Department for International Development for the Working Group on Poverty and Social Policy, Special Programme of Assistance for Africa, February.

Booth, D., J. Holland, P. Lanjouw and A. Herbert (1998) *Participation and Combined Methods in African Poverty Assessment: Renewing the Agenda* (London: Department for International Development, Social Development Division).

Boston, J., J. Martin, J. Pallott and P. Walsh (1996) *Public Management: The New Zealand Model* (Oxford: Oxford University Press).

Bourdieu, Pierre (1980) 'Le Capital Social, Notes Provisoires', *Actes de la recherche en science sociales*, 30 (Paris).

Brohman, J. (1996) *Popular Development: Rethinking the Theory and Practice of Development* (Oxford: Blackwell).

Brown, D. (1998) 'Professional Participation and the Public Good: Issues of Arbitration in Development Management and the Critique of the Neo-Populist Approach', in M. Minogue, C. Polidano, and D. Hulme (eds), *Beyond the New Public Management: Changing Ideas and Practices in Governance* (Cheltenham: Edward Elgar).

Burnell, P. (1994) 'Good Government and Democratisation: A Sideways Look at Aid and Political Conditionality', *Democratisation*, 1 (3): 485–503.

Burnell, P. (1997) *Foreign Aid in a Changing World* (Buckingham: Open University Press).

Cammack, P. (1988) 'Dependency and the Politics of Development', in P. F. Leeson and M. M. Minogue (eds), *Perspectives on Development: Cross-disciplinary Themes in Development* (Manchester: Manchester University Press).

Cammack, P. (1994) 'Political Development Theory and the Development of Democracy', *Democratization*, 1 (3): 353–74.

Cammack, P. (1996) 'Domestic and International Regimes for the Developing World: The Doctrine for Political Development', in P. Gummett (ed.), *Globalization and Public Policy* (Cheltenham: Edward Elgar).

Cammack, P. (1997) *Capitalism and Democracy in the Third World* (London: Leicester University Press).

Canadian Council for International Cooperation (1991) *Two Halves Make a Whole: Balancing Gender Relations in Development* (Ottawa: CCIO).

Carmen, R. (1996) *Autonomous Development: Humanizing the Landscape* (London: Zed Books).

Carney, Diana (ed.) (1998) *Sustainable Rural Livelihoods: What Contribution Can We Make?* (London: DFID).

Carr, John (1998) 'Civil Society and Civil Society Organisations: A Review,' background paper for the British Council, available at http://old.britcoun.org/governance/civil/review/index.htm.

Carvalho, S. and H. White (1997) 'Combining the Quantitative and Qualitative Approaches to Poverty Measurement and Analysis: The Practice and the Potential', World Bank Technical Paper no. 366 (Washington, DC: World Bank).

Cassen, R. (1994) *Does Aid Work?*, 2nd edn (London: Clarendon Press).

Castells, M. (1998) *End of Millennium* (Oxford: Blackwell).

Centre for Rural Development and Training (1998) 'ICITRAP: Training Exercise for Examining Participatory Approaches to Project Management' (University of Wolverhampton).

Cernea, M. (ed.) (1985) *Putting People First: Sociological Variables in Rural Development* (Oxford: Oxford University Press).

Cernea, M. (1992) 'The Building Blocks of Participation: Testing Bottom-Up Planning', World Bank Discussion Paper no. 166 (Washington, DC: World Bank).

Cerny, P. G. (1990) *The Changing Architecture of Politics: Structure, Agency and the Future of the State* (London: Sage).

Chabal, P. (ed.) (1986) *Political Domination in Africa* (London: Cambridge University Press).

Chambers, R. (1983) *Rural Development: Putting the Last First* (London: Longman).

Chambers, R. (1988) 'Sustainable Rural Livelihoods: A Key Strategy for People, Environment and Development', in C. Conroy and M. Litvinoff (eds), *The Greening of Aid. Sustainable Livelihoods in Practice* (London: Earthscan).

Chambers, R. (1992) 'Rural Appraisal: Rapid, Relaxed, and Participatory', IDS Discussion Paper 311 (Brighton: Institute of Development Studies).

Chambers, R. (1994a) 'The Origins and Practice of Participatory Rural Appraisal', *World Development*, 22 (7): 953–69.

Chambers, R. (1994b) 'Participatory Rural Appraisal (PRA): Analysis of Experience', *World Development*, 22 (9): 1253–68.

Chambers, R. (1994c) 'Participatory Rural Appraisal (PRA): Challenges, Potentials and Paradigm', *World Development*, 22 (10): 1437–54.

Chambers, R. (1995) *Poverty and Livelihoods: Whose Reality Counts?* (Brighton: Institute of Development Studies, University of Sussex).

Chambers, R. (1996) 'Paradigm Shifts and the Practice of Participatory Research and Development', in N. Nelson and S. Wright (eds), *Power and Participatory Development: Theory and Practice* (London: Intermediate Technology Publications).

Chambers, R. (1997) *Whose Reality Counts? Putting the First Last* (London: Intermediate Technology Publications).

Chambers, R. (1999) 'Relaxed and Participatory Appraisal: Notes on Practical Approaches and Methods', notes for participants in PRA familiarisation workshops in the first half of 1999, unpublished.

Chandra, R. (1992) *Industrialisation and Development in the Third World* (London: Routledge).

Clark, J. (1991) *Democratizing Development: The Role of Voluntary Organizations* (London: Earthscan).

Clayton, A. (ed.) (1996) *NGOs, Civil Society and The State: Building Democracy in Transitional Societies* (Chippenham: INTRAC).

Cleaver, F. (1999) 'Paradoxes of Participation: A Critique of Participatory Approaches to Development', in B. Cooke and U. Kothari (eds), *Participation: The New Tyranny?* (London: Zed Books).

Cochrane, A. (1995) 'Global Worlds and Worlds of Difference', in J. Anderson, C. Brook and A. Cochrane (eds), *A Global World?* (Oxford: Oxford University Press).

Coleman, James S. (1988) 'Social Capital in the Creation of Human Capital', *American Journal of Sociology*, 94 (supplement): S95–120.

Coleman, James S. (1990) *The Foundations of Social Theory* (Cambridge: Harvard University Press).

Collier, P., P. Guillaumont, S. Guillaumont and J. W. Gunning (1997) 'Redesigning Conditionality', *World Development*, 25 (9): 1399–1407.

Common, R. (1998) 'The New Public Management and Policy Transfer: The Role of International Organisations', in M. Minogue, C. Polidano and D. Hulme (eds), *Beyond the New Public Management: Ideas and Practices in Governance* (Cheltenham: Edward Elgar).

Cook, P. and C. Kirkpatrick (1997) 'Globalization, Regionalisation and Third World Development', *Regional Studies*, 31 (1): 56–66.

Cook, P. and M. Minogue (1993) 'Economic Reform and Political Change in Myanmar (Burma)', *World Development*, 21 (7): 1151–62.

Cooke, B. and U. Kothari (eds) (2001) *Participation: The New Tyranny?* (London: Zed Books).

Cornerhouse (1998) 'Same Platform, Different Train: The Politics of Participation', briefing 4 February.

Cornia, G., R. Jolly and F. Stewart (1987) *Adjustment With a Human Face: Protecting the Vulnerable and Promoting Growth* (Oxford: Clarendon).

Cornwall, A. (1997) 'Men, Masculinity and Gender in Development', *Gender in Development*, 5 (2): 8–13.

Cornwall, A. and S. Fleming (1995) 'Context and Complexity: Anthropological Reflections on PRA', *PLA Notes 24*, October: 8–12.

Crawford G. (1995) *Promoting Democracy, Human Rights and Good Government Through Development Aid: A Comparative Study of Four Northern Donors* (Leeds: Centre for Democratisation Studies, University of Leeds).

Crawford, G. (1998) 'Aid and Political Reform: A Comparative Study of the Development Cooperation Policies of Four Northern Donors, 1990–1994', unpublished PhD thesis, University of Leeds.

Crook, R. C. and J. Manor (1995) 'Democratic Decentralisation and Institutional Performance: Four Asian Experiences Compared', *Journal of Commonwealth and Comparative Studies*, 33 (3): 309–34.

Crush, J. (1995) *The Power of Development* (London: Routledge).

DAC Ad Hoc Working Group (1997) 'Final Report of the Ad Hoc Working Group on Participatory Development and Good Governance' (Paris: OECD).

Dahrendorf, R. (1996) 'Economic Opportunity, Civil Society and Political Liberty', *Development and Change*, 27 (2): 229–49.

Dasgupta, Partha and Ismail Serageldin (eds) (1999) *Social Capital: A Multifaceted Perspective* (Washington, DC: World Bank).

de Haan, A. (1998) ' "Social Exclusion": An Alternative Concept for the Study of Deprivation?', *IDS Bulletin*, 29 (1): 10–19.

de Haan, A. (1999) *Social Exclusion: Towards an Holistic Understanding of Deprivation* (London: Department for International Development, Social Development Division).

Department for International Development (DFID) (1997) *Eliminating World Poverty: A Challenge for the Twenty-First Century* (London: HMSO).

Department for International Development (DFID) (1998) 'Strengthening DFID's Support for Civil Society: Consultation Paper' (London: DFID, May).

Department for International Development (DFID) (1999) Key Sheets for Sustainable Livelihood, http://www.oneworld.org/odi/keysheets/index.html#acrobat.

Department for International Development (DFID) (2000a) *Eliminating World Poverty: Making Globalization Work for the Poor*, DFID white paper (Norwich: HMSO).

Department for International Development (DFID) (2000b) *Governance and Poverty Strategy*, London: Department for International Development.

Desai, R. (1994) 'Second-Hand Dealers in Ideas: Think-Tanks and Thatcherite Hegemony', *New Left Review*, 203: 27–64.

Development Assistance Committee (DAC) (1996) *Shaping the 21st Century: The Contribution of Development Co-operation* (Paris: OECD).

Dhaouadi, M. (1994) 'Capitalism and the Other Underdevelopment', in L. Sklair *Capitalism and Development* (London: Routledge).

Diamond, L., J. Linz and S. M. Lipset (1990) *Politics in Developing Countries: Comparing Experiences with Democracies* (London: Lynne Rienner).

Dolowitz, D. and D. Marsh (1998) 'Policy transfer: a framework for comparative analysis', in M. Minogue, C. Polidano and D. Hulme (eds),

Beyond the New Public Management: Ideas and Practices in Governance (Cheltenham: Edward Elgar).

Drèze, J. and A. Sen (1989) *Hunger and Public Action* (Oxford: Clarendon Press).

Driver, F. (1995) 'Submerged Identities: Familiar and Unfamiliar Histories', *Transactions of the Institute of British Geographers*, 20 (4): 410–13.

Dunleavy, P. and C. Hood (1994) 'From old public adminstration to new public management', Public Money and Management, 14 (3): 9–16.

Elson, D. (1995) *Male Bias in the Development Process* (Manchester: Manchester University Press).

Escobar, A. (1995) *Encountering Development. The Making and Unmaking of the Third World* (Princeton, NJ: Princeton University Press).

ESRC (1999) *The Politics of GM Food: Risk, Science and Public Trust*, special briefing no. 5, ESRC Global Environmental Change Programme (Brighton: University of Sussex).

European Foundation for the Improvement of Living and Working Conditions (1995) *Public Welfare Services and Social Exclusion: The Development of Consumer Oriented Initiatives in the European Union* (Dublin: The Foundation).

Evans, A. (1992) 'Statistics', in L. Ostergaard *Gender and Development: A Practical Guide* (London: Routledge).

Eyben, R. (1998) *The Role of Social Assessments in Effective Development Planning* (London: Department for International Development, Social Development Division).

Eyben, R. (2000) 'Development and Anthropology: A View from Inside the Agency', *Critique of Anthropology* 20(1): 7–14.

Eyben, R. and S. Ladbury (1995) 'Popular Participation in Aid-Assisted Projects: Why More in Theory Than Practice?' in N. Nelson and S. Wright (eds), *Power and Participatory Development: Theory and Practice* (London: Intermediate Technology Publications).

Fanon, F. (1963) *Wretched of the Earth* (New York: Grove Press).

FAO (1999) 'State of the World's Forests 1999' (Rome: Food and Agriculture Organisation of the United Nations).

Farrington, J., D. Carney, C. Ashley and C. Turton (1999) 'Sustainable Livelihoods in Practice: Early Applications of Concepts in Rural Areas', *Natural Resource Perspectives*, 42 (London: Overseas Development Institute).

Ferguson, J. (1990) *The Anti-Politics Machine. Development, Depoliticization and Bureaucratic Power in Lesotho* (Cambridge: Cambridge University Press).

Fine, Ben (1999) 'The Developmental State is Dead – Long Live Social Capital', *Development and Change*, 30: 1–19.

Fowler, Alan (1997) *Striking a Balance* (London: Earthscan).

Francis, P. (1999) 'A "Social Development" Paradigm?' in B. Cooke and U. Kothari (eds), *Participation: The New Tyranny?* (London: Zed Books, 2000).

Freire, P. (1972) *Pedagogy of the Oppressed* (Harmondsworth: Penguin).

Fukuyama, Francis (1995) *Trust: The Social Virtues and the Creation of Prosperity* (London: Penguin).

Gandhi, L. (1998) *Postcolonial Theory: A Critical Introduction* (Edinburgh: Edinburgh University Press).

Gardner, K. and D. Lewis (1996) *Anthropology, Development and the Post-Modern Challenge* (London: Pluto).

Gardner, K. and D. Lewis (2000) 'Dominant Paradigms Overturned or Business as Usual? Development Discourse and the White Paper on International Development', *Critique of Anthropology*, 20 (1): 15–29.

Gaventa, J. and C. Valderrama (1999) 'Participation, Citizenship and Local Governance', background note prepared for workshop on 'Strengthening Participation in Local Governance', Institute of Development Studies, June.

Gendzier, I. (1985) *Managing Political Change: Social Scientists and the Third World* (Boulder, CO: Westview Press).

Gewirth, A. (1978) *Reason and Morality* (Chicago: University of Chicago Press).

Gibbon, P. (1993) 'The World Bank and the New Politics of Aid', *European Journal of Development Research*, 5 (1): 35–62.

Gibbon, P., Y. Bangura and A. Ofstad (eds) (1992) *Authoritarianism, Democracy and Adjustment: The Politics of Economic Reform in Africa* (Uppsala: Scandinavian Institute of African Studies).

Giddens, A. (1990) *The Consequences of Modernity* (Cambridge: Polity Press).

Gill, S. (1998) 'New Constitutionalism, Democratisation and Global Political Economy', *Pacific Review*, 10 (1): 23–38.

Gills, B., J. Rocamora and R. Wilson (eds) (1993) *Low Intensity Democracy: Political Power in the New World Order* (London: Pluto).

Girling, J. (1996) *Interpreting Development: Capitalism, Democracy and the Middle Class in Thailand* (Ithaca, NY: Cornell University, Southeast Asia Program).

Gluckman, Max (1967) *The Judicial Process among the Barotse of Northern Rhodesia*, 2nd edn (Manchester: Manchester University Press).

Godlewska, A. and N. Smith (eds) (1994) *Geography and Empire* (Oxford: Blackwell).

Goetz, A. M. (ed.) (1997) *Getting Institutions Right for Women in Development* (London: Zed Books).

Goldberg, E. (1996) 'Thinking About How Democracy Works', *Politics and Society*, 24 (1): 7–18.

Goldsworthy, D. (1971) *Colonial Issues in British Politics 1945–61* (Oxford: Clarendon Press).

Gore, Charles and José Figueiredo (eds) (1997) *Social Exclusion and Anti-Poverty Policy: A Debate*, Research Series 110 (Geneva: International Institute for Labor Studies).

Granovetter, Mark (1973) 'The Strength of Weak Ties', *American Journal of Sociology*, 78: 1360–80.

Granovetter, Mark (1985) 'Economic Action and Social Structure: The Problem of Embeddedness', *American Journal of Sociology*, 91: 481–510.

Gray, J. (1998) *False Dawn: The Delusions of Global Capitalism* (London: Granta).

Green, M. (2000) Participatory Development and the Appropriation of Agency in Southern Tanzania, *Critique of Anthropology*, 20 (1): 67–89.

Grootaert, Christiaan (1997) 'Social Capital, the Missing Link?', in *Expanding the Measure of Wealth: Indicators of Environmentally Sustainable Development*, Environmentally Sustainable Development Studies and Monograph Series no. 17 (Washington, DC: World Bank).

Grootaert, Christiaan (1999) 'Does Social Capital Help the Poor?', discussion paper (Washington, DC: World Bank).

Grubb, M., C. Vrolijk and D. Brack (1999) *The Kyoto Protocol. A Guide and Assessment* (London: Royal Institute of International Affairs and Earthscan).

Guijt, I. and A. Cornwall (1995) 'Critical Reflections on the Practice of PRA', *PLA Notes*, 24 (2–7 October).

Guijt, I. and M. Shah (1998) *The Myth of Community: Gender Issues in Participatory Development* (London: Intermediate Technology Publications).

Haggard, S. and R. Kaufman (1992) *The Politics of Structural Adjustment* (Princeton, NJ: Princeton University Press).

Hall, S. (1996) *Critical Dialogues in Cultural Studies* (London: Routledge).

Hanifan, L. J. (1920) *The Community Center* (Boston, Mass.: Silver, Burdette).

Hanmer, L., N. de Jong, R. Kurian and J. Mooij (1997) *Social Development: Past Trends and Future Scenarios* (Stockholm: SIDA).

Harriss, J. and P. De Renzio (1997) ' "Missing Link" or Analytically Missing?: The Concept of Social Capital. An Introductory Bibliographic Essay', *Journal of International Development*, 9 (7).

Harrold, P. (1995) 'The Broad Sector Approach to Investment Lending: Sector Investment Programmes', World Bank Discussion Paper 302, Africa Technical Department Series (Washington, DC: International Bank for Reconstruction and Development).

Hausermann, J. (1998) 'A Human Rights Approach to Development: A Discussion Paper Commissioned by the Department for International Development' (London: Rights and Humanity).

Heady, F. (1996) *Public Administration: A Comparative Perspective*, 5th edn (New York: Marcel Dekker).

Healey, J. and M. Robinson (1992) *Democracy, Governance and Economic Policy: Sub-Saharan Africa in Comparative Perspective* (London: Overseas Development Institute).

Healey, J. and W. Tordoff (eds) (1995) *Votes and Budgets: Comparative Studies in Accountable Governance in the South* (London: Macmillan).

Hearn, July (1999) 'Foreign Aid, Democratisation and Civil Society in Africa: A Study of South Africa, Ghana and Uganda,' Discussion Paper 368 (Institute of Development Studies, University of Sussex).

Hecht, S. and A. Cockburn (1990) *The Fate of the Forest* (London: Penguin).

Hecht, T. (1998) *At Home in the Street. Street Children of Northeast Brazil* (Stanford, CA: Stanford University Press).

Held, D. (2000) *A Globalizing World? Culture, Economics, Politics* (London: Routledge and Open University Press).

Held, D. and A. McGrew (eds) (2000) *The Global Transformations Reader* (Cambridge: Polity Press).

Held, D., A. McGrew, D. Goldblatt and J. Perraton (1997) 'The Globalization of Economic Activity', *New Political Economy*, 2 (2): 257–77.

Held, D., A. McGrew, D. Goldblatt and J. Perraton (1999) *Global Transformations: Politics, Economics and Culture* (Cambridge: Polity Press).

Henkel, H. and R. L. Stirrat (1999) 'Participation as Spiritual Duty: The Religious Roots of the New Development Orthodoxy' in B. Cooke and U. Kothari (eds), *Participation: The New Tyranny?* (London: Zed Books, 2001).

Hettne, B. (1990) *Development Theory and the Three Worlds* (London: Longman).

Hill, P. (1986) *Development Economics on Trial. The Anthropological Case for the Prosecution* (Cambridge: Cambridge University Press).

Hirst, P. and G. Thompson (1992) 'The Problem of "Globalization": International Economic Relations, National Economic Management and the Formation of Trading Blocs', *Economy and Society*, 21 (4): 357–96.

Hirst, P. and G. Thompson (1999) *Globalization in Question: the International Economy and the Possibilities of Governance*, 2nd edn (Cambridge: Polity Press).

HM Government (1997) *Eliminating World Poverty: The Challenge for the 21st Century*, white paper on international development (London: HMSO).

Hobart, M. (ed.) (1993) *An Anthropological Critique of Development. The Growth of Ignorance* (London: Routledge).

Hobsbawm, E. (1994a) *The Age of Extremes: The Short Twentieth Century, 1914–1991* (London: Michael Joseph).

Hobsbawm, E. (1994b) *The Age of Empire 1875–1914* (London: Abacus).

Holland, J. and J. Blackburn (eds) (1998) *Whose Voice? Participatory Research and Policy Change* (London: Intermediate Technology Publications).

Hondeghem, A. (ed.) (1998) *Ethics and Accountability in a Context of Governance and New Public Management* (Amsterdam: IOS Press).

Hoogvelt, Ankie (1997) *Globalization and the Post-Colonial World* (Basingstoke: Macmillan).

hooks, b. (1989) *Talking Back: Thinking Feminist, Thinking Black* (Boston, Mass.: South End Press).

hooks, b. (1992) *Black Looks: Race and Representation* (London: Turnaround).

hooks, b. (1994) *Outlaw Culture: Resisting Representations* (London: Routledge).

Hughes, S. (1998) *Companions for Life: Case Studies of Accompaniment*, Developing Good Practice Discussion Series (London: Christian Aid, October).

Hulme, David and Michael Edwards (eds) (1997) *NGOs, States and Donors: Too Close for Comfort* (New York: St Martin's Press in association with Save the Children).

Hulme, D. and M. Murphree (2001) *African Wildlife and Livelihoods: the Promise and Performance of Community Conservation* (Oxford: James Currey).

Hutton, W. (1995) *The State We're In* (London: Jonathan Cape).

Hyden, G. and M. Bratton (eds) (1992) *Governance and Politics in Africa* (London: Lynne Rienner).

IDS (1996a) 'The New Poverty Agenda: A Disputed Consensus', *IDS Bulletin*, 27.

IDS (1996b) 'The Power of Participation: PRA and Policy', IDS policy briefing, August (Brighton: Institution of Development Studies, University of Sussex).

IIED (1988–) *PLA Notes: Notes on Participatory Learning and Action* (formerly *RRA Notes*), various issues (London: International Institute of Environment and Development).

International Labour Office (1994) *International Labour Review*, 133 (5–6), 531–78.

INTRAC (1998) 'Draft: The Participatory Approaches Learning Study (PALS): Executive Summary and Recommendations' (London: Social Development Division, DFID).

Jackson, C. (1996) 'Rescuing Gender from the Poverty Trap', *World Development*, 24 (3): 489–504.

Jackson, C. (1997) 'Post Poverty Gender and Development', *IDS Bulletin*, 28 (3): 145–55.

Jackson, Cecile (1999) 'Social Exclusion: Does One Size Fit All?', *European Journal of Development Research*, 11 (1): 125–46.

Jackson, C. and R. Pearson (eds) (1998) *Feminist Visions of Development: Gender Analysis and Policy* (London: Routledge).

Jacobs, J. (1961) *The Life and Death of Great American Cities* (New York: Random House).

Kabbani, R. (1986) *Europe's Myths of Orient* (London: Macmillan).

Kabeer, N. (1994) *Reversed Realities: Gender Hierarchies in Development Thought* (London: Verso).

Keohane, R. and E. Ostrom (eds) (1995) *Local Commons and Global Interdependence. Heterogeneity and Cooperation in Two Domains* (London: Sage).

Kickert, W. (ed.) (1997) *Public Management and Administrative Reform in Western Europe* (Cheltenham: Edward Elgar).

Killick, A. (1997) 'Principals, Agents and the Failings of Conditionality', *Journal of International Development*, 9 (4): 483–95.

Killick, T. (1995) 'Structural Adjustment and Poverty Alleviation: An Interpretive Survey', *Development and Change*, 26: 305–31.

Knack, Stephen and Philip Keefer (1997) 'Does Social Capital have an Economic Payoff? A Cross-Country Investigation', *Quarterly Journal of Economics*, November: 1251–88.

Kolko, G. (1997) *Vietnam: Anatomy of a Peace* (London: Routledge).

Korten, D. (1990) *Getting to the 21st Century: Voluntary Action and the Global Agenda* (West Hartford, CT: Kumarian Press).

Kothari, U. (1997) 'Identity and Representation: Experiences of Teaching a Neo-Colonial Discipline', in L. Stanley (ed.), *Knowing Feminisms* (London: Sage).

Lane, J. (1996) 'Non-Governmental Organizations and Participatory Development: The Concept in Theory Versus the Concept in Practice' in N. Nelson and S. Wright (eds), *Power and Participatory Development: Theory and Practice* (London: Intermediate Technology Publications).

Lane, J.-E. (ed.) (1997) *Public Sector Reform: Rationale, Trends and Problems* (London: Sage).

Langseth, P. and J. Pope (1998) *Building Integrity to Fight Corruption: Learning by Doing* (Washington, DC: Economic Development Institute for the World Bank).

LaPalombara, J. (1963) 'An Overview of Bureaucracy and Political Development', in J. LaPalombara (ed.), *Bureaucracy and Political Development* (Princeton, NJ: Princeton University Press).

Lawton, A. (1998) *Ethical Management for the Public Services* (Buckingham: Open University Press).

Lazarus, N. (1994) 'National Consciousness and the Specificity of (Post) Colonial Intellectualism' in F. Barker, P. Hulme and M. Iversen *Colonial Discourse/ Postcolonial Theory* (Manchester: Manchester University Press).

Leach, M. and R. Mearns (1996) *The Lie of the Land* (London: James Currey).

Lechner, F. J. and J. Boli (eds) (2000) *The Globalization Reader* (Oxford: Blackwell).

Lee, J. M. (1967) *Colonial Development and Good Government* (Oxford: Clarendon Press).

Lee, N. and C. George (eds) (2000) *Environmental Assessment in Developing and Transitional Countries* (Chichester: Wiley).

Leeson, P. and M. Minogue (eds) (1988) *Perspectives on Development: Cross-Disciplinary Essays on Development Studies* (Manchester: Manchester University Press).

Leftwich, A. (1994) 'Governance, the State, and the Politics of Development', *Development and Change*, 25 (2): 363–86.

Leys, C. (1996) *The Rise and Fall of Development Theory* (London: James Currey).

Little, W. (1996) 'Corruption and Democracy in Latin America', *IDS Bulletin*, 27 (2): 64–70.

Long, N. and A. Long (eds) (1992) *Battlefields of Knowledge: The Interlocking of Theory and Practice in Social Research and Development* (London: Routledge).

Lund, C. (1998) 'Development and Rights: Tempering Universalism and Relativism', *European Journal of Development Research*, 10 (2): 1–6.

Mabogunje, A. L. (1989) *The Development Process: A Spatial Perspective* (London: Unwin Hyman).

Mackay, H. (2000) 'The Globalization of Culture?', in D. Held (ed.), *A Globalising World? Culture, Economics and Politics* (London: Routledge).

Mani, L. (1989) 'Multiple Mediations: Feminist Scholarship in the Age of Multinational Reception', *Inscriptions*, 5: 1–24.

Manning, N. (1996) 'Improving the Public Service', unpublished paper, London, Commonwealth Secretariat.

Marchand, M. and J. L. Parpart (eds) (1995) *Feminism, Postmodernism and Development* (London: Routledge).

Massey, D. (1991) 'A Global Sense of Place', *Marxism Today*, June: 24–9.

Massey, D. and P. Jess (1995) 'Places and Cultures in an Uneven World', in D. Massey and P. Jess (eds), *A Place in the World* (Oxford: Oxford University Press).

Maxwell, Simon (1998) 'Comparisons, Convergence and Connections: Development Studies in North and South', *IDS Bulletin*, 29 (1): 20–31.

Maxwell, S. and R. Riddell (1998) 'Conditionality or Contract: Perspectives on Partnership for Development', *Journal of International Development*, 10: 257–68.

McClintock, A. (1994) 'The Angel of Progress: Pitfalls of the Term "Post-colonialism" ' in F. Barker, P. Hulme and M. Iversen (eds), *Colonial Discourse and Postcolonial Theory* (Manchester: Manchester University Press).

McClintock, A. (1995) *Imperial Leather* (London: Routledge).

McCourt, W. and M. Minogue (eds) (2001) *The Internationalisation of Public Management: Reinventing the Third World State* (Cheltenham: Edward Elgar).

McGee, R. and A. Timlin (1999) 'Participation in Christian Aid', Working Paper, February (London: Christian Aid).

McGrew, A. (2000a) 'Sustainable Globalization? The Global Politics of Development and Exclusion in the New World Order', in T. Allen and A. Thomas *Poverty and Development in the 21st Century* (Oxford: Oxford University Press).

McGrew, A. (2000b) 'Democracy Beyond Borders', in D. Held and A. McGrew, *Global Transformations Reader* (Cambridge: Polity Press).

McMichael, P. (1996) *Development and Social Change: A Global Perspective* (London: Pine Forge Press/Sage).

Meadows, D. H., D. Meadows, J. Randers and W. W. Behrens (eds), *The Limits to Growth: A Report for the Club of Rome's Project on the Predicament of Mankind* (London: Earth Island Ltd.).

Mehmet, O. (1995) *Westernising the Third World* (London: Routledge).

Melo, J. and A. Panagariya (eds) (1993) *New Dimensions in Regional Integration* (Cambridge: Cambridge University Press).

Midgley, J. (1995) *Social Development. The Developmental Perspective in Social Welfare* (London: Sage).

Miege, J.-L. (1980) 'The Colonial Past in the Present', in W. H. Morris-Jones and G. Fischer (eds), *Decolonisation and After: The British and French Experience* (London: Frank Cass).

Miles, M. and J. Crush (1993) 'Personal Narratives as Interactive Texts: Collecting and Interpreting Migrant Life-Histories', *Professional Geographer*, 45 (1): 84–94.

Minogue, M. (2001) 'Should Flawed Models of Public Management be Exported?', in W. McCourt and M. Minogue *The Internationalisation of Public Management: Reinventing the Third World State* (Cheltenham: Edward Elgar).

Minogue, M., C. Polidano and D. Hulme (eds) (1998) *Beyond the New Public Management: Ideas and Practices in Governance* (Cheltenham: Edward Elgar).

Mirza, H. (ed.) (1997) *Black British Feminism: A Reader* (London: Routledge).

Mittelman, J. (2000) *The Globalization Syndrome: Transformation and Resistance* (Princeton, NJ: Princeton University Press).

Mohan, G. (1999) 'Beyond Participation: Strategies for Deeper Empowerment', in B. Cooke and U. Kothari (eds), *Participation: The New Tyranny?* (London: Zed Books, 2001).

Mohanty, C. (1991) 'Under Western Eyes: Feminist Scholarship and Colonial Discourses', in C. T. Mohanty, A. Russo and L. Torres (eds), *Third World Women and the Politics of Feminism* (Bloomington, IA: Indiana University Press).

Mohanty, C. (1992) 'Feminist Encounters: Locating the Politics of Experience', in M. Barrett and A. Phillips (eds), *Destabilising Theory: Contemporary Feminist Debates* (Cambridge: Polity).

Mongia, P. (ed) (1996) *Contemporary Postcolonial Theory* (London: Arnold).

Moore, M. (1993a) 'Declining to Learn From The East? The World Bank on "Governance and Development" ', *IDS Bulletin*, 24 (1): 39–50.

Moore, M. (1993b) 'Introduction', *IDS Bulletin*, 24 (1): 1–6.

Moore, M. (1995a) 'Democracy and Development in Cross-National Perspective: A New Look at the Statistics', *Democratisation*, 2 (2).

Moore, M. (1995b) 'Promoting Good Government by Supporting Institutional Development', *IDS Bulletin*, 26 (2): 89–96.

Moore-Gilbert, B. (1997) *Postcolonial Theory: Contexts, Practices and Politics* (London: Verso).

Moser, C. (1989) 'Gender Planning in the Third World: Meeting Practical and Strategic Gender Needs', *World Development*, 17 (11).

Moser, C. (1993) *Gender Planning and Development Theory Practice and Training* (London: Routledge).

Moser, Caroline (1996) *Confronting Crisis: A Comparative Study of Household Responses to Poverty and Vulnerability in four Poor Urban Communities*, Environmentally Sustainable Development Studies and Monographs Series no. 8 (Washington, DC: The World Bank).

Mosley, P., J. Harrigan and J. Toye (1991) *Aid and Power: The World Bank and Policy-Based Lending*, vol. 1 (London: Routledge).

Mosse, D. (1994) 'Authority, Gender and Knowledge: Theoretical Reflections on the Practice of Participatory Rural Appraisal', *Development and Change*, 25: 497–526.

Mosse, D. (1995) 'Social Analysis in Participatory Rural Development', *PLA Notes*, 24: 27–33.

Mosse, D. (1997) 'The Ideology and Politics of Community Participation', in R. D. Grillo and R. L. Stirrat, *Discourses of Development: Anthropological Perspectives* (Oxford: Berg).

Mosse, D. (1999) 'The Making and Marketing of Participatory Development: A Sceptical Note', in B. Cooke and U. Kothari (eds), *Participation: The New Tyranny?* (London: Zed Books, 2001).

Musch, A. (1999) 'Making and Circumventing Tyranny', paper presented at the conference on 'Participation: The New Tyranny?', IDPM, November.

Myrdal, G. (1968) *Asian Drama: An Enquiry into the Poverty of Nations* (New York: Twentieth Century).

Narayan, D. (1995) 'The Contribution of People's Participation: Evidence from 121 Rural Water Supply Projects', Environmentally Sustainable Development, Occasional Paper, Series no.1 (Washington, DC: World Bank).

Narayan, D. (1997) *Voices of the Poor. Poverty and Social Capital in Tanzania* (Washington, DC: World Bank).

Narayan, Deepa (1999) 'Bonds and Bridges; Social Capital and Poverty', Policy and Research Working Paper no. 2167 (Washington, DC: World Bank).

Narayan, Deepa and Katrinka Ebbe (1997) 'Design of Social Funds: Participation, Demand Orientation, and Local Organizational Capacity', World Bank Discussion Paper no. 375 (Washington, DC: World Bank).

Narayan, D. and L. Pritchett (1997) 'Cents and Sociability: Household Income and Social Capital in Rural Tanzania', World Bank Policy Research Working Paper (Washington, DC: World Bank).

Narayan, D. and L. Srinivasan (1994) *Participatory Development Tool Kit: Materials to Facilitate Community Empowerment* (Washington, DC: World Bank).

Nelson, J. (1992) 'Good Governance, Democracy, and Conditional Economic Aid', in P. Mosley (ed.), *Development Finance and Policy Reform* (London: Macmillan).

Nelson, N. and S. Wright (eds) (1996) *Power and Participatory Development: Theory and Practice* (London: Intermediate Technology Publications).

Nieuwenhuys, O. (1999) 'The Paradox of the Competent Child and the Global Childhood Agenda', in R. Fardon, W. van Binsbergen and R. van Rijk (eds), *Modernity on a Shoestring. Dimensions of Globalisation, Consumption and Development in Africa and Beyond* (Leiden: Eidos).

North, D. (1990) *Institutions, Institutional Change and Economic Performance* (Cambridge: Cambridge University Press).

Norton, A. and B. Bird (1998) 'Social Development Issues in Sector-Wide Approaches', Social Development Division Working Paper no. 1 (London: DFID, May).

Nunberg, B. (1995) *Managing the Civil Service: Reform Lessons from Advanced Industrialised Societies*, World Bank Discussion Paper no. 204 (Washington, DC: World Bank).

Oakley, P. (1991) *Projects with People: The Practice of Participation in Rural Development* (Geneva: ILO).

O'Connor, M. (ed.) (1994) *Is Capitalism Sustainable?* (New York: Guilford Press).

ODA (1993) *Taking Account of Good Government* (London: UK Overseas Development Administration).

ODA (1995a) *A Guide to Social Analysis for Projects in Developing Countries* (London: HMSO).

ODA (1995b) 'Technical Note on Enhancing Stakeholder Participation in Aid Activities' (London: Overseas Development Administration).

OECD (1996) *Shaping the 21st Century. The Contribution of Development Cooperation* (Paris: Organisation for Economic Cooperation and Development).

Ohmae, K. (1990) *The Borderless World: Power and Strategy in the Interlinked World Economy*, (London: Harper Collins).

Ohmae, K. (1995) *The End of the Nation State* (New York: Free Press).

Olson, Mancur (1965) *The Logic of Collective Action: Public Goods and the Theory of Groups* (Cambridge, Mass.: Harvard University Press).

Olson, Mancur (1982) *The Rise and Decline of Nations: Economic Growth, Stagflation, and Social Rigidities* (New Haven, CT: Yale University Press).

Ostergaard, C. S. (1993) 'Values for Money? Political Conditionality in Aid: The Case of China', *European Journal of Development Research*, 5 (1): 112–34.

Panitch, L. (1998) 'The State in a Changing World: Social-Democratizing Global Capitalism?', *Monthly Review*, 50 (5).

Parpart, J. (1989) *Women and Development in Africa* (Maryland: University Press of America).

Parpart, J. (1995) 'Deconstructing the Development "Expert": Gender, development and the "vulnerable groups" ', in M. Marchand and J. L. Parpart (eds), *Feminism, Postmodernism and Development* (London: Routledge).

Pearce, D., E. Barbier and A. Markandya (1990) *Sustainable Development. Economics and Environment in the Third World* (Aldershot: Edward Elgar).

Peet, R. and M. Watts (eds) (1996) *Liberation Ecologies* (London: Routledge).

Penna, D. R. and P. Campbell (1997) 'Human Rights and Culture: Beyond Universality and Relativism', *Third World Quarterly*, 19 (1): 7–28.

Phillips, S. and M. Edwards (2000) 'Development, Impact Assessment and the Praise Culture', *Critique of Anthropology*, 20 (1): 47–67.

Pieterse, J. N. (1998) 'My Paradigm or Yours? Alternative Development, Post-Development, Reflexive Development', *Development and Change*, 29 (2): 343–73.

Pieterse, J. N. (2000) 'After Post-Development', *Third World Quarterly*, 21 (2): 175–91.

Pieterse, J. N. and B. Parekh (eds) (1995) *The Decolonisation of Imagination: Culture, Knowledge and Power* (London: Zed Books).

Pigg, S. L. (1992) 'Inventing a Social Category Through Place: Social Representations and Development in Nepal', *Comparative Studies in Society and History*, 34 (3): 491–513.

Poffenberger, M. (1990) *Keepers of the Forest. Land Management Alternatives in South-East Asia* (West Hartford, CT: Kumarian Press).

Portes, Alejandro and Patricia Landolt (1996) 'The Downside of Social Capital,' *The American Prospect*, 26 (May–June): 19–22.

Portes, Alejandro and Julia Sensenbrenner (1992) 'Embeddedness and Immigration: Notes on the Social Determinants of Economic Action,' *American Journal of Sociology*, 98 (6): 1320–50.

Pratt, M. L. (1992) *Imperial Eyes: Travel Writing and Transculturation* (London: Routledge).

Preston, P. W. (1996) *Development Theory: An Introduction* (Oxford: Blackwell).

Pretty, J. (1995) 'Participatory Learning for Sustainable Agriculture', *World Development*, 23 (8): 1247–63.

Pretty, J. N. and I. Scoones (1996) 'Institutionalizing Adaptive Planning and Local Level Concerns: Looking to the Future', in N. Nelson and S. Wright (eds), *Power and Participatory Development: Theory and Practice* (London: Intermediate Technology Publications).

Putnam, Robert D. (1993a) *Making Democracy Work: Civic Traditions in Modern Italy* (Princeton, NJ: Princton University Press).

Putnam, Robert D. (1993b) 'The Prosperous Community: Social Capital and Public Life', *The American Prospect*, 13.

Putnam, Robert D. (1995) 'Bowling Alone: America's Declining Social Capital', *Journal of Democracy*, 6 (1): 65–78.

Pye, L. (1965) 'Introduction: Political Culture and Political Development', in L. Pye and S. Verba (eds), *Political Culture and Political Development* (Princeton, NJ: Princeton University Press).

Racelis, M. (1992) 'The United Nations Children's Fund: Experience with People's Participation', in B. Bhatnagar and A. C. Williams 'Participatory Development and the World Bank: Potential Directions for Change', World Bank Discussion Paper 183 (Washington, DC: World Bank).

Radcliffe, S. (1994) '(Representing) Post-Colonial Women: Authority, Difference and Feminisms', *Area*, 26 (1): 25–32.

Rahman, M. A. (1993) *People's Self Development: Perspectives on Participatory Action Research* (London: Zed Books).

Rahnema, M. (1997) 'Towards Post-Development: Searching for Signposts, A New Language and New Paradigms', in M. Rahnema (ed.), *The Post-Development Reader* (London: Zed Books).

Rahnema, M. with Victoria Bawtree (ed.) (1997) *The Post-Development Reader* (London: Zed Books).

Rahnema, R. (1992) 'Participation', in W. Sachs (ed.), *The Development Dictionary. A Guide to Knowledge as Power* (London: Zed Books).

Rathgeber, E. (1990) 'WID, WAD, GAD: Trends in Research and Policy', *Journal of Developing Areas*, July: 489–582.

Rhodes, R. (1997) *Understanding Governance* (Buckingham: Open University Press).

Richards, G. A. and C. Kirkpatrick (1999) 'Reorienting Interregional Cooperation in the Global Political Economy: Europe's East Asian Policy', *Journal of Common Market Studies*, 3 (4): 683–71.

Richards, P. (1995) 'Participatory Rural Appraisal: A Quick and Dirty Critique', *PLA Notes*, 24 (October): 13–16.

Rietbergen-McCracken, J. and D. Narayan (1998) *Participation and Social Assessment: Tools and Techniques* (Washington, DC: World Bank).

Rist, G. (1997) *The History of Development: from Western Origins to Global Faith* (London: Zed Books).

Robb, C. M. (1999) *Can the Poor Influence Policy? Participatory Poverty Assessments in the Developing World* (Washington, DC: World Bank).

Robertson, R. (1992) *Globalization: Social Theory and Global Culture* (London: Sage).

Robins, K. (1997) 'What in the World's Going on?', in P. Du Guy (ed.), *Production of Culture/Cultures of Production* (London: Sage).

Robinson, M. (1995) 'Political Conditionality: Strategic Implications for NGOs', in O. Stokke (ed.), *Aid and Political Conditionality* (London: Frank Cass).

Rose, Richard (1998) 'Getting Things Done in an Anti-Modern Society: Social Capital Networks in Russia', Social Capital Initiative Working Paper no. 6 (Washington, DC: World Bank).

Rose, Richard (1999) *New Russia Barometer Trends Since 1992*, Studies in Public Policy no. 320 (Centre for the Study of Public Policy, University of Strathclyde).

Roy, A. (1999) 'The Greater Common Good', *Outlook*, 24 May.

Rutazibwa, Gérard, Jean Nizurugero and Lindiro Kabirigi (1998) 'Etude sur la destruction du capital social et sa restauration dans des sociétés dechirées par la guerre: cas du Rwanda', mimeo (Washington, DC: World Bank).

Sachs, W. (ed.) (1992) *The Development Dictionary: A Guide to Knowledge as Power* (London: Zed Books).

Said, E. (1979) *Orientalism* (New York: Vintage).

Said, E. (1989) 'Representing the Colonised: Anthropology's Interlocutors', *Critical Inquiry*, 15 (2).

Said, E. (1990) 'Narrative, Geography and Interpretation', *New Left Review*, 180 (March–April).

Said, E. (1992) *Culture and Imperialism* (London: Chatto and Windus).

Sampson, S. (1996) 'The Social Life of Projects. Importing Civil Society to Albania', in C. Hann and E. Dunn (eds), *Civil Society: Challenging Western Models* (London: Routledge).

Sandbrook, R. (1993) *The Politics of Africa's Economic Recovery* (London: Cambridge University Press).

Schick, A. (1996) *The Spirit of Reform: Managing the New Zealand State Sector in a Time of Change* (Wellington: New Zealand Treasury).

Schick, A. (1998) 'Why most developing countries should not try New Zealand's reforms', *World Bank Research Observer*, 13 (1): 123–31.

Schoonmaker Freudenberger, K. (1994) 'Tree and Land Tenure: Rapid Appraisal Tools', *Forests, Trees and People Community Forest Manual*, 4 (Rome: FAO).

Schrijvers, J. (1996) 'Participation and Power: A Transformative Feminist Research Perspective', in N. Nelson and S. Wright (eds), *Power and Participatory Development: Theory and Practice* (London: Intermediate Technology Publications).

Schumacher, E. (1993) *Small is Beautiful: A Study of Economics as if People Mattered* (London: Vintage).

Schumpeter, J. A. (1970) *Capitalism, Socialism and Democracy* (London: Unwin).

Schuurman, F. (1993) *Beyond the Impasse. New Directions in Development Theory* (London: Zed Books).

Schuurman, F. (2000) 'Paradigms Lost, Paradigms Regained? Development Studies in the Twenty-First Century', *Third World Quarterly*, 21 (1): 7–20.

Scoones, I. (1994) *Living with Uncertainty* (London: Intermediate Technology Publications).

Scoones, I. and J. Thompson (1994) *Beyond Farmer First: Rural People's Knowledge, Agricultural Research, and Extension Practice* (London: Intermediate Technology Publications).

Sell, S. K. (2000) 'Big Business and the New Trade Agreements: The Future of the WTO', in R. Stubbs and G. R. D. Underhill (eds), *Political Economy and the Changing Global Order*, 2nd edn (Oxford: Oxford University Press).

Seth, S., L. Gandhi and M. Dutton (1998) 'Post-Colonial Studies: a Beginning', *Postcolonial Studies: Culture, Politics and Economy*, 1 (1).

Shelley, M. (1985) *Frankenstein* (Harmondsworth: Penguin).

Shiva, V. (ed.) (1994) *Close to Home: Women Reconnect Ecology, Health and Development* (London: Earthscan).

Shohat. E. (1992) 'Notes on the Post-colonial', *Social Text*, 31/32: 99–113.

Shohat, E. and R. Stam (1994) *Unthinking Eurocentrism: Multiculturalism and the Media* (London: Routledge).

Shrestha, N. (1995) 'Becoming a Development Category', in J. Crush (ed.), *Power of Development* (London: Routledge).

Silver, Hilary (1995) 'Reconceptualising Social Disadvantage: Three Paradigms of Social Exclusion', in Gerry Rodgers, Charles Gore and Jose B. Figueiredo (eds), *Social Exclusion: Rhetoric, Reality, Responses* (Geneva: International Labour Organisation and United Nations Development Program).

Simon, D. and A. Narman (1999) *Development as Theory and Practice: Current Perspectives on Development and Development Cooperation* (London: Addison Wesley Longman).

Skocpol, T. (1996) 'Unravelling From Above', *The American Prospect*, 25: 20–5, http://epn.org/prospect/25/25-cn2.html.

Slater, D. (1995) 'Challenging Western Visions of the Global', *The European Journal of Development Research*, 7 (2): 366–88.

Smith, N. (1994) 'Shaking Loose the Colonies: Isaiah Bowman and the "Decolonization" of the British Empire', in A.Godlewska and N. Smith (eds), *Geography and Empire* (Oxford: Blackwell).

Solow, Robert M. (1999) 'Notes on Social Capital and Economic Performance', in P. Dasgupta and I. Serageldin (eds), *Social Capital: a Multifaceted Perspective* (Washington, DC: World Bank).

Sorensen, G. (1995) 'Conditionality, Democracy and Development', in O. Stokke (ed.), *Aid and Political Conditionality* (London: Frank Cass).

Spivak, G. (1988) *In Other Worlds: Essays in Cultural Politics* (London, Routledge).

Spivak, G. (1990) *The Post-colonial Critic: Interviews, Strategies, Dialogues* (New York: Routledge).

Spivak, G. (1991) 'Neo-Colonialism and the Secret Agent of Knowledge', *Oxford Literary Review*, 13: 1–2.

Spivak, G. (1993) *Outside in the Teaching Machine* (London: Routledge).

Spybey, T. (1992) *Social Change, Development and Dependency* (Cambridge: Polity Press).

Stewart, F., G. Cornia, R. Jolly (1995) *Adjustment With a Human Face* (Oxford: Clarendon).

Stirrat, R. L. (1997) 'The New Orthodoxy and Old Truths: Participation, Empowerment and Other Buzz Words', in S. Bastian and N. Bastian *Assessing Participation: A Debate from South Asia* (New Delhi: Konark).

Stirrat, R. L. (2000) 'Cultures of Consultancy', *Critique of Anthropology*, 20 (1): 31–46.

Stokke, O. (1995a) 'Aid and Political Conditionality: Core Issues and State of the Art', in O. Stokke (ed.), *Aid and Political Conditionality* (London: Frank Cass).

Stokke, O. (ed.) (1995b) *Aid and Political Conditionality* (London: Frank Cass).

Sudarsky, J. and Ed D. Bogota (1998) 'The Barometer of Social Capital (BARCAS): Measuring Social Capital in Columbia', paper presented to Research Committee 18: Political Sociology, Montreal: World Congress of Sociology, July.

Suleri, S. (1993) 'Woman Skin Deep: Feminism and the Postcolonial Condition', in P. Williams and L. Chrisman (eds), *Colonial Discourse and Post-Colonial Theory: A Reader* (Hemel Hempstead: Harvester-Wheatsheaf).

Tandon, R. (1999) 'Ways Forward: Mainstreaming and Upscaling Participation of Primary Stakeholders', presentation made on behalf of the Participation Sub-Group of the NGO Working Group of the World Bank at the concluding session of the International Conference on the Participation of Primary Stakeholders, World Bank, Washington DC, November.

Therien, Jean-Philippe and C. Lloyd (2000) 'Development Assistance on the Brink', *Third World Quarterly*, 21 (1): 21–38.

Thin, N., A. Good and R. Hodgson (1998) *Social Development Policies Results and Learning: A Multi-Agency Review* (London: Department for International Development, Social Development Division).

Thomas, A. and T. Allen (2000) *Poverty and Development in the 21st Century* (Oxford: Oxford University Press).

Thomas, N. (1994) *Colonialism's Culture. Anthropology, Travel and Government* (Oxford: Polity).

Thompson, G. (2000) 'Economic Globalization', in D. Held (ed.), *A Globalising World? Culture, Economics and Politics*, pp. 85–126.

Timmonds, R. and A. Hite (eds) (2000) *From Modernisation to Globalization: Perspectives on Development and Social Change* (Oxford: Blackwell).

Tomlinson, J. (1996) 'Cultural Globalization: Placing and Displacing the West', *European Journal of Development Research*, 8 (2): 22–35.

Townsend, J. in collaboration with Ursula Arrevillaga, Jennie Bain, Socorro Cancino, Susan Frenk, Silvana Pacheco and Elia Perez (1995) *Women's Voices from the Rainforest* (London: Routledge).

Toye, J. (1987) *Dilemmas of Development* (Oxford: Blackwell).

Toye, J. (1993) *Dilemmas of Development*, 2nd edn (Oxford: Blackwell).

Trinh, T. Minh-Ha (1987) 'Difference: A Special Third World Women Issue', *Feminist Review*, 25: 5–22.

Trinh, T. Minh-Ha (1989) *Woman, Native, Other: Writing Postcoloniality and Feminism* (Bloomington: Indiana University Press).

Tripp, A. M. (1998) *Changing the Rules. The Politics of Liberalisation and the Urban Informal Economy in Tanzania* (Berkeley: University of California Press).

UNCED (1992) *Report of the United Nations Conference on Environment and Development, Rio de Janeiro* (New York: United Nations).

UNDP (1993) *Human Development Report* (New York: United Nations Development Programme).

UNDP (1995) *Public Sector Management, Governance, and Sustainable Human Development* (New York: United Nations Development Programme).

UNDP (1998a) *Governance for Sustainable Human Development* (New York: United Nations Development Programme).

UNDP (1998b) *Human Development Report* (New York: United Nations Development Programme).

UNDP (1999) *Human Development Report* (New York: United Nations Development Programme).

UNDP Vietnam (1999) *Fact Sheet: Governance* (Hanoi: United Nations Development Programme).

Uvin, P. (1993) ' "Do As I Say, Not As I Do": The Limits of Political Conditionality', *European Journal of Development Research*, 5 (1): 63–84.

Van Rooy, A. (1998) *Civil Society and the Aid Industry* (London: Earthscan).

Visvanathan, N. (1997) *The Women, Gender and Development Reader* (London: Zed Books).

Wade, R. (1990) *Governing The Market* (Princeton, NJ: Princeton University Press).

Wade, Robert (1996) 'Globalization and its Limits: Reports of the Death of the National Economy are Greatly Exaggerated', in S. Berger and R. Dore (eds), *National Diversity and Global Capitalism* (Ithaca, NY: Cornell University Press).

Warren, M. (1991) 'Using Indigenous Knowledge in Agricultural Development', World Bank Discussion Paper no. 127 (Washington, DC: World Bank).

Waters, M. (1995) *Globalization* (London: Routledge).

WCED (1987) *Our Common Future* (Oxford: Oxford University Press).

Weiner, M. (1990) 'Immigration: Perspective From Receiving Countries', *Third World Quarterly*, 12 (1).

Weiss, Linda (1998) *The Myth of the Powerless State* (Ithaca, NY: Cornell University Press).

Welbourn, A. (1991) 'RRA and the Analysis of Difference', *RRA Notes*, 14 (London: IIED): 14–23.

White, G. (1994) 'Civil Society, Democratisation and Development (1): Clearing the Ground', *Democratisation*, 1 (3).

White, G. (1996) 'Corruption and Market Reform in China', *IDS Bulletin*, 27 (2): 40–7.

Whitehead, A. and M. Lockwood (1999a) 'Gendering Poverty: A Review of Six World Bank African Poverty Assessments', *Development and Change*, 30 (3): 525–55.

Whitehead, A. and M. Lockwood (1999b) *Gender in the World Bank's Poverty Assessments: Six Case Studies from Sub-Saharan Africa* (Geneva: UNRISD).

Williams, P. and L. Chrisman (eds) (1993) *Colonial Discourse and Post-colonial Theory* (London: Harvester Wheatsheaf).

Wilson, P. A. (1997) 'Building Social Capital: A Learning Agenda for the Twenty-first Century', *Urban Studies*, 34 (5–6).

Wiseman, J. (1998) *Global Nations? Australia and the Politics of Globalization* (Cambridge: Cambridge University Press).

Wood, C. (1995) *Environmental Impact Assessment: A Comparative Review* (Harlow: Longman).

Woolcock, Michael (1998) 'Social Capital and Economic Development: Toward a Theoretical Synthesis and Policy Framework', *Theory and Society*, 27: 151–208.

World Bank (1990) *World Development Report 1990: Poverty* (New York: Oxford University Press).

World Bank (1991) *World Development Report 1991: The Challenge of Development* (New York: Oxford University Press).

World Bank (1992a) *Governance and Development* (Washington, DC: World Bank).

World Bank (1992b) *World Development Report 1992: Development and the Environment* (New York: Oxford University Press).

World Bank (1993a) *Global Economic Prospects and the Developing Countries, 1993* (Washington, DC: World Bank).

World Bank (1993b) *World Development Report 1993: Investing in Health* (New York: Oxford University Press).

World Bank (1994a) 'The World Bank and Participation' (Washington, DC: Operations Policy Department, World Bank, September).

World Bank (1994b) *Governance: The World Bank Experience* (Washington, DC: World Bank).

World Bank (1994c) *World Development Report 1994: Infrastructure for Development* (New York: Oxford University Press).

World Bank (1995a) *World Bank Participation Sourcebook*, Environment Department Papers (Washington, DC: Social Policy and Resettlement Division, World Bank).

World Bank (1995b) *World Development Report 1995: Workers in an Integrating World* (New York: Oxford University Press).

World Bank (1996) *World Development Report 1996: From Plan to Market* (New York: Oxford University Press).

World Bank (1997) *World Development Report 1997: The State in a Changing World* (New York: Oxford University Press).

World Bank (1999a) *World Development Report 1998/1999: Knowledge for Development* (New York: Oxford University Press).

World Bank (1999b) *World Development Report 1999/2000: Entering the 21st Century* (New York: Oxford University Press).

World Bank (2000) *World Development Report 2000/2001: Attacking Poverty* (Washington, DC: World Bank).

Wright, S. C. (1996) 'Depoliticizing Development: The Uses and Abuses of Participation', *Development in Practice*, 6 (1): 6–15.

Young, K. (1992) 'Household Resource Management', in L. Ostergaard *Gender and Development: A Practical Guide* (London: Routledge).

Young, R. (1990) *White Mythologies: Writing History and the West* (London: Routledge).

Index